PRAISE FOR *HIGH NO*

"Brave, honest, brilliant, innovative, ar... [gold] medal for the least politically-correct wo... [cal] *Son.*"

--R. James Woolsey, Chairma... ...e Foundation for Defense of Democracies and Director of Central Intelligence 1993-95.

"These symposia are so intellectually fascinating that you will be glued to your seat once you open the first page. *High Noon for America* is one of the most riveting intellectual roller coaster rides you will ever take. This book is a must read."

--Steven Emerson, Executive Director of the Investigative Project on Terrorism.

"A Rabelais, a Swift for our times, Jamie Glazov has his finger on the pulse of our troubled age, and the clarity of vision to offer workable solutions, with an engaging wit and clarity of style that is unparalleled."

--Robert Spencer, author of the New York Times bestsellers The Politically Incorrect Guide to Islam (and the Crusades) *and* The Truth About Muhammad.

"Ever astute and incisive, Dr. Jamie Glazov once again soars above the political barking match that passes for debate in our troubled country. Gathering the key insights of a platoon of our liveliest conservative thinkers, *High Noon for America* is well worth your time and money!"

--Lt. Col. Ralph Peters, U.S. Army (Retd.), author of Lines Of Fire and Endless War.

"*High Noon for America* provides us with a stunning arsenal of intellectual weapons to defend America's minds, our freedom, and our way of life."

--Ion Mihai Pacepa, author of Red Horizons, *republished in 27 countries.*

"*High Noon for America* is better than talking heads, it's talking brains, including many of our finest. It expands consciousness, adds immeasurably to your education, and stimulates us all to rethink our convictions about this highly volatile world. And there's even a guide to the religiously perplexed."

--Michael Ledeen, Freedom Scholar at the Foundation for the Defense of Democracies and author of Accomplice to Evil: Iran and the War Against the West.

High Noon for America:
The Coming Showdown

By Jamie Glazov
Foreword by Theodore Dalrymple

Published by Mantua Books Ltd.
Brantford,   Ontario   N3T   6J9
Email: MantuaBooks@gmail.com
Website: www.mantuabooks.com

Library and Archives Canada Cataloguing in Publication

Glazov, Jamie, 1966-
   High noon for America : the coming showdown / Jamie Glazov.

ISBN 978-0-9869414-3-6

   1. United States--Foreign relations--21st century. 2. United
States--Foreign relations--Arab countries. 3. United States--
Politics and government--2009-. 4. Right and left (Political
science)--United States. I. Title.

JZ1480.G53 2012   527.73   C2012-902615-8

First Printing May 2012

Cover Design by Linda Daly; author photo by Ron Jocsak

To Babushka,
Maria Andreevna Korneeva

Table of Contents

Foreword

Dialogue in which people are unafraid to speak their mind is almost the foundation of the western intellectual tradition. But Jamie Glazov's symposia are different from Plato's in one important respect: he doesn't write or edit them to produce the conclusion that he would like the reader to accept.

Indeed, where the discussants disagree, as often they do (and strongly), the reader will have to make up his own mind who has got the better of it. This will not always be easy for him, because the discussants are often formidably knowledgeable about the important, or vital, matters under discussion, and all of them use rational arguments based upon facts to support their case. It is part of the exhilaration of the best of these symposia that disagreement between the participants is the result of strongly, reasonably and sincerely held views, but expressed with respect for and courtesy towards the other. The discussion is vigorous without being shrill.

This is less common than one might suppose, or than it ought to be. If you look at discussion forums on the internet, you will be surprised by the speed with which abuse takes the place of argument, indeed is the *only* argument. Not only are the discussions in this book on matters such as the relationship between the former Soviet Union and contemporary Russia, the meaning of the downfall of Ceauşescu in Romania, and the possibility of an Islam genuinely at peace with the secular state, fascinating in themselves, but they are conducted in a manner than one might wish to become more general between people with an even wider range of opinion.

Let us hope, then, that Jamie Glazov's symposia become a model imitated wide and far.

Theodore Dalrymple
Retired doctor and psychiatrist, and the author of several books, among them the *Life at the Bottom* and *Anything Goes.*

i

Preface

As the "Arab Spring" sweeps across the Muslim Middle East, it is becoming increasingly evident that far from being a movement that will usher in democracy and liberty (a notion that leftists in the West are enthusiastically propagating), the "Arab Spring" is really just an Islamic Supremacist Winter paving the road toward pro-Sharia regimes taking power throughout the region. This scenario is horrifying in its consequences. The abrogation of the Egyptian-Israeli peace treaty, for example, the cornerstone of Middle East peace for more than three decades, is a major Brotherhood goal, recently restated by Brotherhood leaders in Egypt — and the Brotherhood is now on the way to solidifying power there. President Obama, meanwhile, actively supported the Arab revolts. He withdrew American support for Egypt's Hosni Mubarak at a crucial moment — a betrayal that assisted Mubarak's downfall, and sent the U.S. military to topple Gaddafi in Libya and usher in a pro-Sharia regime with links to al-Qaeda. The Obama administration, with its destructive and anti-American agenda, is facilitating this whole nightmarish process throughout the region. The symposiums collected in Part I, "The War in the Middle East," shed light on this tragic and depressing phenomenon.

Aggravating these disasters evolving in the Middle East, the Russian KGB enters the picture with its malicious tricks and influences. The former Soviet Union engendered much mischief in the Middle East throughout the Cold War. Now, with KGB thug Vladimir Putin in charge of post-Soviet Russia, the tradition continues. Putin's trouble-making in Iran, Syria and vis-à-vis Palestinian terror (among other instigations) is evident — while the Obama administration turns a blind eye. And yet the recent growing demonstrations in Russia against Putin have sparked a glimmer of hope for something new. We now see the possibility for democratic change in Russia. Will democratic forces succeed? If they do, what will it mean, not only for Russia's internal affairs but also for its foreign policy? Part II, "The Evil Empire," deals with these urgent issues, and the distinguished panels assembled make clear why a section on the Evil Empire deserves a significant place between discussions of the Middle East, Islam, and Obama's policy of giving away America's power.

In the context of Obama's efforts to disempower America as much as possible, there is the reality of the United States relinquishing, in several important spheres, its status as a superpower. At the same time, the U.S. remains robust in many realms and is growing in strength in some areas. Therefore, in "Part III: The End of a Superpower?" two experts on this issue go toe-to-toe in a debate over the question: "American Economic and Military Decline?"

The decline of a nation is not easily reversed when its enemies are waging war on it from without and within, and when the nation's culture disallows not only an effective defense against the enemies' assault but even the admission of the enemies' very existence. This is exactly what is happening in terms of Islam's war on the West and the Left's control of the boundaries of Western discourse on this war, which, in turn, incapacitates our society's ability to properly defend itself in the face of Islamic jihad. This phenomenon is the substance of discussion in the collection of symposiums in "Part IV: Islam: The Religion of Peace?"

The Left inflicts destruction on our society by paving the road for our totalitarian adversaries' destructive agenda against us. It is, therefore, urgent and crucial for citizens of the West to understand the Left and its makeup. Without a cognizance of what makes the Left tick, it is impossible for freedom-loving people to battle its pernicious plans. And who better to deconstruct the Left than David Horowitz, the former leader of the New Left, who ultimately gauged the evil of his political faith and departed from it, exposing and fighting it ever since. In "Part V: Leaving the Faith," four great thinkers gather to reflect on Horowitz's fascinating memoir *Radical Son,* celebrating the tenth anniversary of its publication.

Another major problem facing America in the terror war is that it funds its enemies because of its energy dependence. Giving the Saudis billions of dollars for oil, when the House of Saud is one of the major centers of terror and a leading disseminator of the terrorist ideology, is not, to say the least, the most effective prescriptive plan for victory. A distinguished panel of experts attacks this issue in "Part VI: Energy Independence."

The damage that the Left inflicts on society is interwoven with the falsehoods it spouts, falsehoods that often become accepted truths that are not to be questioned by the society at large due to the restricted boundaries of debate that the Left despotically sets up. A powerful example of this phenomenon is the way that progressive myths mold how drug addiction is viewed by society, a telling issue that Theodore Dalrymple has exposed in his book, "Romancing Opiates." In "Part VII: Leftist Lies," a symposium hosts a heated debate with four participants, including Dalrymple himself, on this extremely controversial topic.

In the end, the War on Terror also clearly has its spiritual component. And so the problem of our beliefs is interwoven into the fabric of the challenges we face. The book ends with leaders of spiritual faiths joining a roundtable, in "Part VIII: A Discussion on Faith."

All of these symposiums, on topics ranging from the Middle East to Russia to Islam and the Left's flirtation with our deadliest enemies, make it transparently clear that it is High Noon for America. The highly informed analyses these discussions contain, thanks to the contributions of the recognized and leading experts, clearly reveal that major crises and threats to America are visible on the horizon, with the conflict inevitably, and swiftly, approaching. Do Americans have the capacity and the will to stand up and defend their culture and civilization? This book contains the intellectual weapons with which Americans can arm themselves to begin doing so. The year 2012 will tell if they will rise or fall at the opportunity to save their nation.

Acknowledgements

I am most grateful to all the superstars in this book who gave their time and energy for these symposiums and to Theodore Dalrymple for his kind and thoughtful foreword.

I owe deep thanks to David Horowitz. Thank you David.

To my dear friend Michael Finch, the Chief of Operations at the David Horowitz Freedom Center, thank you for all your encouragement, help and magnanimity of spirit. I am honored to be your friend.

John Corrigan, I cherish your friendship and all your help throughout the years. Thank you also to my dear friend (and Frontpage's contributing editor) Stephen Brown. I am profoundly grateful for all the strength and support you have given me.

I am indebted to Professor Jack L. Granatstein, my academic mentor, who helped me build the foundation on which my career, and books like these, became possible.

To Ouna Matebekwane, thank you for your tenderness, love and support.

I am grateful to Josh Lyon, Anton Wright, Ivan Wright, Levi Mcdonald, Rudy Chavarria and Anna Atell. Thank you for your friendship that sustained my perseverance.

I thank Lynne Rabinoff, my agent, for all her superb help in making the publication of this work possible. I am most grateful to my publisher Howard Rotberg for publishing this book—as well as for his valiant battle to allow conservative voices to be heard.

To Nonie Darwish, I treasure your helping, loving and magnanimous hand during my arrival in a new land.

Thank you Peter Collier, Elizabeth Ruiz, Jeffrey Wiener and Sharon Schuster - my colleagues at the Freedom Center who have stood by me over the years and helped me a great deal. Thank you Stephanie Knudson, another Freedom Center colleague, for your warm friendship.

To my brother Grisha and his family - and especially G-team members Talia and Yuri, thank you. To my sister Elena, my favorite brother-in-law, Kevin, and Maria and Sarah, I am grateful for all your prayers, love and support. Thank you Yuri and Arielle.

To Papochka, looking at me from above: thank you for being a noble knight and a courageous hero — and for your efforts to instill your priceless values in me. To Mamochka, thank you for all the love and wisdom you bestowed upon me. Thank you for teaching me the importance of celebrating the gift of life and of being joyful and grateful in the face of God's beautiful gifts to us. Papa and mom, I love both of you dearly.

And finally, to Babushka, my mom's mom, Maria Andreevna Korneeva.

We were separated when I was 5-1/2 years old, never to see each other again - due to my family's forced emigration from the Soviet Union in 1972 and, then, alas, to the ingredients of Soviet totalitarianism that made seeing each other impossible.

Till this day I remember my overabundance of joy when I was in your company. I recall vividly how much you loved me and how you brought me gifts that instilled such exhilaration in me that I could hardly contain myself. I remember running frantically, with triumphant celebration, towards you, out of breath, down the path in our Moscow apartment building's entrance when you would come to visit us. "Babushka! Babushka!" I would scream as you laughed with open arms, seeing me darting towards you with over-excited anticipation. Those are some of the most beautiful memories of my life - memories that also tug heavily at my heart.

When we were surgically removed from one another by Soviet despotism, you missed us unspeakably and dearly — as we missed you. You had lost your husband in WWII and now you were separated from your daughter and your grandchildren because of the Cold War. Life inflicted a heavy penalty on you — a penalty that I carry in my soul daily thinking of you and what you must have went through.

My mom cried throughout the years longing for you. I remember being a young boy, standing by her helplessly, as she lay on a couch weeping inconsolably, missing you. I would try to comfort her, but it was clear that my caresses and soothing words were not the panacea for her grief. My life-long vendetta against communist ideology and systems were solidified in those moments.

You passed in 1999. I am sorry to say that life's circumstances have not allowed me to return to the homeland of my birth to pay you respect and to express my love and longing for you at your gravesite. But if God, in his mercy, will allow it, and if I can only make it one day to the beautiful place I know you are now, joined as you are in happiness again with granddad, Gregory Rafalski, you will not have much difficulty recognizing me. Because, once again, you will see me sprinting with ecstatic joy towards you — as you did when I was a little boy in our Moscow courtyard. But this time, Babushka, I will run much faster, and when I finally reach you, I will leap into your arms and embrace you with such force that, in that miraculous moment, we will both know that we have touched the face of God.

And I will not let you go.
I love you.
This book is for you.

Maria Andreevna Korneeva

vii

Part I: The War in the Middle East

[1] The Mismanaged War Against Libya

In this special edition of Frontpage Symposium, we have gathered a distinguished panel to explore what American — and Western — interests are served by the coalition's war against Libya. Our guests today are:

Michael Ledeen, a noted political analyst and a Freedom Scholar at the Foundation for the Defense of Democracies. He is the author of *The Iranian Time Bomb*, *Machiavelli on Modern Leadership* and *Tocqueville on American Character*, and he is a contributor to The Wall Street Journal. His latest book is *Accomplice to Evil: Iran and the War Against the West*.

Lt. General Ion Mihai Pacepa, the highest official ever to have defected from the former Soviet bloc. His first book, *Red Horizons,* was republished in 27 languages. In April 2010, Pacepa's latest book, *Programmed to Kill: Lee Harvey Oswald, the Soviet KGB, and the Kennedy Assassination,* was prominently displayed at the annual meeting of the Organization of American Historians held in Washington D.C., as a "superb new paradigmatic work" and a "must read" for "everyone interested in the assassination of President Kennedy."

Dr. Walid Phares, an expert on the Middle East who teaches Global Strategies in Washington DC. His most recent book is *The Coming Revolution: Struggle for Freedom in the Middle East.*

and

Robert Spencer, director of *Jihad Watch* and author of *The Politically Incorrect Guide to Islam (and the Crusades)*, *The Truth About Muhammad, Stealth Jihad* and *The Complete Infidel's Guide to the Qur'an.*

FP: Walid Phares, Mihai Pacepa, Michael Ledeen and Robert Spencer, welcome to Frontpage Symposium.

Robert Spencer, let us begin with you. What is your position on the coalition campaign, with U.S. involvement, against Gaddafi?

Spencer: As the U.S. fired over one hundred Tomahawk cruise missiles into Libya Saturday, the objective seems clear. Barack Obama declared that "we cannot stand idly by when a tyrant tells his people that there will be no mercy." He explained: "Today we are part of a broad coalition. We are answering the calls of a threatened people. And we are acting in the interests of the United States and the world." But he didn't explain how acting forcibly to remove Muammar Gaddafi would indeed be in America's interests. And that is a case that is not as easily made as it might appear to be.

How could removing Gaddafi *not* be in America's interests? It is unlikely that he will be succeeded by Thomas Jefferson. The fact that Gaddafi is a reprehensible human being and no friend of the U.S. does not automatically turn his opponents into Thomas Paine.

Obama has affirmed his support for "the universal rights of the Libyan people," including "the rights of peaceful assembly, free speech, and the ability of the Libyan people to determine their own destiny," but he has never specified who in Libya is working to uphold and defend those rights. He has praised "the peaceful transition to democracy" that he says is taking place across the Middle East, and yet the countries where uprisings have taken place have no democratic traditions or significant forces calling for the establishment of secular, Western-style republics.

Eastern Libya, where the anti-Gaddafi forces are based, is a hotbed of anti-Americanism and jihadist sentiment. A report by West Point's Combating Terrorism Center reveals that over the last few years, more jihadists per capita entered Iraq from Libya than from any other Muslim country - and most of them came from the region that is now spearheading the revolt against Gaddafi.

That may explain why Libyan protesters have defaced Gaddafi's picture with the Star of David, the hated symbol of the Jews, whom the Qur'an designates as the "strongest in enmity" toward the Muslims. There has been a notable absence among the protesters of anything equivalent to "Don't Tread On Me" flags or other signs that what the uprising is really all about is establishing the ballot box and the give-and-take of open-society politics. The Libyan protesters have chanted not "Give me liberty or give me death!," but "No god but Allah!"

Abu Yahia al-Libi, a Libyan who heads up al-Qaeda in Afghanistan, has warmly praised the uprising in his homeland, calling on Libyans to murder the tyrant and crowing: "Now it is the turn of Gaddafi after he made the people of Libya suffer for more than 40 years." He said that removing Gaddafi as well as other Middle Eastern autocrats was "a step to reach the goal of every Muslim, which is to make the word of Allah the highest" - that is, to establish a state ruled by Islamic law.

And America's Tomahawk cruise missiles will have helped bring about such a state in Libya.

Pacepa: I fully agree with Robert Spencer.

There are few people on earth who want to see Gaddafi removed from power more than I do. I could write a book about my reasons, and maybe someday I will. Here I will just say that, after I was granted political asylum by President Carter (1978), Gaddafi set a $2 million bounty on my head because I had revealed his secret efforts to arm international terrorists with bacteriological and other weapons of mass destruction. But my personal animus against Gaddafi is my own policy, and it should not have anything to do with the policy of the U.S. Nor should the personal hatred for Gaddafi on the part of other Americans, such as those whose relatives he killed at the La Belle nightclub in West Berlin (1986), in the Pan Am Flight 103 at Lockerbie (1988) or elsewhere, be raised to the level of U.S. foreign policy.

The U.S. policy toward Libya — and any other country — should defend and promote only the interests of the United States. Unfortunately, the current events taking place in Libya show that our administration does not have any coherent foreign policy toward that country, and that U.S. foreign policy simply blows with the prevailing wind.

The name of the wind propelling the current U.S. policy toward Libya is Sarkozy. The president of France has no real policy toward Libya either, and he is also blowing with the wind—the wind of the 2012 presidential elections, where he is seriously threatened by the socialist Dominique Strauss-Kahn. Rattling sabers has always helped French politicians in the short run-in spite of the fact that France has lost every war it ever started.

Just three years ago, President Sarkozy welcomed Gaddafi and his 400-person entourage on a five-day royal visit to Paris, allowing him to set up his Bedouin tent near the Elysée Palace. "Gaddafi is not perceived as a dictator in the Arab world," Sarkozy explained at the time, adding as further justification: "He is the longest-serving head of state in the region." [1] Now this justification is Sarkozy's reason to go to war against Gaddafi. "France has decided to play its part in history," Sarkozy gravely announced from the steps of the Elysée Palace just before starting the war against Libya. "The Libyan people need our aid and support." [2] But he, and the rest of the Western World, still do not really know who those people are that he decided to protect.

All we know for certain about the "freedom fighters" opposing Gaddafi is that they fight with Kalashnikov in hand, and that Kalashnikovs have no history of promoting freedom. A recent article published in the prestigious *Le Monde* goes a step further, revealing that these "brave Libyan freedom fighters" are dominated by jihadists espousing the same complaints of "Westoxification," accompanied by the Jew-hatred and broader infidel-hatred that permeates the Arab world. [3]

President Obama has also praised Gaddafi in the past. According to press reports, last year, around the time Gaddafi called Obama "our son," the U.S. president earmarked $400,000 for two of Gaddafi's charities. The money was divided between the Gaddafi International Charity and Development Foundation, run by Gaddafi's son Saif, and the Wa Attasimou, run by Gaddafi's daughter Aicha. [4]

Now President Obama is also facing elections, also in 2012, and he is having at least as much difficulty with the electorate as Sarkozy has. A new war would certainly help. Americans are patriots, and their support for our troops might occasion them to move to the back burner their discontent with Obamacare and with this administration's disastrous spending habits.

The U.S. has made it abundantly clear to Gaddafi that he had better not try any more dirty tricks against us. He got the message and has so far been quiet toward us. There are plenty of evil dictators in the world who kill their own people, and whom we do not attack. The United States is not the police country of the world.

War is a matter of life and death. It should be never used as a way to win elections.

Ledeen: A week ago I wrote a little blog wondering what Obama might do to prevent everyone from concluding he's a wimp. I confessed that this thought worried me quite a bit, as it had in the 1970s when Carter's name became inseparably tied to "wimp." Every author falls in love with his own words, but I hope to be forgiven for saying that I was right to worry.

I quite agree with both Robert Spencer and General Pacepa, both of whom remind us of my grandmother's famous bit of folk wisdom, "things are never so bad that they can't get worse." Indeed, both of them raise the truly paradoxical and terrible possibility that we may "win" in Libya, only to find that we have made things worse: worse for American interests, worse for the Libyan people, worse for the whole region, which hardly needs to get even worse.

But that's not my major concern. What gets my juices flowing is the ongoing failure to see the Middle Eastern cauldron in full context, and that we are bringing American power to bear on Qadaffi, but not on the tyrants in Tehran. As almost everyone with a keyboard has said, we don't have a major national interest at stake in Libya, but Iran is our main enemy, and is killing Americans every day. So if you want to act decisively in the Middle East, you should be working for regime change in Iran; Libya is a sideshow.

So it's the wrong war in the wrong place.

That said, I have a lot of sympathy for the view (often attributed to Samantha Power, Susan Rice and Hillary Clinton) that America should support citizens fighting for freedom against tyrants. But that does not mean a suspension of strategic judgment, and a failure to recognize which of those fights is most important.

Bits and pieces: I never liked the no-fly-zone idea, and in fact several weeks ago I said about Libya what I had said years before about Darfur: bomb the air force, destroy the planes of the regime. That takes a few minutes. Then, if you decide you want to support the rebels, or some of them, go ahead. At least you've given them a respite from the slaughter.

More: It's not all bad, you know. This gives hope to the "rebels" we should be supporting — the ones in Syria and Iran. Maybe one of the three Administration Valkyries will call for political support for the dissidents in those two unhappy lands. Obama's video to the Iranians marks a significant change in rhetoric; he's abandoned all that sweet talk about "outstretched hands" and told the young Iranians on the streets that "I'm with you." I don't quite believe it, but he may now find it much more difficult to appease Tehran. Time will tell.

As you see, I keep coming back to the big context, because that's the one that really matters. We're in a big war; the Libya thing is a skirmish.

Phares: We all agree that Colonel Gaddafi is a dictator, that he supported terrorism against the U.S. and France, was responsible for the tragedy of PanAm 103, that he funded, armed and trained radicals in many African countries such as in Mali, Mauritania, Niger, Senegal, Haute Volta, and in a few Middle Eastern countries, including Lebanon. We all are aware that his regime oppressed his people and tortured and jailed his opponents for four decades. I observed Gaddafi ruling Libya unchecked during and after the Cold War before and after 9/11 and he was received by liberal democracies as a respectable leader.

My first question is: Why has the West been silent so long and why is it so late in taking action against this dictator? Of course it had to do with oil. Western elites were morally and politically encouraging him by buying his oil and empowering him with endless cash as Libyan dissidents were dying in jails.

Now, as missiles are crushing Gaddafi's air defense systems and tanks, Western governments should be invited for serious self-criticism for having enabled this regime to last that long. Squeezing or even defeating Gaddafi should prompt a comprehensive review of past decades of Western policies towards this regime and its abuses of human rights. The military operation should not end with the departure of Gaddafi from power. It must open the door for an examination of U.S. and European policies that have aligned themselves with Petrodollars interests for over half a century. Such self-criticism was supposed to start with the removal of the Taliban and Saddam Hussein, but unfortunately, it hasn't taken place yet, precisely because of the mega-influence inside the West and the United States by powerful lobbies representing the interests of OPEC, the Arab League and the OIC.

Besides, questions should be raised about the Arab League and OIC endorsement of an action against Gaddafi's regime. Where were they for decades, when the Libyan dictator used to seize the microphone on their platforms and blast the very democracies they implored to act against him? These organizations catered to the interest of regimes they now are calling for sanctions against. Mr. Amr Moussa, the current secretary general of the Arab League, rises against Gaddafi after having supported him for years, while the latter was oppressing his own people.

In my book, *The Coming Revolution: Struggle for Freedom in the Middle East*, I call all these regimes and organizations a "brotherhood against democracy." They have supported each other against democratic movements and minorities everywhere in the region. From Sudan to Lebanon, from Iraq to Libya, the regional organizations were at the service of these regimes, not of the people. As these revolts are ongoing, these inter-regimes' organizations must be criticized and eventually reformed. Last year, the Arab League and OIC were endorsing Libya's role in the UN Council on Human Rights. Egypt, Tunisia and Libya's representatives at the Geneva UN body were shutting up the voices of Libyan dissidents just a few months ago. Now that the uprisings have crumbled the regimes in Cairo and Tunisia, and Tripoli's ruler is cornered, the negative impact these inter-regime organizations have on dissidents and human rights on international levels must be exposed and their future representation comprehensively reformed.

I do agree with Mr. Spencer that many jihadists have been recruited from Libya, and particularly from its eastern provinces. I also agree with General Pacepa that Western policies towards Gaddafi's regime were incoherent. And I certainly agree with Dr. Ledeen that U.S. policy should support true democratic forces and uprisings in the region from Iran to the Arab world.

In short I would have advised for a different set of U.S. global strategies in the Middle East. We should have backed the Iranian Green Revolution in 2009, the Cedars Revolution as it struggles against Hezbollah, and Darfur in its liberation drive against the jihadist regime in Khartoum. In Egypt, we should have clearly sided with the secular youth and Copts, as they asked for a new constitution. In Iraq, we should have been clear in supporting reformist and secular forces. As far as Libya is concerned, removing Gaddafi is not the question. That should have been done years ago on the grounds of abuse of human rights. The question is who will come next? Clearly, the agenda of the Benghazi leadership is not clear. We know there is a layer of former bureaucrats, diplomats, intellectuals and military dissidents with whom partnership is possible and should be encouraged. But there is another layer below the surface which is made of Islamists, Salafists and in some cases jihadists.

From a simple observation of the latter's narrative on al Jazeera, one major component of the opposition is an Islamist force aiming at taking over in Tripoli. Hence, Washington must partner with the secular-democrats and warn that it won't endorse replacing Gaddafi's Jamahiriyya with a jihadi emirate. Why aren't most liberal Libyan dissidents received in Washington and made visible? As Mr. Spencer said, the U.S. and NATO military has been tasked to open the highways to Tripoli for the opposition, but we need to insure that on that highway we won't see the democracy groups eliminated by the next authoritarians.

FP: Walid Phares, Mihai Pacepa, Michael Ledeen and Robert Spencer, thank you for joining Frontpage Symposium.

Notes:

[1] Joseph A. Harris, "Sarko's War," *The American Spectator*, March 21, 2011.
[2] Idem.
[3] Andrew G. Bostom, "Let Muslim Anti-Terrorist States Police Libya," *Human Events*, March 21, 2011.
[4] "Obama Gave $400,000 To Libyan Charities Run By Gaddafi's Children," *Slapblog.com*, February 24, 2011.

[Jamie Glazov, "Symposium: The Mismanaged War Against Libya," *Frontpagemag.com*, March 23, 2011.]

[2] The Red Arabs

In this special edition of Frontpage Symposium we have assembled a distinguished panel to discuss how and why Arab socialists and Islamists have been preparing for this Mid-East moment for many years. Our guests today are:

Michael Ledeen, a noted political analyst and a Freedom Scholar at the Foundation for the Defense of Democracies. He is the author of *The Iranian Time Bomb, Machiavelli on Modern Leadership* and *Tocqueville on American Character*, and he is a contributor to The Wall Street Journal. His latest book is *Accomplice to Evil: Iran and the War Against the West*.

Pavel Stroilov, a historian who smuggled a vast secret archive of the Gorbachev era out of Russia. Top secret documents concerning the Middle East will be revealed in his forthcoming book *Behind the Desert Storm*, due to be published by Price World Publishing this summer.

Lt. General Ion Mihai Pacepa, the highest official ever to have defected from the former Soviet bloc. His first book, *Red Horizons,* was republished in 27 languages. In March 2010, *The Washington Post* recommended it to be included on the list of books that should be read in schools. A commemorative edition of *Red Horizons* was just issued in Romania to mark 20 years since Ceauseşcu was executed at the end of a trial where most of the accusations came out of this book. In April 2010, Pacepa's latest book, *Programmed to Kill: Lee Harvey Oswald, the Soviet KGB, and the Kennedy Assassination,* was prominently displayed at the annual meeting of the Organization of American Historians held in Washington D.C., as a "superb new paradigmatic work" and a "must read" for "everyone interested in the assassination of President Kennedy."

and

Nonie Darwish, the author of *Cruel and Usual Punishment* and the President of FormerMuslimsUnited.org.

FP: Nonie Darwish, Pavel Stroilov, Lt. General Pacepa and Michael Ledeen, welcome to Frontpage Symposium.

Pavel Stroilov, let us begin with you.

Tell us what you discovered in the Soviet archives concerning the Middle East and what light it might shine on the events in Egypt and in the Middle East in general.

Stroilov: Of course, the Soviet archives are not immediately relevant to the current events in the Middle East; but they do give us a useful insight into the world of Arab socialist dictators, such as Mubarak or Saddam, Assad or Arafat, Gaddafi or all the others. Today's media reports from the Middle East somehow manage to omit nearly all important questions. For instance, any sensible analysis of a revolution should certainly begin from considering the nature of the regime. But in all these 24-hours TV coverages from, say, Libya, how many times have you heard the phrase *Islamic Socialism*? And that is the regime's official ideology. That is also what it is all about - not only in Libya. Likewise, it is not enough simply to say that Mubarak was a dictator and that he was backed by the West. Let me explain:

The Egyptian regime was the first-born 'Arab Socialist' regime; its ultimate goal was to 'overcome the legacy of colonialism' and unite the entire Arab world in a national-socialist super state. As a movement, Arab Socialists are quite similar to Communists and Nazis, and they have been backed by both Nazis and Communists in different periods of their history. The founder of the present Egyptian regime, Col. Nasser, worked with Moscow to export his revolution all over the Middle East - with considerable success. The most notorious of the Egyptian regime's younger brothers were the Baathist regimes in Iraq and Syria, as well as the Palestine Liberation Organization, founded by Nasser as his future puppet government for whatever would remain of Israel and Jordan after a successful socialist jihad.

After several unsuccessful invasions of Israel, Nasser's successor Sadat realized this was a wrong tactic. Make no mistake: this does not make the Egyptian regime genuinely pro-Western or pro-Israeli. At no time, for example, did the Egyptian regime stop supporting one or

12

another of the subversive Palestinian groups; it still supports Fatah today. It was only a question of tactics. For this matter, as the archives show, Moscow in the early 1970s tried to persuade Sadat that another invasion of Israel was a wrong tactic, but he insisted on making one more attempt.

After the assassination of Sadat (by a pure coincidence, as we now know from the archives, the Islamist assassins unwittingly fulfilled a secret plan worked out by the Syrian KGB and Palestinian terrorists, approved by Moscow), he was succeeded by Mubarak, a graduate of a Soviet military academy, who commanded Egypt's air forces in the Yom Kippur War against Israel. The West readily accepted him as a re-incarnation of Sadat. But if Mubarak was another Sadat, why was he not killed like Sadat?

To the Soviets, as the documents show, Mubarak was keen to present himself as a genuine Nasserite whose true loyalty lies with Socialism, and to dissociate himself from his pro-Western predecessor. He described his continuing relations with the West as a cynical game of extracting loans he had no intention to repay, but which alone could keep his regime afloat. He hinted he was just waiting for a convenient moment to stab 'the imperialists' in the back.

So, Mubarak was not the Shah of Iran. He was not even Sadat. The regime he led for years is still institutionally hostile to Israel and the West, and it is still a totalitarian socialist regime based on the Party - army - secret police triangle. One feature that distinguishes it from Communist regimes is that the land is still privately owned. That is because (as Mubarak confided to Gorbachev) Khruschev once told Nasser in strict secrecy not to create collective farms: that experiment, he said, was tried in the USSR and failed.

True, this regime has a peace treaty with Israel; but I think its significance is exaggerated. When did such regimes ever pay any attention to their peace treaties? Mubarak does not attack Israel because he knows he would be beaten — Egypt has been beaten every time it tried.

To be brief, Mubarak's Egypt was a similar regime to Saddam's Iraq, Assad's Syria, of Gaddafi's Libya; a typical 'Red Arab' regime. Today, the world of Red Arabs has reached its natural Year 1989. It has become commonplace to call it 1989 with an air of absurd optimism. Yet, nobody seems to be thinking of how to avoid the mistakes of 1989. The history of 1989 in East Europe is a history of bogus movements, orchestrated revolutions, and cynical power-sharing deals behind the scenes. That was a year when East Europe lost its chance to establish genuine democracy and free market, and was doomed to decades of 'post-Communist' nonsense. In the Middle East, it can be even much worse.

So, the tragedy is not that we have reached this point: that had been inevitable all along, as every socialist regime eventually exhausts its economy and the patience of its people. Anyone with a bit of sense and a bit of interest in the matter had known this day would come. Even I, as I happened to be finishing my book shortly before the events in Tunisia, concluded it by predicting that the Red Arabs were on the way to their downfall (now this has become a platitude and I need a new ending). The tragedy is that the Red Arabs and the Islamists have been preparing for this moment for many years; but the West is, as usual, caught by surprise. All we can think of is supporting El Baradei, best known for his covering up of Iraqi and Iranian nuclear programs, because he is one Arab name we've already memorized (or is there some better reason?). The 'experts', barely concealing their bewilderment, offer us a choice between the hopeless course of supporting a doomed regime and the suicidal course of going along with the future Islamic Republic of Egypt. This much could be worked out without experts.

On close examination, these two options are exactly the same. It is no coincidence that the Muslim Brotherhood is the only organized opposition in Egypt. Mubarak's KGB (or whatever is Arabic for Gestapo) had been working to achieve this for years, ruthlessly stifling any alternative, any embryonic democratic movement, but sparing the Islamist opposition. It is, no doubt, densely infiltrated by secret police informers. And now the events are moving towards the worst-case scenario from 1989: some 'roundtable' negotiations between the regime and the selected opposition groups, leading to some 'transitional' power-sharing deal, giving the Islamists a bridgehead in the government. All those brave boys fighting on the streets, whose only organization is Twitter, will go by the board. By the time of 'elections', the only choice will be between the Red Arabs and Muslim Brotherhood. And the West will warmly welcome every step in this direction as a step to stability. It already does.

Is it too late now to prevent all this? We must at least try — but we are not even trying. The West does not even have a policy. The West does not even bother to do an obvious, fool-proof thing: stand up for one oppressed minority which is immune to both Socialism and Islamism — Christians. As for the 'Arab street', no policy-maker seems even to know what forces there are on the ground and which of them we want to win.

I am sure my colleagues on this panel will have some good ideas on what that policy should be. For my part, I can only warn against four major mistakes made in 1989, which the West is, I fear, about to repeat:

1. 'Stability' is a word we'd better forget — there is no such thing in a revolution. 'Stability' will be the motto of the Islamo-Socialist roundtable, whereas our only potential allies are young street-fighters who demand freedom, not stability.

2. Another word to forget is 'moderate'. Revolutions are never won by moderates; they are won by radicals. The Islamists must not be allowed to 'sell' themselves as the most radical force. Indeed, they are not — they are too closely interlinked with the regime. We should support those who demand a complete dismantling of the regime, putting it on trial, opening all its secret archives, revealing the names of all secret police informers. I bet we would find many Muslim Brothers' names there. This is radical; this is also something the Islamists would not like. Indeed, this is about the only trump card I can see in the hands of Egypt's democrats (if they do emerge as a serious force as I hope).

3. Once you've identified 'our guys in Egypt', don't be shy about supporting them morally and financially — this won't compromise

them. Red Arabs and Islamists will accuse democrats of being Western agents anyway. Winning a revolution is very money-intensive; Iran and others will certainly shower Islamists with money (I guess, it already does). Moral support would also be important — in a turmoil like this, the foreign opinion is seen as something of an impartial arbiter.

4. This revolution won't stop in Egypt, and Libya — it will spread further. We should take a broad view of it. The West has been late in Egypt - but we must, at least, try to influence further developments in the region. Now is the time to start working not just on Egypt's and Libya's revolutions, but on the next one, and on the one after the next. It is one matter if the revolution now spreads to Saudi Arabia, and quite another if it spreads to Iran. We must do our best to make it Iran. This, indeed, may be our last hope to snatch victory from the bearded jaws of Islamists (if you forgive the expression).

Ledeen: Wow, what a great panel! Kudos to you Jamie.

Pavel and his friend Vladimir Bukovsky have done yeoman work in uncovering the real history of the Soviet Empire, and I agree with just about everything he says. My main demurral is when he talks about "bogus revolutions" in Central and Eastern Europe. Yes, there were many of those, but here and there we saw real ones, and some of those succeeded and have endured and even flourished. Poland, Czech Republic, and Slovakia are successes, the Baltics are either doing ok or are still in play, and despite the dark clouds, I haven't given up on Ukraine and Bulgaria. I expect that General Pacepa, one of the great heroes of modern times, will give us a full picture of Romania.

Pavel makes a central point, which is largely overlooked in the frenzy of Egypt coverage (Tunisia has virtually disappeared from "reportage"): it's a regional mass movement. I have often encouraged people to read R.R. Palmer's great masterpiece *The Age of the Democratic Revolution* (written in the 1960s), which deals with the last quarter of the 18th century. In those years there were democratic revolutionary movements all over the civilized world. Most failed. So don't be surprised if most of these fail; that's the template. But we should support the real democratic forces if we know who they are.

That's another good point from Pavel. We haven't been supporting them (to our shame), so it's hard for us to distinguish the good guys from the frauds, and some of the frauds are in the pay of the Iranians and, I rather suspect, the Russians. My heart fell last week when our chief of "national intelligence" said that the Muslim Brotherhood is secular and non-violent, when the opposite is true. On the other hand, the Obama Administration (albeit not the president himself, so far as I can tell) has very strongly endorsed the Iranian opposition and denounced the regime's vicious oppression. Maybe we will yet have a policy supporting revolutionary regime change throughout the region. It started in Iran, inspired Tunisia and Egypt, and is now reverberating all over the Islamic Republic.

Finally, a bit of analytical modesty is in order. We don't know how this will play out. Things are never so bad they can't get worse, and Islamist tyrannies would be worse than the Arab authoritarian dictatorships. It's a fight, and the totalitarian Islamists are probably much better organized and much more resolute than their democratic foes…time will tell.

Darwish: I agree with Michael Ledeen that this is a great panel and I always learn a lot from Russian heroes such as him and Mr. Stroilov. I also agree with him that the current revolution in Egypt is a regional movement that will destabilize the region for quite some time. If democracy wins in the region, the instability and perhaps civil wars will last much longer than if tyranny wins. We can only wait and see, but my fear is that as tyranny falls, the chances for the chaos reaching Israel and the West increases.

Having lived during the socialist dictatorship of Nasser in Egypt, I cannot wait to read Mr. Stroilov's upcoming book. I like Mr. Stroilov's term 'socialist jihad' which indicates how Socialism and Islamism have combined in many parts of the Muslim world.

Despite some rocky history between Socialism and Islamism, they have often cooperated, fed on one another and blended and bonded. It is much more accepted for an Arab rebel to adopt Communism than a pro-Western capitalist ideology. I have heard many Arabs proudly say they are Communists and survive, but those who can dare announce they are supporters of a Judeo/Christian style democracy are nowhere to be found. The former is rarely described as infidel, but that is what the latter is called. The reason is complex but the obvious one is that both ideologies, Socialism and Islam, are totalitarian in nature and both have Western-style, free democracies as their number one enemy.

In the political chaos of the Middle East, Socialism has managed to survive and attract many followers. Almost all Muslim countries have tolerated a side-kick Communist/socialist party which was well connected to the much needed Communist block of the Soviet Union. Arab regimes have always needed the support of the Communist block militarily and politically.

Unlike Western-style democracy, Socialism was closer to Islamism producing a unique blend of the two ideologies in almost all Arab countries. Socialism has served many Muslim leaders well and provided them with yet another layer of tyranny that Islam might have missed. The flags of Iraq and Egypt for instance were very similar indicating the socialist twist of black, white and red stripes; but then to please the Islamists, Saddam tastelessly added the Allahu Akhbar in Arabic in the middle which made the flag represent the blending of the two ideologies.

The reason that Red Arab ideology can survive inside the brutal political environment of Islam was because it did not challenge Sharia Islamic law as much as Western free-style democracy. Red Arabs and Islamists were brought closer together by their Western mutual enemy. That is the state of Egyptian politics today, where the Islamist and socialists have often cooperated; however, this cooperation evaporates as soon as the Muslim Brotherhood is in control.

The self-exiled Egyptian Yusuf Al-Qaradawi arrived in Cairo after the revolution to speak at Tahrir square Friday and socialist activists were prevented from joining him on the stage after his prayer sermon. That is perhaps a message that socialists are no longer needed by the Brotherhood after the revolution. I do not predict that Socialism in Egypt will disappear with a triumph of Islamists, but the dance between the two ideologies will continue to manifest itself.

In that dynamic, the possibility for Egypt's supporters of a Western-style democracy to appear as a force is very weak. This group will immediately be branded as puppets of the West and traitors to Islamic aspirations. For such a group to gain power, tremendous change and growth in Egyptian thinking and education must take place.

Unfortunately, my guess is that the situation in Egypt will get worse before it gets better, and Egyptians need to experience the horrors of life under Islamic Sharia for a Western-style democracy to emerge. The Egyptian culture is still extremely anti-Semitic and anti-American after many decades of indoctrination and propaganda that Islam is the solution. For now the power in Egypt will be with Islamists who will adopt some socialist policies.

Pacepa: I'm also grateful to Jamie Glazov for gathering together such a great panel, and especially for persuading Michael Ledeen to attend this symposium. He is among the few Americans who really understand the three main components of this international crisis: U.S. foreign policy, Islamic terrorism, and the Middle East. For, in my view, the current wave of Islamic "revolutions," which have been long in the making, are turning against the United States primarily because our administration does not have *any* foreign policy to deal with them, does not understand Islamic terrorism, and has no clue about what to do in the Middle East.

I am not an expert on Egyptian matters, but in my other life, as a top figure in the Soviet bloc, I witnessed the Kremlin's secret effort to ignite "liberation revolutions" within the Islamic world, and to turn them against the Kremlin's main enemy, the United States. I have described this effort elsewhere ("Russian Footprints," *National Review Online*, August 24, 2006).

From my vantage point, the Kremlin's long effort to implant a rabid hatred for the U.S. in the Islamic world has now arrived at gestation for the simple reason that the current administration in Washington has been caught with its pants down. It would have been hilarious, if it were not such a deadly serious matter, that this administration could not even make up its mind on how to react *publicly* to recent events in Egypt. And it is outright incredible that the Libyan ambassador to the

U.S. should be begging Washington to condemn his own brutal tyrant, who has already killed hundreds of demonstrators in Tripoli, while our administration still does not know what to say, let alone have any semblance of a foreign policy to deal with the future oil crisis that will surely be generated by the chaotic Islamic uprisings — as things look now, we may soon be paying $10 per gallon for fuel at the pump.

We all want to see democracy succeed in Egypt, Libya and the rest of the Islamic world. The current horrors of anarchy taking place there, however, will not lead to democracy. Democratic revolutions have inspiring national leaders. The demonstrators in Cairo, Tripoli and in the rest of the Islamic countries do not have national leaders.

Just recently, Sheik Yusuf al-Qaradawi, the Muslim Brotherhood's chief theoretician, who is banned in the United States and Britain, returned to Cairo after a 50-year absence to lead Egypt's "democratic revolution." His Muslim Brotherhood's "democratic" motto: "Allah is our objective. The Prophet is our leader. The Qur'an is our law. Jihad is our way. Dying in the way of Allah is our highest hope." According to the Muslim Brotherhood's supreme guide, Mohamed Badie, these objectives could only be attained by "raising a jihadi generation that pursued death as the enemies pursued life." [1]

These Islamic "democratic revolutions" look much like the "democratic revolutions" that took place in my native Romania and the rest of Eastern Europe after World War II. I was there, and I witnessed how things went. None of them had a national leader. All were secretly instigated by Moscow, all were secretly manipulated by Moscow's men, and all were geared toward transforming those countries into Soviet satellites. They all succeeded, because the U.S. administration of that time also lacked any foreign policy that could recognize and deal with the Kremlin's export of revolution. Why were we able to win WWII, but unable to put together a foreign policy to deal with one of its most important aftermaths?

In 1943, the Kremlin manufactured evidence suggesting that Hitler was planning to kidnap President Roosevelt from the American Embassy in Tehran during the Allied Summit to be held there. As a result, Roosevelt agreed that the meetings between the three leaders be held within the "safety" of the Soviet Embassy compound, which was guarded by a large Soviet military unit. [2] Unbeknownst to the American organizers, the Soviet personnel assigned to Roosevelt were English-speaking undercover intelligence officers. With few exceptions, however, they kept their English fluency a secret, so as to be able to eavesdrop. Even given the limited technical capabilities of that day, those officers were able to provide Stalin with hourly monitoring reports on the American and British guests. That helped Stalin gain Roosevelt's confidence. "The cripple's mine!" Stalin reportedly exulted, after Roosevelt chummily referred to him as "Uncle Joe." Unfortunately, Stalin proved right.

In 1944, Gheorghe Dimitroff, president of the Comintern in Moscow, landed in Bulgaria on board a Soviet military plane, in order to lead the Bulgarian "national revolution." On February 2, 1945, he and his "democratic revolutionaries" executed, without any trial, 3 regents, 22 ministers, 68 members of parliament, and 8 advisers to King Boris, after labeling them "enemies of the revolution." During the following months, another 2,680 members of Bulgaria's government were executed by the "democratic revolutionaries," and 6,870 were imprisoned.

Washington was nonplussed. In the same manner, four other "democratic" leaders who had spent World War II in Moscow were dispatched to Eastern Europe to lead their own "national" revolutions: Walter Ulbricht to Germany; Matyas Rakosy to Hungary; Clement Gottwald to Czechoslovakia; Ana Pauker to Romania. Millions of people were killed, and many other millions perished in the "democratic" gulags subsequently created in those countries.

That was the beginning of the end for a democratic Eastern Europe — for a long while. Soon after that, the Kremlin installed a Communist government in China, and it expanded its reign over a third of the world.

President Truman learned his lesson. In 1950 he approved NSC 68/1950, a 58-page top-secret report of the U.S. National Security Council (declassified in 1975), which set forth the strategy of containment, and that became a significant weapon in the Cold War. The NSC described the situation in cataclysmic terms. "The issues that face us are momentous," the document stated, "involving the fulfillment or destruction not only of this Republic but of civilization itself." [3]

We are now facing a similar cataclysmic situation, and we can only hope that President Obama will put together a contemporary version of NSC 68/1950. If not, the American voters will have to take the matter into their own hands and treat it the same way they recently handled the Democratic Party's ill-conceived plans to redistribute our country's wealth — the Democrats were booted out of positions that let them decide where to spend our money.

Americans are a proud people who love their country, and they will do everything in their power to defend it. They know that the peace and freedom of the world depend, as they have for the whole last century, upon the leadership of the United States.

Let's make no mistake: If American leadership goes, so will world peace and stability.

FP: Thanks, Mihai Pacepa.

So what should a contemporary version of NSC 68/1950 toward the Middle East say and do?

Pavel Stroilov?

Stroilov: As a matter of principle, Jamie, I don't want to answer this question. A strategy of containment may be necessary after we have lost - and even then, I'd prefer a counter-offensive. But I do not accept we have already lost. There has been a lot of news from the Middle East; some of it (alas, little) good news. The best, of course, is the revival of protests in Iran. The West must support this in every possible way and support strongly. A change of regime in Iran would change everything in the region. But even the very fact that 'the other Iran' (to adapt a phrase from Russian politics) is seen to be alive and kicking has a huge significance. I agree with Michael: Iran is absolutely central to the whole regional revolution. If there is a major confrontation between the Iranian regime and the Iranian people, regimes and peoples across the region will have to take sides. And it would be very difficult now to manipulate, say, Egyptians to support a regime against the people, contrary to their own recent experience.

A crisis in Iran inevitably means a crisis of Islamism across the region: the Islamists will face a painful dilemma where they cannot defend Iran and cannot condemn it. Remember what happened to communists in the West whenever there was a crisis in the Soviet empire? So it is true to say that the future of the Middle East — nay, the world — is being decided now on the streets of Tehran.

Containment of the Islamic Caliphate may become a subject of some future symposium, which I hope will never need to happen. Now is the time to think of attack, not defense.

Quite rightly, we look at the revolutions of the past to learn lessons for today's Middle East. Let me sum up the historic parallels drawn in this symposium and elsewhere:

- *Russia 1917*: the revolution begins as democratic, then goes increasingly socialist, and ends in a coup where the best organised and most radical group captures power. Can Islamic Bolsheviks win in Egypt? There is certainly a high risk of that. Next in this scenario comes a long and bloody civil war, because the nation won't just surrender its newly won freedom. Russian Whites lost because they were betrayed by the West. If it comes to an Egyptian civil war, the West ought to do better than that.

- *East Europe 1948:* (an original and very perceptive parallel just drawn by Gen. Pacepa): a series of bogus revolutions across the region, orchestrated by Moscow and bringing the region under Moscow's control. Indeed, there are signs that the Middle East revolutions may be coordinated. Each develops along a similar scenario. Each has this odd feature of having no leaders. The sequence is suspiciously logical, too: it starts in the least important country in the region (apologies to all Tunisians), then copied in the most important country (Egypt), and that sets the pace for the entire Arab world (or at least, its socialist part). Who, if anyone, is behind it all? The operation seems too massive for any of the usual suspects. Obviously, Iran is a big player, and I share Michael's suspicions they may be in league with Moscow in this game (as we know they are in some others). But it does not look like they initiated this revolution, even though staging a dress rehearsal in an unimportant testing area at first has always been a KGB trademark. Who else? The Muslim Brotherhood Comintern? Perhaps... Gaddafi blames Al Qaeda, which sounds like cheap propaganda. Mubarak hinted at a Western conspiracy — I wish he was right, but... We badly need a credible conspiracy theory — has anybody got one?

- *Egypt 1952*: a national-socialist military coup overthrows a pro-Western constitutional monarchy. Same place, but a totally misleading parallel. The Kingdom of Egypt was a British-style parliamentary system with free elections, free press, and a very corrupt political class (alas, democracies are also vulnerable to this disease). It was against the faults of democracy, not of tyranny, that Nasser and comrades rebelled. That was not a popular revolution — it was a Lenin-style coup by a small, conspiratorial, professional group, overthrowing a weak democracy to establish a totalitarian regime. What is happening today is the opposite of that, indeed, a counter-revolution to that.

- *Iran 1979*: a revolution welcomed by the West as democratic, which quickly turned out to be Islamist. An obvious, likely, pessimistic scenario today. But there is more to it: for Moscow had been preparing that revolution for over 30 years, and then it was hijacked in an extraordinary twist of history. Major Vladimir Kuzichkin, the KGB man in Tehran in charge of the Soviet fifth column, secretly worked for MI6. He gave them all the names, all the threads; the British shared that with the Shah's secret police; then its archives were captured by Islamists. With this information, the Islamists quickly rounded up their red allies, and hijacked the whole revolution. So I re-iterate my golden rule for revolutions: *follow the secret archives*. They can work miracles. It is important to know who started this revolution; it is more important to know who will hijack it. The archives are the key to that. If made public, they will work for democracy against the Islamists and socialists. If either or both of the enemies get there first, God help us.

- *East Europe 1989*: the most complicated scenario of all. Originally, it was planned as a bogus revolution, to pre-empt genuinely democratic ones. It went out of control; but it failed only partly. The worst trick was the so-called 'roundtables', whereby the regime could select the most convenient opponents to share power with in the transitional period. That corrupted the new democracies from the very start, and undermined the recovery enormously. But Michael is right: at least, few exceptions aside, it is still democracy and a recovery in East Europe. In the Middle East, it can be much worse because the Red Arabs would reserve the 'opposition' side of their roundtables for the Islamists.

The common denominator of all these revolutions is this. Each time, there are some decent democratic forces present with greater or lesser chances of success. Each time, the West betrays them. Alas, this is likely to happen again, in this awfully typical 20th century scenario of replacing a Hitler with a Stalin or vice versa. This is likely; this is not inevitable. We should prepare for the worst. We should do all we can to prevent it.

Thank you Jamie for organizing this, and especially for the privilege of sharing the platform with such distinguished experts.

Ledeen: Thanks to everyone for their remarkable insights. This conversation could easily be expanded into an invaluable little book. I like Pavel's question about conspiracy theories and our need for a new one. As it happens, we have one: the social media did it. And who controls the social media? The Iranian tyrants think they know: the Jews, ergo the West (run by the Jews) plus the Zionist Entity (wall to wall Jews).

Funnily, the Iranian Green Movement knows that the West has abandoned the Iranian democratic revolution long since, so they have had to create their own conspiracy, or, if you prefer, their own network. And reflect on this: as the regime has become increasingly efficient at cutting off (modern) communications — from satellite broadcasts to email to Facebook and Twitter — the opposition is reverting to older forms of communications, frequently involving couriers. And there is a military counterpart to this; I just read an article in the London Telegraph telling of the Chinese Army training a hundred thousand carrier pigeons for military coms in the event their computer-driven network gets fried during combat.

I don't like to call the current turmoil "a revolution," because as yet we have not seen structural change. Not even in Tunisia. So far "it" consists in the removal of a couple of leaders, demonstrations galore, and an internal war in Libya. We're a long way from revolution. And since our governments aren't very good at thinking about more than one problem at a time, let alone acting, and nothing remotely approaching a strategy for "it" has been enunciated or started. Meanwhile, the other actors in the region, like the Saudis, the Syrians and the Iranians, are very much engaged on the ground. I am told that more than 25 top Iranian Quds Force officers are working out of the Iranian Embassy in Tripoli, for example, and you can be sure that the Saudis are assisting their friends in Egypt.

It's a terrific opportunity for us. We are the one truly successful revolutionary country in the world, and the Middle Easterners certainly know that well. We could do a lot. The big problem is our president. Obama doesn't believe in American exceptionalism, and he rather thinks that we are a reactionary imperial power that has to be cut down to size. Can he learn otherwise? Doubtful. Kissinger once said that top leaders leave government with the same culture they carried in, because there is no time for serious reappraisal of basic convictions.

Still, we are very close to seeing a major tectonic shift in Iran. The regime is very frightened-as the arrests of Mousavi and Karroubi demonstrate and the opposition is fighting back more and more. These things are impossible to measure. You have to be there to smell the odor of panic. But the signs are there. If Iran were to fall, the whole world would change.

But if you're a betting man, you'd bet that things will not work out well; that's the historical pattern. Machiavelli: "Man is more inclined to do evil than to do good."

Sigh.

FP: Words of wisdom Michael Ledeen. Nonie Darwish, your turn.

Darwish: I like Mr. Pacepa's statement "to ignite 'liberation revolutions' within the Islamic world, and to turn them against the Kremlin's main enemy, the United States." The uprisings and revolutions going on today in Egypt, Libya and other Arab countries, appear wonderful at the surface. However, under the radar, there are other forces and motivations. Today's Islamic revolutions are not, as in the old days, manipulated by the Kremlin, but by Islamism. Jihadists and Red Arabs have been working against Arab regimes for a long time and the true reason is not because Mubarak and others are dictators.

Muslim dictators are rejected by Islamists because they are standing in the way of Jihadist confrontations with not only Israel, but more importantly with the United States. Islamic jihad has been restrained and choked by Mubarak and some other Muslim leaders. As to the unstable Gaddafi, he has revealed fear and an inability to stand up to the U.S. when he surrendered his WMD after the Iraq war.

Today's Islamists want to get rid of Arab dictators who no longer want to engage in jihad against the West and Israel. Jihadists feel they now have a golden opportunity in the political atmosphere in America today, especially with the Obama administration in office. They want to seize the moment. Many in the Muslim world believe that the Obama administration is on their side and too weak to act aggressively in the best interests of America. This opportunity might be very hard in two or six years under another administration. The moment is here for the Islamists, for they also have a growing assertive and very political and vocal Muslim minorities in the West, together with the existence of sleeper cells and home grown Islamic terrorists whose loyalty is dedicated to the Muslim world and its agenda.

In case of any future confrontations with an outside Islamist threat, America will have to deal at the same time with a fifth column: internal Islamic terrorism. The Muslim uprisings to overthrow dictators that we are seeing today are not just motivated by the brutality of the tyrants to some, but more importantly because these dictators are blocking the jihadist aspirations against America, Europe and Israel. Islamism and Red Arabs feel the time is ripe to confront the United States and they must act now.

There are factors within the U.S. that are also inviting outside hostility, especially from Islamists. America is sharply divided against itself. The world today is no longer divided between Red/Totalitarian regime nations vs. free Western Capitalist nations. The Cold War divide of nations of East vs. West, tyranny vs. freedom, is not what the U.S. is facing now. The divide now exists *within* nations. America might have won the Cold War, but that war has now been replaced with a war within the boundaries of America over the same philosophical values that divided the two superpowers in the Cold War.

The Cold War is now residing within America and its destructive dynamics are raging in full gear dividing Americans against each other rather than against what should be their mutual enemy: Islamism. The number one enemy of the Socialist Left in America, which denies there is any threat from Islamism, is the traditional Judeo/Christian culture of America and the American capitalist system as we know it. In this internal war going on in America today, Islam is the winner and the current revolutions in the Middle East are clearing the way for their dictators who are considered the stumbling block for jihad to be activated in full swing. Removing Mubarak and perhaps the Saudi regime will certainly expedite the pending confrontation with the West and Israel.

The uprisings in the Middle East are being done in the name of freedom and democracy, but what they will achieve is the new phase in American history of war on the outside and from within. The age of jihad and civil wars has begun.

Pacepa: What a great symposium. We seem to all be on the same wave length. I agree with Michael Ledeen that its substance deserves to be expanded in a book, and I hope he will write it.

We are certainly not dealing with Islamic "democratic revolutions." The evidence shows that we are facing a military-ideological war carried out with Soviet/Russian weapons by Islamic fundamentalists, who seem to be dreaming of erasing Israel from the map and building a multinational Islamic empire that would control the rest of the world by manipulating the Arabs' vast oil and natural gas resources.

During the 2006 Lebanon War, also called the 2006 Israel-Hezbollah War, most of the Hezbollah weapons cases captured by the Israeli military forces were marked: Customer: Ministry of Defense, Syria. Supplier: KBP, Tula, Russia. [4]

The European Union-sponsored Gulf Research Centre, which provides journalists an inside view of the Gulf Center Region, found out that Hezbollah's military forces were heavily armed with "Soviet-made Katyusha-122 rocket, which carries a 33-lb warhead." Hezbollah is also armed with Russian-designed and Iranian-made Fajr-5 rockets with a range of 47 miles, enabling it to strike the Israeli port of Haifa, and with the Russian-designed Zelzal-1 rockets, which could reach Tel Aviv. The Gulf Research Center established that Hezbollah also possessed the infamous Russian Scud missiles, obtained from Syria, as well as the Russian anti-tank missiles AT-3Sagger, AT-4Spigot, AT-5 Spandrel, AT-13 Saxhorn-2, and AT-14Spriggan Kornet. [5]

Now let me return to the need for the U.S. to have a contemporary NSC 68/1950. That 58-page strategy for winning the Cold War devised a powerful *ideological* offensive against Communism, which was a deadly threat "not only to this Republic but to civilization itself." [6] NSC 68/1950 argued that the propaganda used by the "forces of imperialistic communism" could be overcome only by the "plain, simple, unvarnished truth. [7] The Voice of America, Radio Free Europe, and, the following year, Radio Liberation (soon to become Radio Liberty) became part of the U.S. ideological offensive. For those who still wonder how the U.S. won the Cold War, here is the view of the second post-Communism president of Romania, Emil Constantinescu:

Radio Free Europe has been a lot more important than the armies and the most sophisticated missiles. The "missiles" that destroyed Communism were launched from Radio Free Europe, and this was Washington's most important investment during the Cold War. [8]

The missiles that will destroy radical Islamic fundamentalism and its anti-American terrorism should be fired by a new U.S. *ideological* offensive similar to that which helped us win the Cold War. We are facing a similar cataclysmic situation, one that cannot be overcome by abandoning our own allies in the Islamic world, or by "no fly zones." The Kremlin spent half a century spreading the lie throughout the Islamic world that the U.S. was a war-mongering, Zionist country financed by Jewish money and run by a rapacious "Council of the Elders of Zion" (Moscow's derisive epithet for the U.S. Congress), the aim of which was to ignite a new war in order to transform the rest of the world into a Jewish fiefdom. We need to put that lie to rest by again spreading the "plain, simple, unvarnished truth."

Unfortunately, President Obama does not seem to be a Truman. So, I end by repeating what I said at the beginning of our symposium: Americans are proud people who love their country, and they will do everything in their power to defend it. If their president continues simply to vote "present," the American voters will take the matter into their own hands.

FP: Nonie Darwish, Pavel Stroilov, Lt. General Pacepa and Michael Ledeen, thank you for joining Frontpage Symposium.

Notes:

[1] Arnaud De Borchgrave, "Gullible Amnesia," *The Washington Times*, February 22, 2011.
[2] At that time Iran was "protected" by Soviet troops, which together with British troops had invaded the country in August 1941 in "Operation Countenance," to secure Persian oil fields and supply lines for the Soviets fighting against Axis forces on the Eastern Front. The British troops withdrew in September 1941. The Soviets refused to recall their troops until May 1946.
[3] Gary B. Nash, Julie Roy Jeffrey, John R. Howe, Allen F. Davis, Allan M. Winkler, Charlene Mires, and Carla Gardina Pestana, *The American People, Concise Edition Creating a Nation and a Society*, combined volume, 6th Edition (New York, Longman, 2007).
[4] Adrian Blomfield, "Israel humbled by arms from Iran," *The Telegraph*, August 15, 2006.

[5] Paul Weitz, "Hezbollah, Already a Capable Military Force, Makes Full Use of Civilian Shields and Media Manipulation", *JINSA Online*, August 12, 2006, retrieved from the original (http://web.archive.org/web/20080107090241/http://www.jinsa.org/art icles/articles.html/function/view/categoryid/158/documentid/3504/hist ory/3,2360,655,158,3504), on January 9, 2008.

[6] Gary B. Nash, Julie Roy Jeffrey, John R. Howe, Allen F. Davis, Allan M. Winkler, Charlene Mires, and Carla Gardina Pestana, *The American People, Concise Edition Creating a Nation and a Society*, combined volume, 6th Edition (New York, Longman, 2007).

[7] Elizabeth E. Spalding, *The First Cold Warrior: Harry Truman, Containment, and the Remaking of Liberal Internationalism* 1 (University Press of Kentucky, 2006).

[8] Nestor Ratesh, "Radio Free Europe's Impact in Romania During The Cold War," prepared form the Conference on Cold War Broadcasting Impact, AStanford, CA, October 13-15, 2004.

[Jamie Glazov, "Symposium: The Red Arabs," *Frontpagemag.com*, March 11, 2011.]

Part II: The Evil Empire

[3] The Shadow of the KGB

Frontpage Symposium has gathered a distinguished panel to discuss the nature of Putin's authoritarian regime and its true roots. Our guests today are:

Adam Burakowski, the author of *Carpathian Genius. The Dictatorship of Nicolae Ceauşescu 1965-1989* and co-author of *1989 - Autumn of Nations*, a book that compares the process of Communism's fall in different states of Central and Eastern Europe. He received a Ph.D. from the Warsaw-based Institute of Political Studies of Polish Academy of Sciences.

Vladimir Bukovsky, a former leading Soviet dissident and author of *To Build a Castle* and *Judgment in Moscow*.

Pavel Stroilov, a historian who smuggled a vast secret archive of the Gorbachev era out of Russia.

Lt. General Ion Mihai Pacepa, the highest official ever to have defected from the former Soviet bloc. His first book, *Red Horizons,* was republished in 27 languages. In March 2010, *The Washington Post* recommended it to be included on the list of books that should be read in schools. A commemorative edition of *Red Horizons* was just issued in Romania to mark 20 years since Ceauşescu was executed at the end of a trial where most of the accusations came out of this book. In April 2010, Pacepa's latest book, *Programmed to Kill: Lee Harvey Oswald, the Soviet KGB, and the Kennedy Assassination,* was prominently displayed at the annual meeting of the Organization of American Historians held in Washington D.C., as a "superb new paradigmatic work" and a "must read" for "everyone interested in the assassination of President Kennedy."

Robert Buchar, an associate professor and author of the Cinematography Program at Columbia College in Chicago. A political refugee from former Czechoslovakia, he is the producer of the documentary, *Velvet Hangover*, which is about Czech New Wave filmmakers, how they survived the period of "normalization" and their reflections on the so-called Velvet Revolution of 1989. He is the author of the new book, *And Reality be Damned... Undoing America: What The Media Didn't Tell You About the End of the Cold War and Fall of Communism in Europe.* The book is based on a documentary feature he is currently working on, *The Collapse of Communism: The Untold Story.*

Konstantin Preobrazhenskiy, a Senior Fellow at the Gerard Group International and a former KGB agent who became one of the KGB's harshest critics. He is the author of seven books about the KGB and Japan, two of which are *The Spy Who Loved Japan* and *KGB/FSB's New Trojan Horse: Americans of Russian Descent.*

J. R. Nyquist, writes a column on global strategic issues for Financial Sense Online (financialsense.com), and is also president of the Strategic Crisis Center, Inc. (StrategicCrisis.com).

Olga Velikanova, an Assistant Professor of Russian History at the University of North Texas. She was among the first scholars to work with declassified Communist Party and secret police archives. Her research about everyday Stalinism, the cult of Lenin and Russian popular opinion has been broadcast by the BBC, Finnish and Russian radio and TV, as well as the History Channel in Canada. She is the author of *Making of an Idol: On Uses of Lenin, The Public Perception of the Cult of Lenin Based on the Archival Materials* and *The Myth of the Besieged Fortress: Soviet Mass Perception in the 1920s-1930s.* She is a recipient of many awards from different international research foundations.

and

David Satter, a senior fellow of the Hudson Institute and a visiting scholar at the Johns Hopkins University Nitze School of Advanced International Studies (SAIS). He was Moscow correspondent of the *Financial Times* of London from 1976 to 1982, during the height of the Soviet totalitarian period and he is the author of *Age of Delirium: the Decline and Fall of the Soviet Union,* which is being made into a documentary film. His most recent work is *Darkness at Dawn: The Rise of the Russian Criminal State.*

FP: Adam Burakowski, Vladimir Bukovsky, Pavel Stroilov, Lt. General Ion Mihai Pacepa, Robert Buchar, Konstantin Preobrazhenskiy, J. R. Nyquist, Olga Velikanova and David Satter, welcome to Frontpage Symposium.

During most of the last century, U.S. policies were heavily centered around the Soviet Union, and yet today our government seems to almost ignore Russia, even though it is still an aggressive dictatorship armed with nuclear weapons.

Mihai Pacepa, you have provided a profound foundation for our discussion by giving Frontpage the following statement: "The United States spent forty years and trillions of dollars to fight Soviet Communism, whose criminal political police killed over 70 million people within the Soviet bloc alone. Now that same Communist political police — with a new nameplate at its door — is running the Kremlin, and Russia is seen as our friend. Over 6,000 former officers of the KGB, which shot millions to keep Soviet Communism in power, are now members of Russia's federal and local governments, and nearly half of all other top governmental positions are held by other former KGB-ists. [1] The United States would certainly not even think about establishing diplomatic relations with a Germany run by former Gestapo officers. In 2002, however, NATO welcomed Russia as an honorary member and junior partner into that alliance set up by the United States for the purpose of containing Soviet expansion. There is still a widely popular belief in the United States and Western Europe that the evil Soviet legacy was uprooted in 1991, when the Soviet Union was abolished, just as the Nazi legacy was extirpated in 1945, when World War II ended. But was it?"

Take it from here.

Gen. Pacepa: No, it wasn't. To explain why, we should first correctly define the Soviet Union, which has been regularly described as a dictatorship based on the mass appeal of the Marxist ideology and on the strong arm of the Communist Party. In other words, the Soviet Union has been regarded, both in the West and within its own borders, as a form of government that, although dictatorial, ruled the country through a political party and based its decisions on a political ideology. Only a handful of people who were working in extremely close proximity to the top Soviet and East European rulers, as I once did, knew that after Lenin died, Soviet Union devolved into a one-man totalitarian dictatorship.

Stalin, who succeeded Lenin, grew up as the son of a drunken cobbler in the far reaches of the Transcaucasus, and he was unencumbered by any experience with Marxism, Western social democracy or party politics. For Stalin, Lenin's Party was just a "yakkity-yak," a place where people sat around beating their gums. Stalin hated public debate; secrecy was the element in which he thrived, like a fish in water. To Stalin the normal structure for a country was the autocratic Russian police state, and he started running the Soviet Union secretly, with the help of his political police.

Stalin began his reign by ordering his political police to secretly expel his main rival for the Soviet throne, Leon Trotsky, from the country without letting anybody find out about it. When the deed was done, Stalin gave his political police a *"pokhvalnaya gramota"*, i.e., a *magna cum laude.* Trotsky and his guards were the only passengers on board the Soviet ship *Iskra* when it sailed out of Odessa bound for Istanbul in January 1929, carrying Trotsky into exile.

Stalin had already changed the name of his political police from *Cheka* to State Political Directorate (*Gosudarstvennoye Politicheskoye Upravleniye*, GPU), a revealingly descriptive name, and he turned his new instrument of power against the Communist Party itself. Within a few years, all members of Lenin's Politburo at the time of the 1917 Communist Revolution were shot as Western spies. The man named by Lenin in his testament as the most capable of the younger generation, Georgy Pyatakov, was also shot. With the party under his belt, Stalin ordered his political police to frame as German spies the Red Army's chief of staff, Marshal Mikhail Tukhachevsky, the man responsible for modernizing the Red Army, and seven other top military commanders. After their hasty execution, Stalin's secret police liquidated 70 out of the 80 members of the Supreme Military Council and an estimated 35,000 other Red Army officers.

Once firmly seated in the saddle, Stalin promoted the chief of his political police, Nikolay Yezhov, as his main lieutenant and began an era of terror unequaled since Ivan the Terrible. In all, some seven million people lost their lives during those purges, including most of the Soviet Communists who had fought for Lenin's revolution and numerous foreign Communist leaders as well. Yezhov's name has been preserved for history in the word *yezhovshchina*, the popular name for the cruel purges of 1936-38. In a truly Byzantine scenario, those who had carried out the purges and could claim that they had only acted on Stalin's orders were themselves then liquidated. By the time the purges came to an end in December 1938, thousands of political police officers had also disappeared. Yezhov himself, the ugly dwarf who gave his name to the whole *yezhovshchina*, was never heard from again after January 1939.

In 1978, when I broke with Communism, the Communist Party played no greater role in the Soviet Union — or in the rest of the Soviet bloc — than did Lenin's embalmed corpse in the Kremlin mausoleum. Lenin's Communism was transformed into a *samoderzhaviye*, the traditional Russian form of totalitarian autocracy in which a feudal lord ruled the country with the help of his personal political police. After the August 1991 *coup* in Moscow, the Communist Party lost its official power as well, and nobody within the country really missed it. Until Lenin came along, Russia had never had a real political party anyway.

The Soviet political police, however, survived, by repeatedly changing its name-from KGB to MSB, to MB, to TsSR, to FSK, to FSB-to make the West and Russia forget that, in the end, it was the same Stalinist political police, which had killed over 20 million people to protect a feudal government in the middle of the 20th century.

During the old Cold War, the KGB was a state within a state. Now the KGB, rechristened FSB, *is* the state. The Soviet Union had one KGB officer for every 428 citizens. The "democratic" Russia has almost twice as many: one police officer for every 297 citizens. [2] The fate of millions of people killed or terrorized by the Soviet political police is still locked up behind the Lubyanka's walls. Hangmen do not incriminate themselves.

KGB General Aleksandr Sakharovsky, who headed the Soviet espionage service, the PGU, for an unprecedented 14 years, repeatedly told me that, "every society reflects its own past." Sakharovsky, who was a Russian to the marrow of his bones, believed that someday "our socialist camp" might wear an entirely different face, Marxism might have been turned upside down, and even the Communist Party itself might have become history, but that would not matter. Both Marxism and the party were foreign organisms that had been introduced into the Russian body, and sooner or later they would have to be rejected in any case. One thing, though, was certain to remain unchanged for as long as the Russian motherland was still in existence: "our *gosbezopasnost*" (the state security service). Sakharovsky used to point out that "our *gosbezopasnost*" had kept Russia alive for the past four hundred years, "our *gosbezopasnost*" would guide her helm for the next five hundred years, "our *gosbezopasnost*" would win the war with "our number one enemy, American imperialzionism," and "our *gosbezopasnost*" would eventually make Russia the leader of the world.

So far, Sakharovsky has proved to be a dependable prophet. His successor at the PGU, Vladimir Kryuchkov, who later became chairman of the KGB and authored the August 1991 coup that briefly deposed Soviet leader Mikhail Gorbachev, clearly shared the same fanatical belief in Russia's *gosbezopasnost*. Kryuchkov's successor, Yevgeny Primakov, who was an undercover KGB officer under Sakharovsky, rose to become Russia's prime minister. Most notably, Vladimir Putin was the very chief of the entire *gosbezopasnost* before being appointed Russia's president. It is like democratizing Germany with Gestapo officers at its helm.

It will not be easy to break Russia's five-century-old tradition of *samoderzhaviye*. Nevertheless, man would not have learned to walk on the moon, if he had not first studied what the moon was really made of and where it lay in the universe. I hope this Symposium will help.

Satter: I agree with Gen. Pacepa that Russia has not repudiated the legacy of the Soviet Union. In fact, there was little attempt. A few statues were removed (although there was an effort to return the statue of Dzerzhinsky to Lyubanskaya Square in 2002), a couple of cities were renamed as well as a few streets but Russian society never faced the meaning of communist crimes and the roots of Communism in centuries-old Russian traditions.

I think there were three things that needed to be done (but were not done) in order to free Russia of the legacy of Communism. First, there needed to be a juridical condemnation of Communism. The 1991 law on rehabilitation, which was passed just as the Soviet Union was about to disappear, is the only place in Russian legislation that it is possible to find such a condemnation. It does not exist anywhere else although there was a need on the part of the state to pass broad judgment on this period of Russian history and to make an attempt to condemn, if only posthumously, those who played key roles in it.

Second, there needed to be an explicit apology from the government to the victims of Communism, acknowledging their suffering and the state's responsibility. This also was not done. The victims were "rehabilitated." The state absolved them of guilt and granted them some meager privileges but at all times it was the state which exercised the right to forgive. At the same time, the state made no effort after the perestroika period, to discover and memorialize the places of mass burial. When they were found and memorialized, it was due to the efforts of private individuals (and, in a few cases, local governments.)

Finally, the Russian state needed to make public the lists of KGB informers as was done in East Germany. Of course, this would have destroyed relationships and damaged peoples' lives. But the alternative was to preserve the institution of informers for use in the future and to allow society to fool itself about the extent to which the regime planted informers everywhere. Ultimately, revealing the names of informers who played such a terrible role in Soviet history would have had a purifying effect on the moral atmosphere, making it much harder for a future regime to resort to totalitarian methods again.

Taken together, these steps would have constituted a real break with the past. But they were not taken. Instead, the psychological patterns of hundreds of years were able to reassert themselves, in particular, the traditional Russian disregard for the value of the individual. It was therefore a sad inevitability that the security services, which enforce the degradation of the individual, would come to the fore, as they did in a remarkably short period of time.

Burakowski: Like Gen. Pacepa, I also come from a Central-East European state, which suffered under communism and Russian occupation for a long time — and the legacy of this sad period is still alive in both our countries. I agree with Gen. Pacepa that the world is paying too little attention to what is happening in Russia. Since the Soviet Union was dissolved, and its "international" emblem with hammer and sickle over the globe (stressing global aspirations of Communism) was discarded, the world has not only forgotten about communist crimes (even the very recent ones), but also started underestimating Russia itself. Nowadays the world treats Russia as just one of the not particularly important countries, like e.g. Mexico or Saudi Arabia. In my opinion this attitude helps the Kremlin rulers in their game of erasing the past.

The steps proposed by Mr. Satter are necessary if Russia wants to one day become a truly democratic and — which is probably more easy — peaceful state. But who would be willing to implement them? Are there any political or even social forces in Russia that are interested in condemning the communist crimes? Of course there are, but in my opinion they are too weak now, as they have been for the last twenty years.

How the Russian government deals with the recent past is clearly visible in the case of the Smolensk plane crash, where Polish President Lech Kaczyński and about ninety other high-ranking state officials, military officers and politicians died in conditions that are yet to be properly investigated. The catastrophe is treated by the Russian officials as a thing of the remote past, even though the event took place as recently as April 10th this year. The remnants of the wreck still lie in Smolensk and the Russians hardly pay any attention to it. "This is the past and the past should be immediately forgotten" reads the hidden message of the Kremlin rulers.

Nyquist: The real question before us has two parts. First, what is the nature of the current regime in Moscow? Second, what are its intentions? According to Gen. Pacepa, the Soviet regime devolved into a one-man totalitarian dictatorship. The methods used by the dictator and his secret police were criminal, including: unprecedented confiscations of property, kangaroo courts, and mass executions. This dictatorship system might be described as a gang of thieves, rapists and murders. Obviously these thieves, as a class, will not peacefully part with their ill-gotten gains. And they have many tricks for holding onto power. While the West grew comfortable, they advanced in the science of deception and destruction. I completely agree with Gen. Pacepa and David Satter's suggestion that the Soviet "legacy" continued after 1991. There is no doubt of this. We must not deceive ourselves or evade the truth. Removing the Soviet label from the Soviet system did not change the criminal nature of the country's ruling personalities and structures, especially the secret police.

Having established that Russia is run by a criminal regime, we must ask what this regime's intentions are? *This is the key question.* And this is the question our leaders and pundits continually evade. It was the late SVR defector, Sergei Tretyakov, who warned us (only a short while ago) that the Russian KGB leadership wants to destroy America. He said that Americans were naive about Russia. And he was in a position to know. We have other warnings, as well, from Russian patriots who see what has happened. Modern history has taught us what criminal states are like, and what we may expect from them. It is disappointing that Western statesmen have formed a partnership with Moscow. It is disappointing to see the U.S. president flying to Moscow, pretending that the KGB will keep its bargains. This is a very dangerous game, and I don't believe our leaders know what they're doing.

Burakowski and David Satter suggest that the Soviet "legacy" continued after 1991. There is no doubt of this. We must not deceive ourselves or evade the truth. Removing the Soviet label from the Soviet system did not change the criminal nature of the country's ruling personalities and structures, especially the secret police.

Preobrazhenskiy: I also wish the list of the KGB collaborators were published. But I am afraid it will be too long. Everybody appointed to a more or less important position has to become a KGB agent. Oh, how many world-famous names we would see on this list! All spheres of human activity would be presented, from the Russian Orthodox Church to the criminal world. The KGB has informants everywhere.

Of course, the most honorable place must be occupied by the outstanding Soviet scholars. Yes, very many of them were involved in scientific and technical espionage, managed by the Directorate "T" of the KGB Intelligence. Some world-famous academicians were signing their reports there using code names.

Yes, the glorious Soviet Academy of Sciences was established mostly for espionage. All the administrative staff of its "international department" has consisted of officers of the Direct rate "T". Those officers were dispatching Soviet scholars to the West for studies and international congresses. Only one formality was required for it: to become a KGB collaborator. It was hard to refuse: "You do not want to help your Motherland? If you are not a patriot, you cannot go abroad."

Now, many of the outstanding Russian scholars have moved to the West. But their personal files have been kept in Lubyanka forever. And if we touch the mammoth Russian Army? There are hundreds of thousands of KGB informants. Shall we find enough paper for our list? Many of them would put their names on our list voluntarily, with pride.

Some people in Moscow have proudly confessed to me about their being KGB agents. They considered it a patriotic duty. Most of them were the priests of the Moscow Patriarchate. And now these priests have come to America after merging with ROCOR, Russian Orthodox Church Abroad, in 2007. It was a brilliant victory for the KGB. And I heard how one of their bishops was telling his American flock the following: "To be Orthodox means to be a Russian patriot." How many of such "patriots" would come to our list very soon?

But why are we looking for the KGB collaborators only among Russians? There are plenty of them in the West too. Oh, how many "sincere friends of the Soviet Union," "progressive politicians" and "independent Western journalists" would find their names on our list. But what shall we do with the thousands of Japanese and German prisoners of WW2, recruited by NKVD in the prison camps in Siberia? They were forced to become agents using hunger and tortures; but still in the post-war era, they have greatly promoted Soviet influence in Germany and Japan. Some of them kept working for the KGB almost until today. In the KGB archive, I have read many denouncements written by the Japanese prisoners in calligraphic characters: "Sergeant Yamamoto spoke with disrespect about Comrade Stalin and said that there is hunger in the Soviet Union".

And what about some African political activists and leaders? Many of them have studied in the USSR. Did KGB recruit them or miss these potential recruits? The KGB Intelligence always had a department covering the collaborators among heads of foreign states. It was not so hard to achieve: many Western politicians were recruited in their younger years. For this purpose, the KGB founded a special youth organization, "Sputnik." On paper, it was affiliated with Komsomol, a Communist youth organization, but in fact it totally belonged to the KGB. It has invited thousands of young Western politicians to visit the USSR and enjoy life there for free.

Mostly they were socialists and other leftists, but conservatives were involved as well. Having been brought up in the delicate Western society, they easily got into all KGB catches like prostitutes, illegal currency operations and other pleasant temptations. But there was one more thing — a clear obligation by the KGB to help a recruited young Western politician to become a high level person in his country as a KGB agent. And this promise mostly came true, in many countries.

Recently, Putin made the tactic much clearer: he is personally working with foreign leaders as an intelligence officer. This is only a small part of the categories of KGB collaborators. In fact, they cover a certain part of the world population.

The idea of disclosing the list appeared in the early 1990s, almost together with the court action against the Soviet Communist Party. How happy and hopeful I was, when it began in 1992. But, to my bitter disappointment, it vanished very quickly. It was destroyed by the burden of the enormous Communist lobby in Russia, as I guessed. But there was one more side interested in its closing: the democratic West. Its secret contacts with Soviets could cause a scandal. Vladimir Bukovsky has told about it in one of his TV interviews. Well, in case of necessity, the West can find understanding with Russian governments much easier than with Russian dissidents.

Today, the West is kneeling before Russia. It is very vulnerable to Russian influence, dependent on Russian gas and oil, infiltrated with Russian spies. It has shown its spiritual weakness. That is why it has stopped defending Russian dissidents and fighting for human rights in Russia.

Russian influence has penetrated even into our symposium. We are speaking about "former" KGB officers ruling Russia. Why are we so sure that they are "former"? Did they show us their retirement documents? For the KGB officer to become a "former" means to become poor, to get deprived of service privileges. They are all acting, including Putin. His age allows him to stay on the military service. But Russian propaganda has made us repeat these lies automatically, like parrots.

Putin makes the West suffer his painful tests one by one. The latest one was the strange death of Polish President Kaczynski in Russia this summer. There were very many suspicious circumstances in this plane crash, but the West has preferred not to irritate Russia because of Poland. The West has "swallowed" this incident, as Russians say. What will it swallow next?

Velikanova: As a professional historian I would like to note that recent historical studies introduce a much richer and more polychromatic picture of the history of Stalinism and the political police than the former security officers in this symposium present in our discussion. Their opinions confirm that conspiratorial thinking remains the core of the security police mentality even among its former members who no longer serve the institution. Unfortunately, numerous KGB officers, who in the 1990s entered state and administrative positions, brought with them this pattern of black and white thinking to modern Russian politics.

We can see the evidence of such simplified views in domestic Russian politics (the proclivity to solve problems by force, not through negotiations and compromise, spy-trials in Putin's Russia, witch-hunting on gastarbeiters, etc.) and in foreign affairs (suspicion in relations with neighboring countries and the search for enemies, be it the U.S. or Georgia). I do not think that a confrontational approach preached by a discussant, who regrets that the U.S. president negotiates with Moscow, is a productive approach in contemporary international relations. The old proverb "bad peace is better than good war" represents a more constructive and flexible approach.

In regard to international pressure on the Russian government, the Russian liberal opposition may expect that the West declares its position in some crucial collisions like Khodorkovsky's affair, Litvinenko's case or journalists' and human rights activists' murders, but the transformation of the political climate in the country is a domestic affair and a job for the opposition itself. In regards to domestic politics, I agree with the position of Dr. Satter, especially about the necessity of the judicial condemnation of Communism. But such a formal statement and an acknowledgment of state responsibility for millions of victims is impossible without the research work of historians based on the archives. The way the present regime hides from historians and from the public the secrets about the crimes of the communist system by the hands of the security police reveals the continuity between the contemporary regime and Stalin's regime.

Despite Russian President Medvedev's demand to declassify all documents on repressions, the FSB Central Archives and President Archives are still closed to outsiders. I will mention just two examples. 116 volumes of the notorious Katyn case (massacre of Polish officers in 1940) out of 183 volumes are still secret and not accessible for Russian and Polish historians. [3] The FSB Archives declined my recent request to ascertain the number of victims of Stalin's first mass operation in 1927. This information is 83 years old. To separate themselves from the shameful Soviet past, contemporary rulers should first open wide the doors of the archives.

Another necessary condition for the Russian Nuremberg-style trials is an independent court system. In principle, the opposition, public organizations and historians are able now to prepare the formal process. However, no existing court in Russia (all obedient to the Kremlin) would accept such a proposition and next, the verdicts of such trials are open-ended.

As for the publication of the KGB informers' list (Why only the KGB? How about VChK, OGPU, NKVD informers?), I do not think that this would have a purifying effect on society. Eventually, everybody knew about V. V. Putin's career in the KGB, but it did not prevent Russian citizens to vote for him in 2000, in 2004 and to support him today. Furthermore, how would public opinion distinguish between the victims who were recruited under torture, as Mr. Preobrazhensky showed, and voluntary agents, like V. V. Putin? As we know now, it was common practice when OGPU consciously arrested innocent people in order to recruit them in exchange for freedom.

More pragmatic was the idea of post-Communist lustration — policies of limiting the participation of former police officers in civil service positions — promoted by Galina Starovoitova in the 1990s. However, in 1998, this potential candidate for the presidency was killed in the staircase of her home by a former GRU (Military Intelligence) officer.

Anyway, it's too late now for such lustration.

FP: Thank you, Dr. Velikanova.

I think that the West has a moral obligation to take a public and official stand on the side of the dissidents who are oppressed by the Putin thugocracy. What a tragedy that brave and courageous freedom fighters are killed, beaten and imprisoned in Russia while Obama fails to utter even one word on their behalf. We know that U.S. and international pressure on despotisms like the Soviet Union and Castro's Cuba have, in the past, eased the torment and persecution of brave dissidents like Natan Sharanksy and Armando Valladeres and eventually won their release. It is crucial that we let persecuted dissidents know that they are not forgotten, that we are with them in their plight, and that we will pressure and confront their persecutors. Let us not demoralize them with shameless silence.

I also think that whatever the consequences would be of publishing the list of KGB informers, that it must be done for its own sake, to give respect to the historical record and to ascertain who was an informer — notwithstanding why and how — and who they informed on and what they disclosed. We will know many of the trees by their fruits.

Buchar: Well, what Mr. Satter is suggesting needs to happen — juridical condemnation of Communism, an implicit apology from the government to the victims of Communism, and the need to make public the lists of KGB informers. It makes perfect sense but, let's face it, it is just wishful thinking. It's a fairy tail. How is it supposed to happen? It will never happen. And if it does, it will be just another part of the deception game that we have witnessed in other former satellite states.

Let me bring as an example how this was done in former Czechoslovakia. The juridical system stayed intact on purpose, protecting players from the former regime. It was part of the deal. An apology from the government to the victims of Communism is not going to happen because former communists are embedded in all political parties and in the government. When the list of informers or agents comes out, it's doctored before the release. Important names are omitted, taken away from the archives while others are planted in to deceive public.

Look at the infamous "Fund Z" ordered by Vaclav Havel when files of all persons involved in politics during the Velvet Revolution were sealed and moved to an undisclosed location. People critically involved in the process usually die under strange circumstances. And if the idea of post-communist lustration sounds good to some, it proved to be a farce as well. Files were doctored, false certificates were issued to people of special interest and exceptions were allowed in the name of "national interest and security".

The system will never "fix" itself from inside, the same way as the so-called fall of Communism was never a result of rising people's power. In other words, as Mr. Burakowski said, who is going to implement the really democratic changes? The KGB itself? In the meantime, the clock is ticking. Two out of ten residents of Prague are now Russians. Russians are influencing and controlling businesses, buying real estate, controlling organized crime and influencing politics.

As Jeff Nyquist mentioned, we know by now what is the nature of the current regime in Moscow. Under these circumstances, no change can come from outside. And if it comes from inside, it will be just another move on the chessboard of the big deception game. I agree with Jeff that the key question here is what the Russian regime's real intentions are. But this is the million dollar question and we may never know the answer till it will be too late.

Robert Gates admitted to me that we never had any inside information from Moscow's inner circle. And I am sure we never will. But what we can investigate to some extent is why Western democracies, and the U.S. government in particular, are refusing to address this issue. Why is the media treating this issue like a highly toxic substance? The "useful idiots" Mr. Preobrazhenskiy mentioned should be exposed. A new book *DUPES* written by Paul Kengor just came out, finally revealing to the American public, among other things, Ted Kennedy's secret dealing with the Soviets. [4]

Some six years ago I asked a former CIA counter intelligence director if Kennedy's dealing with Soviets shouldn't be called the treason. He replied, "Yes, but Kennedy is untouchable." Well, how many "untouchable" politicians are in our government and why is the whole issue of secret dealing with Soviets/Russians is "untouchable"? What is the strategy? Is there any strategy? Does anybody care that we are under attack? What is our defense, if any?

By the way, did you ever hear the American media mentioning that the Russian Mafia is charging Mexican drug lords 30 percent for laundering drug profits from sales in the United States? It looks like the FBI counter intelligence is finally willing to admit that there is a "Russian problem" but the question remains what to do about it and if it's not too late to stop this avalanche in motion. Historically speaking, there is no evidence that "bad peace is better than good war" ever worked.

FP: Robert Buchar, thank you for your contribution.

Vladimir Bukovsky and Pavel Stroilov, we have agreed that both of you would offer a comment under a joint byline. What wisdom would you like to offer to our discussion?

Bukovsky/Stroilov: With the greatest respect to Gen. Pacepa, neither the Soviet regime nor the present KGB regime in Russia has anything to do with the history of Tzars' monarchy (samoderzhavie). One could have as well suggested that Ceauşescu followed the example of Vlad the Impaler. Nor is it correct that KGB, in Soviet times, enjoyed any degree of autonomy from the Communist Party — it always remained, as Lenin defined it, the armed detachment of the Party, the Party's 'avenging sword' which, until 1991, remained tightly controlled.

There is nothing peculiarly Russian about what happened then, with the KGB corporation becoming the strongest surviving splinter of the Soviet system, the best organised gang of marauders, who subsequently captured power. Rather, it was the most grotesque illustration of what happened all over the world, as a result of our failure to condemn Communism at a Nuremberg-style tribunal. The old Soviet clients, Petens and Quislings of the Cold War, were left in a position to write its history, and consequently remained both opinion-makers and decision-makers. We see them in power everywhere, be it in the Al Queda or in the White House. You have a Marxist administration in America, and any attempt to investigate their past reveals excessive communist connections. Like in Russia or anywhere, this has nothing to do with historic traditions, but everything to do with our failure to conclude the Cold War as we should have done.

The entire world is still overwhelmed with the Soviet legacy, and any serious investigation of Putin's crimes would inevitably lead back to the Communist Party of the Soviet Union, and put it in the dock where it belongs. Far from being impossible for the passage of time, a Nuremberg-style trial of Communism remains the only way for the world to begin a recovery from the horrors of the 20th century. No matter how hard we tried to do it differently, 10, 20, 30 years later, the logic of criminal justice brings us back to the same point: we cannot go on until we find out the truth of what had happened. Passage of time notwithstanding, Cambodia had to put the Red Khmers leaders on trial over 30 years after their crimes and Poland had to put its communist leaders on trial now. Sooner or later, Russia and others will have to follow suit. Without that, any effort to recover would be wasted, just like it has been in the past 20 years.

FP: Pavel Stroilov and Vladimir Bukovsky, thank you.

Let us begin our second and final round.

Mihai Pacepa, your thoughts on the first round?

Pacepa: I want to thank Mr. Bukovsky and Mr. Stroilov for giving me a chance to expand on the Kremlin's historical *samoderzhavyie*. I have high respect for Mr. Bukovsky's heroic fight against Soviet Communism, and I fully understand his and Mr. Stroilov's emotional attachment to Russia — I, too, have warm feelings for my native country. But if we want to help normalize Russia, we should base our analysis on historical reality, not on emotions. And the historical reality is that Russia's current KGB dictatorship was not born in a vacuum. It is rooted in the traditional Russian cult of the ruler and precisely in the history of the tsars' autocracy (*samoderzhavyie*), despite any belief to the contrary on the part of Mr. Bukovsky and Mr. Stroilov.

In my other life, I — unfortunately — rose to the top of both the Soviet bloc's Communist hierarchy and the KGB's community, and I myself became a small cog in the Kremlin's autocratic system of government. In spite of what Lenin may originally have intended, the political police was neither "the armed detachment of the party," nor "the party's avenging sword." It was the ruler's primary and personal instrument for protecting and promoting his own power. There was no way for the KGB — or the Romanian *Securitate* — to be subordinated to the Politburo or any other collective leadership of the Party while at the same time carrying out the leader's instructions to monitor the microphones installed in the offices and homes of the Party leaders. "Only the Comrade is taboo when it comes to bugging," KGB chief Andropov told me when I began supervising a super-secret *Securitate* unit that was charged with electronically monitoring the top party and government officials. The "Comrade" was Brezhnev. "Only Nikolay Andreyevich is taboo for you," Andropov added. "Nikolay Andreyevich" was Ceausescu.

In 1972, Andropov bragged to me that a party membership card was no longer enough for someone to be promoted to the top of the party or the government, and that a person's secret affiliation with "us" had become the passkey to prominence. Brezhnev himself had already sworn in, as "deep-cover" intelligence officers, 18 out of the 26 Soviet deputy ministers of foreign affairs and of foreign trade, along with a dozen ambassadors. Those "deep-cover" officers were to be secretly remunerated with tax-free salary supplements, in exchange for obeying "our" military (i.e., intelligence) regulations and orders. That would discipline the party and government apparatus, and it would also put an end to the theft and bureaucratic chaos that had become Soviet plagues.

The concept of the "deep-cover" intelligence officer, Andropov explained, was as Russian as the Kremlin's onion domes. The tsarist *Okhrana* had planted its deep-cover agents everywhere: in the central and local governments, in political parties, labor unions, churches and newspapers. Roman Malinovsky, a deep-cover *Okhrana* agent secretly infiltrated into Lenin's Communist Party, became the chairman of the Bolshevik faction in the *Duma* and edited the newspaper *Pravda*. Andropov was famous for not wasting his breath on chitchat. "All of our sister services should now fall into step," he told me bluntly.

A couple of weeks after I was granted political asylum in the United States in July 1978, the Western news media reported that my defection had unleashed the greatest political purge in the history of Communist Romania. Ceausescu had fired one third of his cabinet members, demoted four politburo members, and replaced 22 ambassadors. All were deep-cover intelligence officers whose military documents and pay vouchers I had regularly signed off on.

Since Romania's political police archives began opening a couple of years ago, information on hundreds of other ranking party activists and government employees who had become deep-cover intelligence officers has come to light. If the KGB archives are ever opened — without being sanitized — they will certainly tell a frightening story.

Andropov's deep-cover officers propelled him onto the Kremlin throne, crowning a five-century tradition of secret *samoderzhaviye*. That tradition started in 1564, when Ivan the Terrible began ruling the country with the help of his *Oprichnina*, meaning "separate court", which was in effect a secret political police force answerable only to him. When Peter the Great ascended to the throne at the end of the 17th century, he set up his own political police, the *Preobrazhenskiy Prikaz*, so secretly that the exact date of its creation is still a mystery. Peter unleashed his new instrument of power against everybody who spoke out against him, from his own wife to drunks who told jokes about his rule. Peter even entrusted the *Preobrazhenskiy Prikaz* with luring his own son and heir, the *tsarevich* Aleksey, back to Russia from abroad and torturing him to death.

Similarly, months after Tsar Nicholas I took the throne, he established the Third Section of his Imperial Chancellery as his secret police, and he institutionalized political crime in Russia. His 1845 Criminal Code, which laid down draconian penalties for all persons guilty of arousing "disrespect for sovereign authority or for the personal qualities of the sovereign," became the core of the Soviet Criminal Code, and generated the Soviet gulags. At the time of the October Revolution, the tsar's political police was called the *Okhrana*, founded in 1881 by Alexander II, and had the power to search, imprison and exile on its own sole authority, a power inherited by all its successors — from the *Cheka* to the KGB and beyond.

Lenin, who spent most of his mature life in 19th century Europe, home to many political parties, was determined to eradicate Russia's traditional *samoderzhaviye*. In his *What Is To Be Done?*, written in 1902, Lenin stated that in the future Soviet state there would be no place for a police force, much less for a secret police. [5] But in October 1917, when Lenin returned to Russia, he found a chaotic country, and he was constrained to continue the *samoderzhaviye* tradition. His *Cheka*'s coat of arms, consisting of a shield representing the protection of the Communist tsar against traitors, and a sword for drawing across those traitors' necks, harks back to the *Oprichnina*'s symbol, a dog's head for sniffing out traitors and a broom for sweeping the country clean of them — not to anything out of Karl Marx or social-democratic Europe. The shield and the sword is still the coat of arms of today's successor to the KGB, the FSB.

Lenin's new political police, conceived as the armed detachment of the party, was the Soviet Union's fastest expanding organization; it started out with only 23 men, but within a year it numbered over 200,000 employees. A 1993 book (*Deadly Illusions,* New York: Crown, 1993) by British researcher John Costello and Russian intelligence officer Oleg Tsarev, stated that, according to original documents found in KGB archives, in 1921 Soviet Russia counted more *Cheka* officers than party members. [6]

After Lenin died, his political police stopped being "the armed detachment of the party." Stalin, who wanted to become an unchallenged tsar, subordinated the political police to himself — just as all the tsars before him had done — and turned it against the most important creation of Lenin's revolutionary life, the Bolshevik Party. Stalin, who feared competition, started by ordering his political police to liquidate his main rivals. Leon Trotsky, recommended by Lenin to become leader of the party, was exiled, and later barbarically killed. The first chairman of the Comintern, Grigory Zinovyev, was framed as a Zionist spy and shot. The man named by Lenin's testament as the most capable of the younger generation, Georgy Pyatakov, was also shot. Most members (98 out of the 139) of the Central Committee elected at the XVII Party Congress, hailed as the "Congress of the Victorious," were also shot as spies. [7] By 1939, seven million party members had lost their lives at the hand of Stalin's political police, which, behind a facade of Marxism, took secret precedence over the original tools of ideology and the Communist Party for running their country.

On December 31, 1999, Russia's president, Boris Yeltsin, shocked the world by resigning. "I shouldn't be in the way of the *natural course of history,*" he explained. "I understand that *I must do it* and Russia must enter the new millennium with new politicians, with new faces, with new intelligent, strong, energetic people." [8] Yeltsin decreed that Article 92 Section 3 of the Russian Constitution would be triggered, under which the power of the Russian president would be transferred to Prime Minister Putin at noon on December 31, 1999. [9] For his part, Putin signed a decree pardoning Yeltsin "for any possible misdeeds." Yeltsin had in recent months come under a cloud of scandals for bribery, and Putin granted him "total immunity" from prosecution, from search and from questioning for "any and all" actions committed while in office. Putin also gave Yeltsin a lifetime pension and a state *dacha*. [10]

To me, it had all the appearances of a KGB palace putsch. Indeed, soon after Putin became president, former KGB officers took over thousands of governmental positions. To Ted Koppel of ABC television, Putin explained that the KGB men were needed to root out graft. "I have known them for many years and I trust them. It has nothing to do with ideology. It's only a matter of their professional qualities and personal relationship." [11] Lies. Blunt lies. That was the beginning of a new, open era of *samoderzhaviye*. As of June 2003, some 6,000 former KGB officers were holding important positions in Russia's central and regional governments. Today, over half of Russia's federal and local governmental positions are held by former KGB officers, and 70% of her current political figures have been affiliated, in one way or another, with the KGB. [12]

I share the view of Mr. Bukovsky and Mr. Stroilov that the virus of Marxism has began infecting the United States. But Marxism and its nauseating, Stalinesque cult of personality are not rooted in the history of the United States, and those evils are being rejected. Most Americans already realize that, if the current Democratic Party has its way, it will transform the United States into a Marxist country in all but name, and during the last November elections they cut this party's wings. The Russians, however, decided in the last *three free elections* to entrust the helm of their country to the KGB, which had killed over 27 million Russians.

Now some Russians are blaming the United States for not having tried these KGB hangmen. The United States did indeed win the Cold War, but, unlike other wars, that one did not end with a formal act of surrender and the defeated enemy throwing down his weapons. Therefore, the U.S. was not in a position to organize any kind of Nuremberg trial for the Soviet criminals. But the Russians could have done so, as did the Romanians, who at least executed Ceauşescu. He was sentenced to death not because he was a modern Vlad the Impaler, but because he had been educated in Moscow and become a Romanian Stalin who transformed their country into a monument to himself.

A new generation of Russians is now struggling to give their country a new identity. I hope our Symposium will help them. I also hope that Mr. Bukovsky will really be able to run for president of Russia.

Satter: It is understandable that many Russians do not want to dignify the KGB and its predecessors, the Cheka and the NKVD, by treating them as part of the Russian tradition. But as Gen. Pacepa makes clear, the connections are hard to ignore. Of course, the terror unleashed by the Cheka was far more extreme both in extent and depravity than anything undertaken by the Okhrana.

Between 1825 and 1917, 3,932 persons were executed for political reasons in the Russian Empire. The overwhelming majority (3,741) were executed between 1906 and 1910 when the regime was fighting revolutionary terror. The Bolsheviks exceeded this figure in four months. On September 3, 1918, the Bolshevik regime introduced the Red Terror, based on hostage taking and liquidation according to class. In the next 60 days, the Cheka killed anywhere from 10,000 to 15,000 persons. Symptomatic was the fate of the St. Petersburg clown Bim Bom who, in 1918, made a few jokes at the expense of the new regime during his act. Cheka operatives burst on to the stage. The audience thought this was part of the act but Bim Bom realized what was happening and tried to flee. As the spectators looked on in horror, he was gunned down. The Cheka also introduced a level of torture and sadism that had not been shown by the Tsarist police.

Nonetheless, the behavior of the first Soviet secret police was not unrelated to Russian traditions. The use of provocateurs, the penetration of society by informers and the resort to savage violence against whole categories of the population all have their roots in

Russian experience. In fact, the resort to terror is an inherent possibility in any culture that disregards the dignity of the individual and the denigration of the individual is the red thread that runs through Russian history from Russia's emergence as a unified modern state to the present day. The repressive methods of the Tsars were limited by the effects of Orthodox Christian culture, and, in a seemingly stable society, the need to resort to them was diminished. The practices of the Oprichniki under Ivan the Terrible, however, always existed as a potential and when the political circumstances conferred a huge advantage on the side prepared to act with maximum savagery, there was no commitment to the value of the individual in Russia capable of standing in the way.

The persistence of a secret police tradition in Russia raises the question of whether there is any point in trying to influence Russian society from outside. The mere fact that Stalin nearly came in first in a recent poll to name history's greatest Russian is a sign that Russians lack a commitment to their own political self defense.

Despite Russians' often discouraging lack of concern for their own welfare, however, I think that there are several reasons why the West cannot react passively to manifestations in Russia of secret police rule. In the first place, domination of the country by the security services leads to intellectual and moral stagnation that makes Russia the scene of possible future horrors. The recent race riots in Moscow instigated by young fascists is only the inevitable result of the deliberate fostering of political support for a corrupt and dictatorial regime with the help of youth groups like "Nashi" ("Ours") that draw a strict separation between Russians and everyone else.

Secret police rule in Russia needs to be resisted by the West also because it leads to an aggressive and unpredictable Russian foreign policy. If Russia is run by a KGB oligarchy in that oligarchy's own interests, the rulers will have a permanent vested interest in rallying the population against the threat from the West. This means that campaigns against U.S. missile defense and support for Iran are not accidents. They spring inevitably from the need of the leadership to maintain a state of tension in the world in the interest of its own preservation.

Finally, the West needs to resist Russian KGB led authoritarianism in order to preserve the possibility of democracy in Russia in the future. All too often ignored is the need of the West to create moral capital with the citizens of repressive regimes. In the case of Russia, this should be done in anticipation of the day which must come when the present regime loses all legitimacy in the eyes of the population. At that time, it will be important that Russians do not believe that the regime had Western collaborators. In this regard, nothing is more self defeating for the U.S. than such ill advised joint commissions as Gore-Chernomyrdin and McFaul-Surkov.

Despite the statements of so called "realists" the world really is intertwined and the triumph of the secret police anywhere is full of danger for the moral consensus on which civilization depends. This is nowhere more true than in the case of the triumph of arguably the most blood stained security police in history, the Russian KGB.

Burakowski: I agree to some extent with Mr. Bukovsky and Mr. Stroilov in that the Communist regime in Russia was not a continuity of the Russian tradition, but rather something completely new. Communism did not originate in Russia, and the consequent dictators made tremendous efforts to eradicate the traditional values of the pre-revolution society. The Orthodox Church was destroyed, the clergy killed and persecuted. Whole classes of society (e.g. rich peasants), as well as part of more independent communities, were virtually extinguished. The industry and commerce were nationalized, private property banned. Moreover, the cultural legacy of Russia, or at least the major part of it, was condemned. At the same time, national values and aims were changed to international ones. The main goal of the USSR was to bring proletarian revolution to everywhere in the world and, at least until a moment in time, the communist parties were following the directions from Moscow even if their local interests were against it. Take for example the Indian communists: after the USSR allied with the UK during the Second World War, they rapidly became loyal to London and gave up all the anti-colonial claims - this move cost them a lot of credibility among society which, back then, was in major part anti-British. The goal of the communist revolution overruled their basic survival instinct. The same thing happened in Russia itself — the worldwide victory of the revolution was more important than national interests. This was something completely unknown to Tsarist Russia.

But Gen. Pacepa and Mr. Satter are also right when they stress that some methods of Russian communists were just extended methods used by the ancien régime. It is not only secret services, but also some propagandistic claims, presenting Russia and the Soviet Union, as a guarantee of world peace and order. The same slogans were used in the 19th century, in the debate on Europe and Russians having a role in dealing with "hooligans" like Napoleon Bonaparte.

Still, I wouldn't call today's Russia a mixture of Tsarist and communist regimes. I see it as a new form of autocracy with global aspirations, but with no ideology behind it. It appears to be purely power-oriented, aimed only at economical and political expansion. There are no ideological goals, neither national nor universal. This is probably a better situation for the world than it was before, since communism is, in my opinion, the most evil idea that appeared on this Earth. But at the same time, no clear goal of the present regime means also no limitations. The rulers of today's Russia have nothing to propose to anybody, they just want to expand, to dominate and to execute their power in every corner of the world, where it is only possible.

Let me end with rather a sad conclusion. The glorious Roman Empire eventually fell, about fifteen hundred years ago, but we still see its remnants everywhere. It's all around us, in the code of law, in architecture, in arts, even in the language. The presence of the Roman legacy is overwhelming. In my opinion the legacy of the USSR and communism may also prove to be extremely long-lived. Communism affected the thinking, the mentality of entire nations and generations. But, contrary to the Roman Empire, the Soviet Empire has not created anything positive, so the remnants of it could only be negative. I cannot exclude that centuries from now people will still believe in some lies invented by the communists, and some offspring of the KGB will still be active.

Nyquist: In discussing the nature of the Russian regime people sometimes fall into disagreement about the legacy of autocracy and secret police rule in Russia. Obviously, the Soviet state represented a break with the tsar's autocracy in terms of fundamental values, and in its bloodthirsty ruthlessness. But the legacy of the autocratic regime was nonetheless significant; and, as Gen. Pacepa points out, the importance of the political technology of the secret police is a key element of the whole. When you fight against something there is always the danger of acquiring its characteristics. Lenin called into existence a conspiratorial revolutionary party, because conspiracy was necessary in the face of the tsar's secret police. Perhaps we can all agree that the Soviet regime was a political hybrid which borrowed from the Russian past to supplement the nightmare of a communist present.

Many excellent points have been made in our discussion, including the idea that the KGB has corrupted the very language we are using right here, right now. We are confused about basic concepts, definitions — about the nature of Communism. In his remarkable explanation, I believe Gen. Pacepa was making a key point: namely, we should not credit Communism as an idea. Karl Marx did not believe in Communism. He was a cynical man who didn't believe in anything, and the same may be said of Mao and Stalin, or any of the truly effective "Communist" leaders. Karl Marx wanted to be dictator of Germany, and created his ideology for the sake of building a new kind of power — mainly for himself. He was not a humanitarian, but a would-be political murderer who failed to take office. Marx once said there was nothing grander under heaven than the mind of a criminal. Is it any wonder that Marxist regimes belong more to the lumpen proletariat — to criminals like Stalin and Kang Sheng — than to the real working class? And is it any wonder that such a regime should degenerate into a criminal police regime, working hand-in-hand with its own global mafia?

Mao said that "Marxism-Leninism is better than a machine gun." He did not mean that Marxism-Leninism is true. A machine gun is not truth. It is a weapon. So I say again: We should not credit Communism as an idea, but only as a weapon. Each decade after 1917 the weapon was modified according to the requirements of the moment. So flexible is this weapon, and so ready to dispense with outward labels and names, that even when people have been inoculated after living under totalitarianism, the totalitarian organism mutates and re-infects them once again. As previously indicated, this organism is not an idea but an emerging criminal class whose cynicism is as limitless as their ambition. By fixating on Communism as an idea, many of us have lost our way upon the deceptive surface of a phenomenon that continually redefines and re-invents itself: From the dictatorship of the proletariat to the state of the whole people it is the same criminal organization at work. Now they are talking about "one common European home" and "Europe from Brest to Vladivostok." It is merely the latest incarnation of an old criminal program; namely, to rule Europe.

The intentions of a regime may be read in its strategy, in its movement toward certain preliminary positions. This is not merely a Leftist movement. The KGB has infiltrated and influenced the European new Right, the American conspiratorial Right, the Islamic fundamentalist Right, and countless organizations representing every shade of opinion. People across the political spectrum are beginning to repeat ideas that were current in *Pravda* during the 1960s. *This cannot be a coincidence.* And what are the regime's intentions? The answer should be obvious: To remove the one thing on earth that holds it in check; and that is the United States of America. Ask yourself why Russia currently arms China, Iran, Venezuela, Syria and other anti-American regimes? Why has Russia facilitated the proliferation of nuclear, biological and missile technology to anti-America states? What is behind Russia's role as the capital of international organized crime, money laundering and drug trafficking? There is a great snake, with the name anaconda, that coils around its victim and crushes the victim's bones in order to prepare the way for digestion. This is what I believe the KGB is doing today.

It was earlier suggested that we must engage and negotiate with this predatory monster. The unstated justification for "engagement" is because Moscow is holding hostages — political dissidents and average citizens who want a normal life. If we do not negotiate with the criminals, the hostages will be harmed. Not only this, but the regime's nuclear arsenal makes hostages of us all. While police in most countries refuse to negotiate with hostage-takers, the basis of the West's global policy is exactly the opposite, thereby making weapons of mass destruction the most attractive tool in the totalitarian toolbox.

Meanwhile, we have convinced ourselves that negotiation and appeasement are unavoidable. How else can we avoid a nuclear war? It is a clear case of extortion and nuclear blackmail, effective and ongoing. Ask yourself: When will it end? How will it end? Over time, the blackmailer erodes the strategic position of his victim. Finally, his victim becomes helpless. Moscow can then exterminate the most troublesome hostages, which may include entire nations — especially if those nations threaten to emerge from helplessness. Please remember: This is a regime with no morality, for which mass killing is a form of reassurance. It is proof, writ large, that the regime's power is effective and real.

I do not think we have appreciated how flexible, resilient and persistent a totalitarian formation can be. Forming a partnership with such a regime leads to a process that gradually weakens the West through compromise. Reagan had the right idea when he waged economic warfare against the Soviet regime during his first term. He made a mistake when he began to deal with the "evil empire" in his second term. It was through this process of engagement that we saved the totalitarian formation in Russia. By now, at long last, this must be clear.

Preobrazhenskiy: I agree with Bukovsky's/Stroilov's opinion that the high price of moral self-destruction with which the West is paying Russia is a result of our failure to condemn Communism at a Nuremberg-style tribunal. It is a result of Western political correctness. And I am afraid the West has been punished forever, as the KGB will never yield the state power to anybody in Russia. And there is nobody to take it there. Russian opposition is weak; the FSB is playing with it as a cat plays with a mouse.

Also I agree with Dr. Burakovsky saying that the people in the Kremlin today have no ideological goals, anything to propose to anybody; they just want to expand, to dominate and to execute their power in every corner of the world. Unfortunately, not so many people in the West have allowed themselves to understand this.

I fully support Dr. Buchar's opinion that the principle "bad peace is better than good war" never worked. This principle is translated into the current Western political language as "real politics." It is a hypocritical policy of closing our eyes on Russian interior situation. It is helping Putin to accomplish the hidden aim of his program, which is: "Oil for democracy."

Western hypocritical policy is returning back there as a boomerang and it damages their own democracy. The destruction of Western democracy and lowering it to the Russian level is Putin's main goal. And he is achieving it very successfully. Western democracy is really fading under Russian influence now.

The core of world democracy is rooted in America. There is no wonder that Russia wants to diminish America first and foremost. I think Dr. Nyquist is quite correct saying that Russia wants to remove the one thing on earth that holds it in check; and that is the United States of America. But does America realize it? That is the question.

Velikanova: Some visions of Russia presented here have survived from the Cold War period. Since then the world, Russia itself and the balance of forces in the world have changed drastically. The Communist idea has been very much discredited by the failure of the Soviet experiment. The role of modern Russia in the alleged "world anti-American conspiracy" is too much exaggerated in the minds of the esteemed discussants. At the end of the 20th century Russia was relinquished of its role as the major opponent to the Western civilization by other challengers. The world now faces much greater dangers from radical Islamic groups than from KGB agents (even at the head of Russian government). However, with different views on the nature of the modern Russian political regime expressed in our discussion, we all agree that the West is obliged "to resist Russian KGB led authoritarianism."(Satter) The problem is by what methods. I want to focus on that now.

There are several potential means in the arsenal of the Western governments. First, there is a moral pressure on Russian government through the official condemnation of the most outrageous cases like Mikhail Khodorkovsky's trial, the impunity in many cases of journalists' murders (for example, the Anna Politkovskaya case), or the case of Sergey Magnitsky's death. Such Western denunciations of the corrupt, Russian legal system and violations of human rights do take place. Of course, we can doubt how effective such measures are in the case of insensitive Russian leaders, who now play a game of "kind and cruel interrogators"(KGB tactic of interrogation), turning the intelligent face of Dmitry Medvedev to the West and the KGB face of Vladimir Putin to the Russian dissidents and citizens.

Another tool is legal. The European Court of Human Rights in Strasbourg often remains the last hope for justice for many Russian citizens. The European Court has now the largest amount of the complaints originating from Russia. As a result, the Russian government has to pay huge penalties to the victims of injustice according the European Court verdicts. The claims of foreign shareholders in *Yukos* (Khodorkovsky's oil company) are under investigation in the international court now. The cases of "spy" exchanges (example: the summer exchange of alleged "spy," scholar Igor Sutiagin for Russian spies in the U.S.) are also channels to defend innocent victims of Russian Themis, but at the same time, very individual and irregular.

One more instrument of showing a firm stand is the recent precedent of the Senator Cardin list. When the lawyer S. Magnitsky, who had exposed the $230 million corruption affair in the Police Ministry (MVD), died in prison after being deprived of medical care, Senator Cardin in the spring of 2010 demanded that the State Department *"immediately cancel and permanently withdraw the U.S. visa privileges of all those (60 officials) involved in this crime, along with their dependents and family members."* This motion was approved.

This new tactic of the Western governors was enforced in response to the shockingly harsh verdict pronounced by the Moscow puppet court to M. Khodorkovsky and P. Lebedev on December 30, 2010. The European Parliament recently recommended to the Western governments to block visa privileges to the officials involved in this caricature trial. Moreover, the European Parliament suggested to block their accounts in the Western banks and to enforce sanctions on their property abroad. This tactic can be more successful as it strikes material interests of the corrupted officials. They like to invest their dirty incomes into European or American assets. I hope that other similar, more or less "elegant" sanctions could be found in resisting the authoritarian politics of modern Russian government.

In the arsenal of international means available to states, there are also economic sanctions as a very severe instrument. Should Britain forbid BP to deal with *Rosneft'*, which had been a beneficiary of the *Yukos* (state raider's) bankruptcy? (As for private business, realists can't expect that it would miss profit while defending human rights in Russia.) It's obvious that the Western governments prioritize more pragmatic politics of cooperation and negotiation with the Russian "monster" (in words of Mr. Nyquist) in diplomatic and strategic spheres and demonstrate a kind of the shyness in the humanitarian field.

Outside the inter-state and private business sector, there are strong public resources, which play a huge role in defending human rights in authoritarian countries. The public can do a lot by raising its voice to express the opinion on the Russian affairs and the stand of American politicians toward it. We can't neglect the function of public opinion in pressuring the governments. One example of this occurred in 2009, when Russian president Dmitry Medvedev created the Commission to Counter Attempts to Falsify History to the Detriment of Russia's Interests. It was a Stalinist-like state intervention into the historical profession and an imposition of boundaries on historical study with the goal to promote the state view on the Soviet past. Due to the critique in the Russian and Western medias, including the statements of the American Historical Association and the Association for Slavic, East European, and Eurasian Studies, the Russian government on January 15, 2010 declined the bill suggesting that "falsification of history and rejection of the role of the USSR in the victory over Nazism" should be a criminal offense introduced by the party *United Russia*.

Here I would like to confirm my position and support the FP comment that the Western governments should strengthen the politics of moral and judicial pressure on Russian authorities. But the main job of the condemnation of Stalinism and its legacy should be done at home, by the Russians themselves.

Buchar: The failure to condemn Communism at a Nuremberg-style tribunal will haunt us forever. But on the other hand this could never happen anyway because it wasn't part of the scenario and either side didn't have any desire to do it. It wasn't on the agenda of international finance obsessed with the idea of globalization. It wouldn't be good for business.

There is no question that the destinies of nations are shaped by the history, traditions and peoples' mindset. I think that everyone has realized by now that democracy can't be exported or forced on any nation only because we believe in it. Every nation has to grow to it gradually on its own and there are no shortcuts. Free elections can't bring any good if bad guys and manipulated masses are in the majority. Identities of nations are shaped by its citizens.

The problem for Westerners to recognize who/what the danger is comes from the inability to define it the way everybody can understand. When I was living in communist Czechoslovakia we had one universal label for our enemy. We called it "Bolshevik." Marxism, Communism, Socialism, secret police, Chekism, all our enemies, were simply "Bolshevik." Westerners need exact definitions. Obviously, the ideology of Communism seems to be dead now for the majority of people. They have no idea what Cheka stands for, and nobody can grasp what the danger really is and why we still should fear Moscow. In the meantime, memories of the past are fading out fast. Czech journalist Sasa Uhlova set up recently an experiment posting on Facebook the question "What are your memories of Communism"? The overwhelming majority of responses were positive memories! Twenty years after the "fall" of Communism people are remembering mostly positives and forgetting all negatives. After the fall of the communist regime, the Communist Party was seen as the party of "retired people," the party that will slowly dissolve or "die out". What a surprise. Twenty years later here comes the resurrection, and the Communist Party is growing by thousands every year, gaining young people 20-40 years old.

It is obvious, I guess, that the old objective, the worldwide victory of the revolution is, in a way, still alive and well. It didn't go away. It just morphed a bit. It may, perhaps, lose its ideological goals, but the global aspiration didn't disappear. As Adam Burakowski mentioned, thinking and mentality of entire nations and generations were affected by communism, which leaves them extremely vulnerable to further manipulation.

Olga Velikanova believes that the role of Russia in the alleged "world anti-American conspiracy" is too much exaggerated in our minds, saying the world now faces much greater dangers from radical Islamic groups. I would suggest a look back and a realization of who seeded the anti-Americanism in Islamic world. People forget that it was the KGB who after WWII ended up spending a lot of effort to take over the German intelligence network in the Arab world and that infiltrated intelligent services there. It was the KGB that started to manipulate them to advance the Soviets' own agenda.

It was Moscow's Institute of International Relations that made in the 1960's the Middle East the key to be the breaking back of Western imperialism. The KGB flooded the Arabic world with agents penetrating even the Islamic clergy, supporting everybody so long as they were strongly anti-American. It was the Kremlin that established in early 1970's "socialist Division of Labor" and jumpstarted the Islamic Terrorist war against the United States. Ion Pacepa can talk about that for a whole day.

I would also point out that while everybody talks all the time about the KGB, there is also the GRU, the organization with six times more agents worldwide than the KGB has. The moral pressure itself can't swing this tide from its path. So, I guess, the key million dollar question remains: Can anything be done to slow down, to detour, to stop this pressure to change this course to weaken, breaking America down and making it into another EU and opening the door for creating a new world order of "peaceful" global management?

FP: Vladimir Bukovsky and Pavel Stroilov, last words go to you.

Bukovsky/Stroilov: This has been a lengthy discussion, mostly of Russian history, and we hardly hope many American readers will reach our final remarks. Yet, the issue is not unimportant. If today's Russians are right to call Putin's regime an "occupation," if we are right that Putin's junta is a surviving gang of marauders from the worldwide Marxist crusade, then something can be done about it. If we are talking about a historic tradition, so deeply rooted in Russian genes, stars, or wherever your fancy places it, that even the Bolshevik revolution could not destroy it - nothing can be done.

We can assure Gen. Pacepa that our analysis is not in the least colored by emotion, patriotic or otherwise (this kind of criticism is, indeed, very novel to both of us). On the contrary, it is the theory linking KGB to historic traditions that is irrational and mystical, like President Nixon's fantasy about the ghosts of Russian Tsars wandering in the Kremlin and influencing Soviet foreign policy. How, in practice, could the tradition of Ivan the Terrible survive to influence Putin? As Adam Burakowski rightly points out, the Bolsheviks outlawed any Russian traditions whatsoever and physically destroyed whole classes where they could have taken root. They did not construct a "hybrid" of Russia and Marxism; they deliberately constructed a Marxist anti-Russia. The plain historical fact is that we inherited the KGB not from the Tsars, but from the Soviets. Generally speaking, it has much in common with Oprichnina or even Okhranka. But it has just as much in common with Vlad the Impaler or those who crucified Jesus Christ.

The "historic traditions" theory has been disproved time and again over many decades — even Vladimir here wrote much about it in his 1989 book *USSR: From Utopia to Disaster.* And yet, alas, it does not die - because it is convenient to everyone. With this theory, the intellectuals don't have to recognize the KGB and gulag as legitimate children of their utopia. Moscow's sympathizers invoke it in mitigation, like a provincial lawyer who invokes the hard childhood of his client in mitigation of his crimes. Putin and company simply love it, because it gives them historic legitimacy where they have none. Those nations who were lucky enough to survive the 20th century without being taken over by communists are flattered by the implied superiority of their civilization. Those who were taken over by communists can forget the inconvenient fact that, Moscow's influence notwithstanding, most communist crimes in, say, Romania, were committed by Romanians and not Russians. In brief, all of us are relieved of our responsibility, since all responsibility is now laid on one man: Ivan the Terrible. And he no longer cares. Nor can we put him on trial. It makes much more sense to blame Adam and Eve, who started all this mess by eating the apple.

Romantic and nationalist thinkers of the 19th century fancied some vague national gods whose whims determine the national destiny. But in the material world, the theory that tyranny or freedom are matters of historic tradition, and therefore either of them comes naturally to a nation, does not hold water. You cannot find any credible explanation why English, Americans or Swiss seem to like democracy, whereas Russians, Arabs or Chinese seem to like dictatorship. Attributing this to national "traditions" or "mentality" is just as well as attributing it to stars, gods, or ghosts.

In practical terms, this is dangerous nonsense. It is nonsense, because no nation can naturally prefer tyranny to freedom. No man — and therefore no nation — likes to be arbitrarily imprisoned, tortured, robbed (taxed), or silenced. Not even Russians, some will be surprised to learn. People can let Putins and Obamas come to power out of apathy or out of illusions; but no nation ever consciously chooses a despotic government. Tyranny only wins by coercion, intimidation, deception; and then maintains itself by force. Otherwise, indeed, it would not need to be tyranny.

And that theory is dangerous, not simply because it leads to disastrous mistakes in dealing with such regimes as today's Russia, China, Iran or Egypt. Above all, it leads the West to complacency and false sense of security about its own future. If the freedom comes to Americans just as naturally as dictatorship comes to Russians, there is no need to make an effort and defend your freedom from Obama, Osama, or indeed Russia. And then, when the tyranny comes to disprove your elegant theories, it will be too late.

If you look at the history of any nation without cherry-picking for your theories, you won't see people clinging to their historic traditions. You will see everlasting battles between tradition and innovation, between believers and skeptics, and indeed, between freedom and tyranny. They come in different shapes; but in no age, in no land had this battle ever ceased. For the past hundred years, it has been one worldwide battle. It goes on today in Russia and America, like it goes on in Iran nd China; and we all share responsibility for its outcome.

Notes:

(1) Garry Kasparov, "KGB State," *The Wall Street Journal*, September 18, 2003, Commentary.

(2) Yevgenia Albats, *The KGB: The State Within a State,* (New York: Farrar, Straus, Giroux, 1994), pp.23.

(3) Novaya Gazeta, November 8, 2010.

(4) Paul Kengor, "DUPES", ISI Books, p.497

(5) V.I. Lenin, *The State and Revolution.* (London: Allen & Unwin, 1919), ch. 5, pts. 2 and 3.

(6) John Costello and Oleg Tsarev, *Deadly Illusions* (New York: Crown, 1993), p. 24.

(7) "*Izvestiya TseKa KPSS*" (Reports of the Central Committee of the CPSU), No.3, March 1989.

(8) Barry Renfrew, "Boris Yeltsin Resigns," *The Washington Post*, December 31, 1999, 6:48 a.m.

(9) Matt Drudge Report, December 31, 1999, 11:00 AM UTC.

(10) Ariel Cohen, "End of the Yeltsin Era," *The Washington Times*, January 3, 2000, Internet Edition, cohen-20000103.

(11) Michael R. Gordon, "Putin, in a Rare Interview, Says He'll Use Ex-K.G.B. Aides to Root Out Graft," *The New York Times*, March 24, 2000, Internet edition, p. 2.

(12) According to Gary Kasparov, "KGB State," half of the Russian governmental positions are held by former KGB officers. *The Wall Street Journal*, September 18, 2003.

[Jamie Glazov, "Symposium: The Shadow of the KGB," *Frontpagemag.com*, Feb. 11th, 2011.]

[4] Secrets of Communism's "Collapse"

The mystery of the 1989 revolution in Eastern Europe remains unsolved even 20 years later, buried in the secret communist archives. Was it a genuine triumph of democracy or a clever plot orchestrated from the Kremlin to avoid a real triumph of democracy?

The events in Romania were the most dramatic of all: the street battles which left over a thousand dead, the hastily arranged trial and execution of the communist tyrant Nicolae Caeusescu, and a National Salvation Committee emerging as the new democratic government. However, the top secret archival documents from the Soviet Bloc suggest that the National Salvation Committee and its leader, Ion Iliescu, were secretly backed by the Soviet Union and even requested a Soviet military intervention during the revolution.

What does this mean?

Our guests today are:

Adam Burakowski, the author of *Carpathian Genius. The Dictatorship of Nicolae Ceauşescu 1965-1989* and co-author of *1989 - Autumn of Nations* (a book that compares the process of Communism's fall in different states of Central and Eastern Europe. He received a Ph.D. from the Warsaw-based Institute of Political Studies of the Polish Academy of Sciences.

Vladimir Bukovsky, a former leading Soviet dissident, author of *To Build a Castle* and *Judgment in Moscow.*

Pavel Stroilov, a historian who smuggled a vast secret archive of the Gorbachev era out of Russia.

Lt. General Ion Mihai Pacepa, the highest official ever to have defected from the former Soviet bloc. His first book, *Red Horizons,* was republished in 27 languages. In March 2010, *The Washington Post* recommended it to be included on the list of books that should be read in schools. A commemorative edition of *Red Horizons* was just issued in Romania to mark 20 years since Ceauşescu was executed at the end of a trial where most of the accusations came out of this book. In April 2010, Pacepa's latest book, *Programmed to Kill: Lee Harvey Oswald, the Soviet KGB, and the Kennedy Assassination,* was prominently displayed at the annual meeting of the Organization of American Historians held in Washington D.C., as a "superb new paradigmatic work" and a "must read" for "everyone interested in the assassination of President Kennedy."

and

Robert Buchar, an associate professor and author of the Cinematography Program at Columbia College in Chicago. A political refugee from former Czechoslovakia, he is the producer of the documentary, *Velvet Hangover*, which is about Czech New Wave filmmakers, how they survived the period of "normalization" and their reflections on the so-called Velvet Revolution of 1989. He is the author of the new book, *And Reality be Damned... Undoing America: What The Media Didn't Tell You About the End of the Cold War and Fall of Communism in Europe.* The book is based on a documentary feature he is currently working on, *The Collapse of Communism: The Untold Story.*

FP: Adam Burakowski, let me begin with you.

What can you tell us about the events in Romania in the 1989 revolution?

Burakowski: The fall of Ceauşescu was unavoidable once Gorbachev came to power in 1985 and new political trends appeared in Moscow, and then all over the Soviet empire. The style of leadership of the Romanian dictator — his omnipresent megalomania, government — fueled personality cult, manifested at numerous state celebrations with fake enthusiasm of the masses — all that was incompatible with the just emerged idea of the face-lifting of Communism in the so-called perestroika. Ceauşescu had significantly contributed to damaging the image of Communism, and at that moment of time, his rule in Romania really did not pay off for the Kremlin.

The Soviets made many attempts to get rid of him in a peaceful way. As early as in 1985, Bucharest speculated as to who could be nominated to replace Ceauşescu. Even in the highest echelons of power, names were mentioned of Ceauşescu's son Nicu, prime-minister Constantin Dăscălescu and others, including the then not too prominent director of one of the publishing houses in the Romanian capital, Ion Iliescu. In May 1987, during his visit to Bucharest, Gorbachev himself tried to incite the reformist sentiments among apparatchiks, but he failed.

The 14th Party Congress in November 1989 marked the last unsuccessful attempt at removing Ceauşescu from power in a legal and peaceful way. The leader was re-elected with a unanimous vote and it became clear, that he would not retire without a heavy fight. When the revolution began in Timişoara, Ceauşescu was not surprised. He was awaiting it and thought he was prepared to face it. But then a part of his closest collaborators betrayed him, misleading him about the real situation in the country — a fact that could suggest some secret agreements made before.

The document that I published in "Revista 22" and then in "Adevărul" does not prove Iliescu's ties to the Kremlin *before* December 1989. It seems that the request for military intervention was his own, a spontaneous idea. Unlike other apparently similar situations from history, when a request for Russia's military help came from another country, it was in fact planned and orchestrated by the Russians themselves — suffice it to mention Hungary in 1956, Czechoslovakia in 1968, and also Poland in 1972 (the Targowica Confederation). It doesn't seem to have been the case with Iliescu. He seems to have just felt insecure and turned to a power, which he considered friendly and willing to help. It does not exclude, however, his possible earlier contacts with Soviet officials.

Just imagine what could have happened, if the Soviets had not rejected Iliescu's plea. A total disaster, not only for Romania, but for other communist countries as well.

FP: How would it have been a disaster for Romania and other Communist countries? What do you mean? Any why do you think the Soviets rejected Iliescu's plea?

Burakowski: A possible Soviet military intervention would have demolished the "peaceful" image of the Soviet Union and perestroika. Please have in mind that the Brezhnev Doctrine was officially denied and a new trend was launched. It was the so-called Sinatra Doctrine which excluded any military intervention in any country of the Soviet Bloc and it was published in late October 1989, i.e. two months before Iliescu's plea. It does not really matter if the Soviets had intervened in favor of the "good" National Salvation Front or "bad" Ceauşescu — it would have significantly damaged the image of all the changes in Central and Eastern Europe.

In addition to that, it could have created a "martyr" legend of the Romanian dictator, which could have caused enormous confusion all over the Soviet Bloc, including among the inhabitants, who would have then understood the political transformation even less than they understood at that time. Disinformation would have flourished even more than it did.

Despite all of the mentioned above, we could not even imagine how many people would have lost their lives if the Soviets had fulfilled what Iliescu wanted and intervened in Romania with the troops.

On the other hand, Iliescu and his people managed to survive and keep he power in their hands without any military help. On December 25, the Ceauşescu couple was executed and the shootings in all the cities ceased. There was no need of military intervention and it seems that the Soviets were conscious of that fact. That is why they rejected the plea.

FP: Pavel Stroilov, what do you bring to the table about all of this and that is your take on Adam Burakowski's comments and interpretations?

Stroilov: The document Adam refers to is a real eye-opener in many respects. Yes, it certainly ruins whatever reputation Iliescu once had as a democrat and a patriot; but there is more to it.

Amid all that turmoil in Romania, on December 24, 1989, State Secretary Baker suddenly announced on television that the United States would have no objections if the Soviet troops enter Romania to help the rebels. Until recently, I thought this was just another of those Baker's blunders — after all, he was famous for many irresponsible, foolish and pompous statements. Today, however, we can see what was behind it. Undoubtedly, the conspirators realized the Soviets would not intervene to help them without a green light being given by the West. So they talked both to the Soviets and to the Americans, trying to present the potential Soviet invasion as an internationally endorsed peace-making mission. Amazingly, Moscow did not buy it, but Washington did.

Why did the Soviets refuse? I don't think they were particularly worried about the Western reaction, or faithful to their 'Sinatra doctrine'. The latter was all in Gorbachev's propaganda department. In other places, in other circumstances, Gorby's troops had no problem killing people in the name of Socialism: Georgia in 1989, Azerbaidjan in 1990, Lithuania in 1991, etc. But this particular operation — the 'velvet revolution' in Eastern Europe — was a different matter.

The whole idea was to keep the hand of Moscow hidden. In the documents I have copied from Soviet archives, you can see how that plan was worked out. One records the speech made by Gorbachev at the Politburo meeting on October 6, 1988, where he said that socialism is in a profound crisis, so all the Communist regimes had to introduce Perestroika-style reforms in order to survive. Then he says: *A number of countries have followed our example, or even preceded us on the road of deep reforms. Others, such as the GDR, Romania or North Korea, still fail to recognize the need for such reforms - but the reasons for that are rather political, since the present leadership is unwilling to change anything. In reality, all those countries need change. We don't say this publicly, lest we are accused of an attempt to impose Perestroika on the friends, but the fact is: there are clear signs of a forthcoming crisis, so radical reforms are required all over the socialist world. In this sense, the factor of personalities becomes of huge significance. [...] Those who stubbornly refuse to follow the call of the times only push the illness deep inside and greatly aggravate its future course.*

That concerns us very directly. We may have abandoned the rights of the 'Big Brother' of the socialist world, but we cannot abandon our role of its leader. Objectively, it shall always belong to the Soviet Union, as the strongest country of Socialism and the birthplace of the October Revolution.

While ruling out any military solutions, Gorbachev wanted the Politburo to work out a clear strategy in case of a serious crisis, so as to keep East Europe under control without a military intervention. This task was given to a special commission chaired by Alexander Yakovlev. Several other documents indicate that the commission kept working in the early months of 1989, but alas — its final recommendations and the subsequent Politburo decision are shrouded in secrecy. Yet, the subsequent events speak for themselves.

There is a lot of evidence to suggest that the coup against Caeusescu in 1989 was secretly directed from Moscow. It is known that at least some of the key figures in the National Salvation Committee (such as Gen. Militaru or Silviu Brucan) had been secretly in touch with the Soviets for years. After the revolution, the new government took a very pro-Soviet line, especially in confidential negotiations with Moscow (in public, they pretended to be more independent).

For instance, there was the question of Moldova — the part of Romania annexed by the USSR under the Soviet-German pact of 1939. Iliescu confidentially assured Moscow that he would not do anything that could undermine the position of Moldova as an integral part of the USSR, but asked Gorbachev to excuse him if his public statements suggest a more independent approach. Another document suggests that Iliescu's government wanted to establish new 'strategic' links between the USSR and Eastern Europe to replace the collapsed Warsaw Pact. According to the transcript, in May 1990 Gorbachev said to the Bulgarian Communist leader Lilov: *'[Iliescu] takes balanced, reasonable position; he is prepared for constructive collaboration.*

However, I think we should not make the closeness of our approaches too public.'

It is also revealing that both Iliescu and Gorbachev are still in complete denial about all these matters. They even deny that they knew each other before 1989, although they were at university together in the 1950s. After Adam's document was published, Gorbachev specifically came to Romania, on Iliescu's request, to deny he was asked to send troops in 1989. Likewise, the late Alexander Yakovlev always maintained that the Politburo had no discussions or decisions concerning Eastern Europe in 1989 — none whatsoever (it was not then known that Yakovlev himself was in charge of working out those decisions).

So, we are not talking about different interpretations of events - the evidence is overwhelming, while all the main participants are in total denial. After all, about a thousand people were killed in those events — so it would take a lot of courage for Gorbachev, or Iliescu, or Baker to tell the whole truth and accept their share of responsibility.

FP: Lt. General Ion Mihai Pacepa, what is your reading of what Adam Burakowski and Pavel Stroilov are telling us here in our discussion?

Pacepa: First, I want to congratulate Dr. Jamie Glazov for organizing this symposium on Communist Romania's move to democracy, which was a unique event and contains important lessons. The 1989 fall of the Kremlin's viceroys in Eastern Europe was generally so peaceful that it enriched our political vocabulary with the expression "velvet" revolution. The only exception was in my native Romania, where the change was bloody: 1,104 dead and 3,352 wounded.

I also want to express my respect for Mr. Stroilov's commitment to exposing the unseen face of the Kremlin. I have strong evidence to agree with his conclusion that Moscow had a hidden hand in overthrowing Ceausescu as well.

The so-called Romanian revolution of 1989 was in reality a popular rebellion stolen by a handful of Communists educated in Moscow, who tried to preserve Romania in the Soviet fold. In the 1970s, when I

77

was Ceauşescu's national security adviser, I supervised a super-secret intelligence unit, the U.M.0920/A, tasked with counter-espionage against the Soviet Union. It was unique in the Soviet bloc. The fear that the Kremlin wanted his scalp was Ceauşescu's Achilles heel. U.M.0920/A had somewhat over 1,000 officers. It was housed in a large building located on Rabat Street, near Ceauşescu's residence, and was listed as the "Institute for Marketing," a cover organization created and run by the DIE for that specific purpose. After I broke with Communism I publicly exposed U.M 920/A, which was renamed UM0110 and got a new boss, Gen. Victor Necolicioiu.

According to information obtained by U.M. 0920/A, in August 1969, two years after Ceauşescu had condemned the invasion of Czechoslovakia, and a few days after he had invited President Richard Nixon to visit Romania against Moscow's wish, the Kremlin launched operation *Dnestr*. Its task was to replace Ceauşescu with a Communist more loyal to Moscow. The Kremlin was afraid that Ceauşescu's trumpeted independence from Moscow might exacerbate popular demand in the Soviet Republic of Moldavia for reunification with Romania, and start an uncontrollable wave of nationalist fervor in the other Soviet republics. The Kremlin also feared that the Romanians' hatred of Ceauşescu might turn their minds toward hating Communism itself. The launching of *Dnestr* was preceded by the extraordinary cancellation of a widely publicized visit that General Secretary Leonid Brezhnev and Premier Aleksey Kosygin had been scheduled to make to Romania.

In my second book, *The Kremlin's Legacy*, published in 1993, I detailed operation *Dnestr*. In an updated Romanian edition of *Red Horizons*, published in June 2010 to celebrate 20 years since Ceauşescu was executed, I dedicated some 60 pages to *Dnestr*. Here is a very short synopsis of what I knew about that operation until 1978, when I broke with Communism.

As part of *Dnestr*, the KGB and the GRU (Soviet military intelligence) persuaded three ranking party activists and seven officers in the Romanian *Securitate* and the army to join a palace coup against Ceauşescu when the time was ripe. The most important party activist was Ion Iliescu, a Politburo member who had matured politically in

Moscow and bore the middle name Ilich, given to him by his father, who had placed his whole life in the service of the Comintern and who had idolized Vladimir *Ilyich* Lenin (Iliescu's 1972 recruitment was recorded on tape, as described in *The Kremlin's Legacy.*). The most important of the seven generals was Nicolae Militaru, deputy minister of defense. (His 1978 recruitment, recorded on tape, was described in *Red Horizons*, published in 1988.).

None of the persons discovered by U.M. 0920/A as having been recruited by Moscow under its *Dnestr* operation was ever tried for espionage. Concerned not to anger the Kremlin, Ceausescu ordered that each case be individually "neutralized" without incurring Moscow's wrath. Ion Ilich Iliescu was released from his position at the top of the Communist Party and moved to a regional post. General Militaru was forced to retire. All, however, remained under constant surveillance by U.M.920/A.

In 1978 I broke with Communism, and I do not know what happened with *Dnestr*. But the similarities between its provisions and the December 1989 events were remarkable. Only a few hours after the Romanian uprising forced Ceausescu to flee in his helicopter, retired general Nicolae Militaru showed up at the Bucharest television station, now in the hands of the rebels, and appointed himself chief of the country's armed and security forces. During the night of December 22, Ion Ilich Iliescu created the National Salvation Front stipulated in *Dnestr,* and appointed himself to head it. At 2:00 p.m. on December 23, Romanian television announced that the National Salvation Front had asked the Soviet Union for military help, invoking the pretext that "unidentified foreign terrorists" in Romania were trying to reinstate Ceausescu. That was exactly what *Dnestr* had called for: to find a pretext for Soviet military intervention, which would occur, should the coup not succeed on its own.

The Soviet Embassy promptly entered the picture, publicly stating that the lives of its personnel were endangered. In Moscow, a few hours later, the Soviet television newscast *"Vremya"* confirmed that Ceausescu was being supported by "foreign mercenaries," and that the Kremlin had already told Iliescu that it would provide the military help he had requested. Misinformed and uninspired, as it has been during all those years when it praised Ceauşescu to the sky, the United States Department of State immediately avowed that Washington would take a sympathetic view of Soviet military intervention in Romania.

In the end the Kremlin was spared both the political and the financial cost of a military adventure in Romania. On that same December 23, Iliescu announced that Ceauşescu had been arrested the previous day, and a spokesman for the National Salvation Front promised that he would be given a public trial. Nevertheless two days later, on Christmas Day, 1989, Romanian television came on the air with the news that the Ceauşescu couple had been already tried, sentenced to death and executed by a military firing squad that same day. The Western media speculated that Ceauşescu was immediately killed to prevent him from exposing Moscow's hand in the December events. I can only confirm that, before 1978, when I broke with Ceauşescu, I reported to him all the details of the *Dnestr* operation. So did my boss of those days, Gen. Nicolae Doicaru, who was found dead soon after Ceauşescu was killed. Doicaru's family got his body back in a sealed coffin.

On March 1, 1990, three months after Ceauşescu's show-trial, Romania's new government announced that the officer who presided at it, Gen. Gica Popa, had committed suicide. The government ruled out an autopsy, and did not release the general's body to his family. Popa's wife, who saw her husband only at his funeral, asserted that his body showed violet marks at both wrists. According to her, after the trial of Ceauşescu her husband had qualms of conscience, and intended to contact the U.S. Embassy.

There is quite enough circumstantial evidence showing that the liquidation of Ceauşescu was carefully prepared. Ten other generals involved in the events of December 1989 died under conditions not yet determined.

In real life, it often happens that a person may go out to find wool and come home shorn, as they say in Romania. Neither Gorbachev nor his intelligence services were able to predict that their efforts to hold Romania within the confines of *glasnost* and *perestroika* would in the end — to use a Marxist image — dig their own graves. The

Romanians, freed from Ceauşescu's boot, began demolishing the barriers the Communists had spent over 40 years erecting between themselves and the rest of the world, as well as between individual Russians. Now Romania is a member of NATO, and a new generation of intellectuals is struggling to give her a new national identity.

Buchar: First let me say it's an honor for me to be invited here together with such distinguished people. The information they are bringing into the open is fascinating, but not surprising. One has to keep in mind that all of this was carefully planned for a long period of time. The name of Anatoly Golitsyn is such a taboo till today, yet he brought to the West information about the Soviets planning these changes back in 1962. Then another defector, Gen. Jan Sejna in 1968, said the same thing. But nobody in the West listened or wanted to hear it.

It looks like this mind-blowing operation was carefully planned for some thirty years. The Soviets used Ceauşescu as a guinea pig to test how to create the Communist leader likeable to the West. At the same time, they created a little monster, because Ceauşescu's ego became so big it crossed the point of no return. However, Moscow's plans had contingency for all alternatives. After all, the swift execution of Ceauşescu and his wife broadcasted on TV in vivid colors sent the chilling message to all "hard-line" Communists across Eastern Europe that any resistance to change was futile. The situation in Romania was quite unique because Ceauşescu was running the country with an iron fist as a ruthless dictator. That type of environment didn't give much opportunity to develop any dissent like the Soviets did in some other countries — like in Czechoslovakia, for instance, where the KGB used the so-called 'Prague Spring' to build the echelon of new leaders for the future.

FP: Vladimir Bukovsky, what do you bring to the end of this first round?

Bukovsky: Thank you, Jamie.

Let me start with a fresh Polish joke about a conversation between two pigs in a barn:

Pig #1: "You know, I cannot believe that they are feeding us and looking after us just because they are kind. They must have some ulterior motive. In the end, they will probably kill and eat us."

Pig #2: "Oh, stop this. To hell with your conspiracy theories!"

The debate about the 1989 revolutions over the past 20 years has been developing along more or less the same lines.

A few years ago, when Iliescu was still the president, I mentioned in an interview to a Romanian newspaper that he and his 'National Salvation Committee' were secretly backed by Moscow. Even at that stage, the evidence was already overwhelming, so I felt free to refer to that as an established fact and did not expect any controversy. But suddenly, Iliescu went out and threatened to sue me for libel in a Romanian court. I replied I would be happy to have the evidence tested in court, but invited him to sue me in Britain. After all, we have the most draconian libel laws in the world. Iliescu calmed down and soon lost the election.

Indeed, the known facts and documents leave me in no doubt that the whole so-called 1989 revolution was simply a Soviet operation. However, even I did not suspect that Iliescu was so close to Moscow that he actually asked for a Soviet invasion. In this sense, Adam's discovery opens a whole new dimension to the history of those events. There are, in particular, a lot of questions to be asked about the role of the West: how much did State Secretary Baker know about the Soviet backing for the revolution? Why did he join that invitation for a Soviet invasion? But one thing is now abundantly clear: Iliescu and his committee were little more than just Soviet puppets. Throughout history, it was typical for Soviet-sponsored subversives in any country to request a Soviet invasion when they lost control of events.

Yet, even being caught with smoking guns, our opponents are still in denial. I remember how I met the late Alexander Yakovlev, — who, as Pavel tells us, was the architect of the 1989 revolutions — at a conference some fifteen years ago. By that time, he was supposed to have become a great democrat and a high authority on matters of Soviet history. Without knowing anything about his personal role except that he was a Politburo member, I asked him about the 1989 revolutions: what was the original Soviet plan? How did it get out of control? Did the Politburo take any advance decision on what should be done in East Europe?

"There was no decision," Yakovlev replied.

"Look," I said, "I have seen the Politburo documents about the withdrawal from Afghanistan. That decision was worked out very carefully in order to preserve the pro-Soviet regime, because, as you, comrades, noted, that regime "was associated with us in the eyes of the world." Surely East Europe could not be seen as less important, and left to its own devices? You must have had at least some plan about it?"

But Yakovlev was adamant: there had been no plan, no decision, no discussion of that issue by the Politburo. All happened by itself.

At that point, we were approached by Radek Sikorski (at that time, he was not the Foreign Minister of Poland yet), who also had a question for Yakovlev:

"Alexander Nikolayevich, I wanted to ask you for a very long time: when exactly have you stopped believing in Communism?"

"Do you think I am an idiot?" Yakovlev asked. "I never believed in Communism in my life."

Amazed, Radek turned to me and said in English:

"It looks like the whole f...ng Soviet Union was governed by anti-Communists!"

Now we learn, from Pavel's documents, that not only did the Politburo have a plan, but Yakovlev personally was in charge of its preparation. After Adam's document was published, Gorbachev specifically came to Romania on Iliescu's request; the two of them staged a press conference and denied everything. It was reported in the Romanian media that the cost of Gorbachev's visit was about a million dollars, but the Communists always have enough money for propaganda (from whatever sources).

I guess Romania is the main reason why Gorbachev and Yakovlev denied their responsibility for the 1989 revolutions. After all, over a thousand people were killed there. Still, our opponents have hardly anything to say on the substance of the matter — you cannot argue against the documents. All they can do is dismiss all the evidence as a "conspiracy theory." Sadly, though, when multiplied by all the power and money of the neo-Communist Establishment, even this cheap propaganda trick works.

Nowadays, the "conspiracy theorist" label is being used in the same manner as "enemy of the people" under Stalin. Nobody ever gave a clear definition of a conspiracy theory, and yet, it is a perfect way to silence dissenting voices without any debate on the substance of the matter. We seem to admit that conspiracies do happen and sometimes succeed, so much so that we even recognize them in criminal law. It is quite respectable, for example, to blame the 9/11 tragedy on an al-Qaeda conspiracy. This is not a conspiracy theory, but any alternative theory is. So, a conspiracy theory is simply a view which does not fit into the margins of what is acceptable to the Establishment, simply a deviation from their propaganda line.

It is time to admit that, because conspiracies sometimes occur, a conspiracy theory may happen to be accurate, just like any other theory. In the case of the Romanian revolution, the "conspiracy theory" is simply the only possible explanation of the known facts. The only alternative theory, aggressively advanced in several academic works and a documentary movie, attempts to explain everything with a conspiracy of Western secret services. Their "evidence" is limited to some empty claims by two or three people, supposedly former French secret agents; and the whole theory is so inconsistent that it hardly merits a serious consideration. Yet, nobody calls it a conspiracy theory.

So, gentlemen, 20 years after the Soviet empire collapsed, we are still in a position when the truth about our history is being jammed by communist propaganda. Even if, as Gen. Pacepa says, the Communist regime has dug its own grave, it will continue to haunt our countries until we nail a wooden stake through its heart. One would expect that Adam's discovery would cause a political storm in Romania; instead, we only saw the panic reaction from Iliecu and Gorbachev amidst the general indifference. Meanwhile, during the same few weeks, the Communists had an immensely important victory of blocking a long-awaited lustration law in the Romania's Constitutional Court.

Alas, as I said many times before, we did not win the Cold War. No war is over until the minefields and unexploded bombs are cleared away, unless gangs of marauders and surviving enemies are disarmed. Above all, no war is over until its crimes are investigated and condemned, and the truth about its history is revealed and accepted. So far, in the world in general and Romania in particular, we only see Communists writing history and dictating the conditions of peace. The most optimistic comment I can make about this is that there is still a long way to go.

FP: Adam Burakowski, what are your thoughts for this second and final round?

Burakowski: As Pavel rightly pointed out, Iliescu and his people did indeed go to great lengths in order to hide their ties to Moscow. Still, they did not fully succeed in doing so. Some of their actions were just too obvious, like the Romanian-Soviet friendship pact signed in April 1991 — just months prior to the collapse of the USSR. The pact met with strong criticism in Bucharest, among other things, for its recognition of the existing northern border of Romania.

The pro-Russian policy was abandoned later by Iliescu himself. In 2000, when the post-Communist party regained power in Romania, many political analysts feared that it would reverse the pro-Western trend established by Emil Constantinescu and consequent governments of the coalition around the Romanian Democratic Convention. This, however, did not happen. Iliescu realized that the integration with Western structures — NATO and European Union — should continue. Our knowledge of the Romanian December is now deeper than it was in the 1990's, when first books on the topic were published. Some theories from that time have since been confirmed by new evidence, others discarded. Recently the bodies of the Ceauşescu couple have been exhumed. I personally doubt whether this particular examination will reveal any new clues, but most certainly, any investigation efforts around the December events should be encouraged and supported. Because there remains a lot to be cleared up.

I agree with Vladimir, that we constantly face attempts to hide the truth. Many of these attempts are primitive and easy to see through, but when they are boosted by media propaganda, they begin to gain undue credibility, significantly harming the public awareness of what happened 20 years ago and what is happening now.

Democracy should be built on the truth. People, not just in Romania, deserve to know the real circumstances of the 1989 events. Why was there more bloodshed after the overthrow of Ceauşescu than before it? How did it happen that following so much bloodshed, hard-headed post-communists took over the power (quite unlike in the bordering Hungary, where not a single shot had been fired)? Why was the pro-western policy, as the only possible way to cut the ties with the country's totalitarian past, introduced in Romania so late? These are only some of the questions that need to be asked repeatedly. I would like to express my gratitude to Dr. Jamie Glazov for organizing this discussion. It's been a privilege to me and, I hope it will be an encouragement to researchers out there to explore and solve the mysteries of the past, so we can all draw a lesson.

Stroilov: I am very grateful to Gen. Pacepa for the kind words. May I, in turn, express my admiration for everything he has done to reveal the truth about the communist regime in Romania and its role in the Cold War. I regard his *'Red Horizons'* as the single most important source on those matters. What he has told us in this discussion about the 1989 revolution and the parallels with the plan 'Dnestr' is also very revealing.

Paradoxically, having spent years and years trying to uncover the truth about the final stage of the Cold War, we on this panel still seem to underestimate the importance of our own work. It cannot be the case that, while the history of Communism is being distorted and falsified, at present the recovery is going on just fine. I agree with Vladimir:

recovery is simply not possible without revealing the whole truth about the past. While the Iliescus of this world are lying about their Communist past, I shall never believe a word of what they say about their ostensibly democratic present.

With respect, I cannot agree with Adam that the fears of Communist restoration after Iliescu's return to power in 2000 turned out to be wrong. The EU membership or even NATO membership do not guarantee democracy. On the contrary, today's European Union is a notoriously anti-democratic, socialist structure. It is a direct continuation of the Soviet plan for a 'Common European Home,' where Eastern Europe would be sandwiched between a Soviet Russia on one hand and a socialist United Europe on the other. According to the documents (Vladimir and I published many of them in 'EUSSR. *The Soviet Roots of European Integration*'), this plan was extensively discussed between Gorbachev and the Western Left (especially the French) in the late 1980s. The architects of the European Union, such as Mitterrand or Delors, were very careful to make the design compatible with Gorbachev's plans. The guarantee of control over the rebellious Central Europe – from United Germany to Romania to Yugoslavia — was a very important consideration in those discussions. So, if Iliescu was pro-Soviet and then suddenly turned pro-EU, it tells us more about the EU than about Iliescu. If he is pro-Western now, this only means something is very wrong with the West. The EU we know is simply a clever device for the Iliescus of the East and the West to preserve their unearned position of power.

After all, what is the meaning of 'pro-Western' after the U.S. State Secretary joined Iliescu's treacherous request for a Soviet invasion of Romania? Was that a 'pro-Russian' idea or a 'pro-Western' idea? And what is the meaning of 'pro-Western' today, when the United States is fighting a losing battle against Marxist reforms by its own government? Can we still seriously say that the free world has won the Cold War?

The problem is by no means purely Romanian; it is global, and has always been so. Even after the end of the Cold War, the Communists have suffered some losses but survived as an international Mafia. The real question is: how much has survived of the free world?

87

We have sown 'post-Communism'; now we harvest neo-Communism, which has turned out to be a very serious threat. The Second Cold War has already started. The question is: do we, in the East and the West, have the strength to resist?

And of course, if we are to fight, we should start by opening our eyes. Like 20 years ago, no recovery is possible until we face the truth about the past. The instincts of the neo-Communist Establishment are still Orwellian: whoever controls the past controls the future. So, indeed, the greatest rebellion in today's world is to put two and two together. That is what we have tried to do in this symposium and in our work over years; hopefully, with some success.

Thank you, Jamie. Thank you, gentlemen.

Pacepa: I fully agree with Mr. Bukovksy: "It looks like the whole f...ing Soviet Union was governed by anti-Communists." Of course, there were no Nazi admirers to be found in Germany after World War II, either. And what about Communists in Romania? A lie! There were none. If things go wrong in Moscow and Bucharest these days, it is because of people like Bukovsky, Preobrazhenskiy and Pacepa. They betrayed their motherland. They are the evil. They are "traitors" and "absolute loafers," as President Putin called former KGB general Oleg Kalugin, a director of the International Spy Museum in Washington D.C., who was sentenced to fifteen years in jail by Moscow during the same year of 2002, when NATO welcomed Putin's Russia as an honorary member in that alliance.

A few months ago, when the world celebrated 20 years since the Soviet empire collapsed, Romania's government refused to cancel a 1974 death sentence given by Ceauşescu's "justice" to a respected American citizen, Constantin Răuţă. The Supreme Court, whose masters are now chauffeured around in American limousines, continue to preach that Mr. Răuţă should be executed because he committed the "crime" of cooperating with Romania's main enemy, the United States.

Mr. Răuţă is a respected American scientist, who over the past thirty years worked on major U.S. aero-spatial projects such as HUBBLE,

88

KOBE, EOS and LANDSAT. He was also involved in the development of various space defense systems, making a substantial contribution to the defense of the United States and her NATO allies. But he is still a "traitor" for the Romanian government.

Mr. Răuță is not an isolated case in Romania. Rather, he seems to be the rule. In the past five years, 6,284 people sentenced by the Communists for fighting Communism have asked to have their sentences canceled, but only three have succeeded — because of Western media pressure.

How is it possible for Communists still to be calling the shots in a NATO country twenty years after Communism collapsed there?

Professor Tom Gallagher, one of the world's leading experts on contemporary Romania, who teaches the evolution of post-Communist states at Bradford University in the U.K., concluded that Romania had moved from rigid [Communist] egalitarianism to super-inegalitarianism run by corrupt ex-Communists who merely pay lip-service to democracy. This "new predatory elite" has "widened the gap between a parasitic state and a demoralized society." In Prof. Gallagher's view Romania is not yet a democracy, because "a functional democracy cannot be based on lies, denial and amnesia." This is also the subject of his book *Romania since Communism: The Denial of Democracy* (Hurst, 2004), which concludes that "a Romania under the control of corrupt ex-communists threatens to be a dangerous force for regional instability."

Let me put it my own way. Today we know how a democracy could be changed into a Communist tyranny, but we are still learning how to reverse that *nightmare*. Post-Ceausescu Romania has been transformed in staggering and unprecedented ways, but it remains a Soviet-style police state.

In 1978, when I broke with Communism, Romania had one major intelligence service, the *Securitate,* staffed with ca. 16,000 operations officers. Now it has six (SRI, SIE, UM 0962, STS, SPP, DGIA), which have absorbed most of the former *Securitate* officers and its *modus operandi.* According to the Romanian media, these six ghosts of Communism are bloated with over 30,000 officers. The SRI (domestic counter-intelligence) alone, covering a population of 22 million, has ca. 12,000 officers. Its French equivalent, the DCRI (*Direction Centrale du Renseignement Intérieur*), covering a population three times as large, has 6,000. Its German counterpart, the BfV (*Bundesamt für Verfassungsschutz*), which covers 82 million people, has only 2,448 officers. If the United States were to apply the Romanian ratio, the FBI would have ca. 190,000 agents, not the 12,156 agents it has today.

Hangmen do not incriminate themselves. Over 500,000 Romanian patriots who were killed or terrorized by the Communist *Securitate* are still not rehabilitated. At the same time, thousands of former *Securitate* officers and hundreds of thousands of its informants and collaborators, who wrote the bloodiest era in Romania's history, are still shielded by a veil of secrecy-quite a few of them are the *nouveaux riches* now running the country.

This is the legacy of the Kremlin's "Dnestr" operation, during which Communists loyal to Moscow (Ion Ilych Iliescu, Nicolae Militaru, Sergiu Celac, Silviu Brucan,) initiated the killing of Ceausescu, and took control of Romania. The Kremlin had a similar "Dnestr" plan for every bloc country. In 1990, I found a *Stasi* extension of the "Dnestr" plan for East Germany in the newly-opened *Stasi* archives.

The *Stasi* extension was called Plan OibE (*Offiziere im besonderen Einsatz* — officers on special assignment), and it defined the *Stasi's* ultra-secret tasks in the event that "the [Communist] Socialist Unity Party of Germany were to lose its power." Known to a few insiders as the "order for survival," Plan OibE was signed by State Security minister Erich Mielke on March 17, 1986, and registered as Top Secret Document 0008-6/86. The plan provided that 2,587 undercover *Stasi* officers, whose identity was extremely tightly held, would on signal move into high-level positions in the German Democratic Republic (2,000) and its embassies (587). The speed with which the East German government collapsed evidently did not allow for Plan OibE to become fully operational. But it is noteworthy that most of the new politicians who rose to prominence in Germany after Communism's collapse were secretly affiliated with the *Stasi*. Among them: Lothar de Maziere, the first democratically elected East German prime minister; Ibrahim Böhme, a founder of the eastern Social Democratic Party; Wolfgang Schnur, the founding leader of the Democratic Awakening, a once burgeoning political party, which collapsed after Schnur's exposure as a *Stasi* asset.

In 1996, West German chancellor Helmuth Kohl described the whole German version of the "Dnestr" plan in his book *Ich wollte Deutschlands Einheit* (I Wanted German Unity). It is worth reading. I also strongly recommend *And Reality Be Damned by Robert Buchar*, a distinguished participant in this Symposium. His book offers a bird's eye view of the 1989 collapse of Communism in Eastern Europe and of its consequences, as seen by former CIA chief, now defense secretary Robert Gates, by national security expert Joseph D. Douglas and by many other experts on Communism and Soviet Russia.

I also want to suggest to Dr. Glazov to hold a similar Symposium on today's Russia. The success of the "Dnestr" plan in Romania may make life miserable for that country's population, but it can scarcely be said to threaten world peace. The spectacular success of the "Dnestr" plan in Russia might, however. Today over 6,000 former officers of the KGB, which killed tens of millions during the Soviet years and terrorized a third of the World's population, are running the country's federal and local governments, and nearly half of all top governmental positions are now held by former officers of the KGB. The Soviet Union had one KGB officer for every 428 citizens. Putin's Russia has one FSB officer for every 297 citizens. We are facing the first intelligence dictatorship in history, and Dr. Glazov's *Frontpage* could make history by focusing on it.

FP: Well, I have my next symposium to put together.

Robert Buchar, your final comments?

Buchar: Very interesting discussion indeed. It is so important to bring as much information to the public as possible. Not just about Romania or today's Russia, as Mr. Pacepa suggests, but about all former Eastern Block countries one by one to connect the dots and point out the similarities. Every country had its own scenario, but when we look at it site by site then the big picture becomes obvious.

The biggest problem we are all facing is the total blackout of media on this issue, globally. No media outlet is willing to challenge the official version of the story regardless of the evidence presented. Why is that? This has bothered me deeply for a long time now since I am trying for years to finish the documentary film on this topic. Then, recently, I was reading Jamie's interview with Michael Ledeen about Iran and here it was loud and clear: "We deny it because when we admit it, we have to do something about it. Better do nothing."

Mr. Ledeen's definition, even though he was talking about slightly different problem, is right on the mark. It's politically incorrect to question already established history. Too much is at stake. As a result, the worldwide neo-Communist movement is spreading like a cancer with the goal to destroy Western civilization and nobody is willing to mention it. Besides, it would be bad for business. And meanwhile, the "first intelligence dictatorship," as Mr. Pacepa put it, is working in overdrive — just look at the Russians' activities in former Eastern Europe countries and in the EU, not to mention in the U.S. and in other parts of the world.

What this symposium is doing, Jamie, is extremely valuable. After all, there are just very few places where this topic is seriously discussed. Besides Jamie Glazov here at FrontPage Magazine, there is Jeff Nyquist at strategiccrisis.com and that's about it.

While the consequences of the fall of Communism are accelerating and spreading around the globe at an exponential rate, the big question that comes to my mind is if people really want to know what happened twenty years ago. Do they really want to learn the truth? I am not so sure they do. It really doesn't matter if they are in Eastern Europe or America. How does one open the eyes of people in a consumer society today? The problem seems to be so distant, almost abstract. Their perception of reality was already shaped and massaged by the media. After all, people prefer to believe what they want to believe. They want to go shopping, be entertained and have a good time. Maybe they will awaken one day, but it may be too little too late. As Vladimir

Bukovsky said, we have a long way to go. My concern is if we have enough time left to reach the end of the road.

Thanks to Dr. Jamie Glazov and all participants of this symposium for making this discussion possible. Let's hope we will meet again soon.

FP: Thank you, Robert.

Vladimir Bukovsky, last word goes to you sir.

Bukovsky: If you come to Romania nowadays, the first thing you notice are the Lukoil petrol stations on every corner, Lukoil being one of those Russian huge oil corporations controlled by the Siloviki mafia. If you start making enquiries, you will discover that a big part of Romania's oil industry — and many other industries as well — is controlled by Moscow either directly or through more complicated schemes involving third parties and countries. Mind you, Romania's oil is no small matter: for example, it used to be the key to victory in the Second World War. So, what kind of national independence is this if Romania is strategically dependent on Russia? How can Romania have a genuine democracy if the country is, to a high extent, owned by a foreign authoritarian regime?

Before the latest presidential elections in Romania, the socialist candidate, Mircea Geoana, was caught secretly talking to Moscow about financing his campaign, in exchange for the further lucrative opportunities he would open for Russian businesses after becoming president, and an improvement of relations 'reset'-style. If the media reports were accurate, this means that Geoana simply offered himself for sale to the Kremlin. Even after this scandal was exposed, the election was still very closely fought, and the fate of Romania hung in the balance. What kind of democracy is this, where at least one of the major parties is little more than a Russian fifth column, and every election presents a very real threat to the country's independence and freedom?

Finally, what kind of national independence is this if the country remains divided, just as it was divided by Comrades Stalin and Hitler? Romania's eastern border, drawn by the Soviet invaders, is still considered sacred. The fate of Moldova was decided by Gorbachev and Iliescu behind closed doors just after their fake revolution; but even twenty years later, nobody dares to suggest reconsidering those decisions. Throughout those years, Moldova lives under a constant threat of a Russian takeover, while Romania is under enormous pressure, from the east and from the west, to do nothing. Just a few weeks ago, Russia expelled a Romanian diplomat, absurdly accused of implementing a covert plan for a takeover of Moldova.

The success of the Operation Dnestr has deprived Romanians of a chance to restore their own sovereign democracy and, symbolically, to reclaim their lawful eastern border on the Dnestr.

All of these realities are the links of the same chain: Russia's subversion of Moldova, Russia's fifth column in Romanian politics, the enormous political influence of Communists in both parts of the divided country, the lustration laws being blocked, the truth about history being suppressed, and, indeed, the Sovietization of the EU and the West.

All of these are direct consequences of our failure to secure a decisive victory in the Cold War twenty years ago, but even more so of our reluctance to face the truth about what happened.

FP: Adam Burakowski, Vladimir Bukovsky, Pavel Stroilov, Lt. General Ion Mihai Pacepa and Robert Buchar, thank you for joining Frontpage Symposium.

[Jamie Glazov, "Symposium: Secrets of Communisim's 'Collapse'," *Frontpagemag.com*, Sept. 23, 2010.]

[5] Remembering the Dissident: Alexander Solzhenitsyn

Alexander Solzhenitsyn died several months ago, on August 3, 2008, at the age of 89. Frontpage Symposium has gathered a distinguished panel to discuss the significance of the dissident's life and work. Our guests are:

Natan Sharansky, a former Soviet dissident and political prisoner who is the co- author (with Ron Dermer) of *The Case For Democracy: The Power of Freedom to Overcome Tyranny and Terror.* Mr. Sharansky has been awarded the Congressional Gold Medal of Freedom for his courageous fight for liberty. He formerly served as Minister for Jerusalem and Diaspora Affairs in the Israeli government.

Richard Pipes, a Professor Emeritus at Harvard who is one of the world's leading authorities on Soviet history. He is the author of 19 books, the most recent being his new autobiography *Vixi: Memoirs of a Non-Belonger.*

Pavel Litvinov, a Russian physicist, writer, human rights activist and former Soviet-era dissident.

Yakov Krotov, a Russian Orthodox priest, who is not in the established Russian Orthodox Church. He is a historian, essayist and freelance journalist who leads a live broadcast on "Radio Liberty" in Moscow titled "From the Christian Point of View." Christians of all denominations, people of all faiths and non-believers participate in the program.

Dr. Natalia Sadomskaya, a former Russian dissident. She is an anthropologist who worked in the 1960s in the Mikhlukho-Makhlay Institute of Ethnography. She participated in the first dissident demonstration on Pushkin Square against the arrest of Siniavsky and Daniel and also signed letters of protest against the arrest of Aleksander Ginzburg. In 1974 she immigrated to the United States with her husband and Russian dissident Boris Shragin. In America, she taught Cultural Anthropology at Amherst College, Queens College (CUNY) and Columbia University (N.Y). In 1994, she returned to

Russia. She taught Social Anthropology at the Russian State University for the Humanities.

Lt. Gen. Ion Mihai Pacepa, the highest official ever to have defected from the Soviet bloc. In 1989, Ceausescu and his wife were executed at the end of a trial where most of the accusations had come word-for-word out of Pacepa's book *Red Horizons,* republished in 27 countries. He is the author of *Programmed to Kill: Lee Harvey Oswald, the Soviet KGB, and the Kennedy Assassination.*

David Satter, a senior fellow of the Hudson Institute and a visiting scholar at the Johns Hopkins University Nitze School of Advanced International Studies (SAIS). He is the author of *Darkness at Dawn: The Rise of the Russian Criminal State.*

Yuri Yarim-Agaev, a former leading Russian dissident and a member of the Moscow Helsinki Group. Upon arriving in the United States after his forced exile from the Soviet Union, he headed the New York-based Center for Democracy in the USSR. He is a Distinguished Visiting Fellow with the Hoover Institution.

and

Dr. Theodore Dalrymple, a retired physician (prison doctor and psychiatrist), a contributing editor to *City Journal* and the author of the new book, *Not With a Bang But a Whimper: The Politics and Culture of Decline.*

FP: Natan Sharansky, Pavel Litvinov, Dr. Natalia Sadomskaya, Richard Pipes, Yakov Krotov, Lt. Gen. Ion Mihai Pacepa, David Satter, Yuri Yarim Agaev and Dr. Theodore Dalrymple, welcome to Frontpage Symposium.

David Satter, let's begin with you. What were your thoughts upon Solzhenitsyn's death?

Satter: On learning of Solzhenitsyn's death I had a sense of the end of an era. I grew up politically with Solzhenitsyn. As a teenager in the 1960s, I once asked my father whether it was true that there were slave labor camps in the Soviet Union. He said that if they had existed, we would have the accounts of survivors. After Solzhenitsyn and the publication of "One Day in the Life of Ivan Denisovich," it was no longer possible to say that there were no first-hand accounts.

Many people, including millions of Soviet citizens, were deceived about the atrocities of the Communist regime. More than anyone else, Solzhenitsyn dispelled those fatal illusions. His contribution to literature and to truth is indelible. I also, however, on learning of Solzhenitsyn's death felt a sense of sadness that in his later years, he strayed from the path of universal values and supported the Putin regime. In this, he demonstrated spiritual weaknesses that were not so evident in the years when he valiantly resisted Soviet totalitarianism.

Solzhenitsyn made a monumental contribution to the destruction of Soviet communism. Many episodes from his books are simply unforgettable — the telephone call in the opening scene in *The First Circle*, Eleanor Roosevelt's visit to the Butyrka Prison, the discovery of a prehistoric salamander in an ice lens by starving prisoners in *The Archipelago Gulag*. This rare artistic talent was used to bear witness to some of the greatest crimes of the century. In this way, Solzhenitsyn combined great art and riveting political relevance.

In his later years, however, Solzhenitsyn exhibited many of the traits that he criticized in his books. He fought for freedom and told Russians "live not by lies" when it was a matter of opposing communism but praised Putin who waged a genocidal war in Chechnya and re-imposed censorship. He told the West to interfere in Soviet affairs in the 1970s but when the West interfered too much 30 years later, he joined the hierarchs of the Russian Orthodox Church, many of them former KGB informers, in casting doubt on the universal validity of human rights.

I believe that ultimately Solzhenitsyn's political views are far less important than his work and his contribution to the fall of Communism. It is his masterpieces that will be remembered and his political views will be only a footnote just as Dostoevsky's bizarre political pronouncements are a footnote to his immortal works. As Russia reverts back to dictatorship, however, Solzhenitsyn's own political evolution should not be completely ignored. Russia's great weakness is its failure to value the truth for its own sake.

Solzhenitsyn struck a blow against this tendency in his opposition to Soviet totalitarianism which promoted an ideology that he came to reject. It would have been better for his legacy and better for Russia if he could have brought himself to denounce the new tyranny that is developing in Russia today.

FP: Thank you, Dr. Satter.

Lt. Gen. Ion Mihai Pacepa, your thoughts on Solzhenitsyn? And what do you make of the man who struck such a blow against Communism, and in such a courageous and heroic way, ending his life by supporting the Putin regime. How do we understand this?

Pacepa: There is little I can add to Dr. Satter's comments, with which I am in full agreement. Perhaps, however, I can look at Solzhenitsyn the man from a slightly different angle.

To fully understand why such a legendary fighter against political terror ended up supporting Putin's terrorist regime, one should first take a closer look at the country that produced Solzhenitsyn. In 1854, Tsar Nicholas I confined Russian sociologist Petr Chaadayev as insane because of his unorthodox, but realistic, view of his country:

"Russia is a whole separate world, submissive to the will, caprice, fantasy of a single man, whether his name be Peter or Ivan, no matter — in all instances the common element is the embodiment of arbitrariness. Contrary to all the laws of the human community, Russia moves only in the direction of her enslavement and the enslavement of all the neighboring peoples. For this reason it would be in the interest not only of other peoples but also in that of her own that she be compelled to take a new path."

Russia's recent arbitrary invasion of Georgia and recognition of her Abkazia and Ossetia provinces as independent countries make Chaadayev's definition timeless.

Ninety years later, Solzhenitsyn also rebelled against the "fantasy of a single man," this time named Stalin, and he was also confined as insane. Chaadayev died in the insane ward. Solzhenitsyn survived, but he remained in that "whole separate world," called Russia, for he was as Russian as the balalaika. In 1970, when he got the Nobel Prize, Solzhenitsyn refused to go to Oslo to receive it, fearing he might not be allowed to return to his Russia.

After he was exiled in 1974 and eventually settled in Vermont, Solzhenitsyn continued to live in that "separate world" called Russia. He never stopped fighting Soviet terror, but he then also began fighting the pro-Western Russian dissidents for being too supportive of individualism and pluralism. "Russia," Solzhenitsyn argued, had "its own path, rooted in national identity, traditional faith, and community rather than individual rights and secular democracy." [1]

When the Soviet Union collapsed, Solzhenitsyn rushed back to his Russia. There he labeled Gorbachev's concessions to democracy as anarchy, and he blasted Yeltsin for dismantling the Russian state. Solzhenitsyn never understood American democracy. The only form of government he really knew was the historically Russian *samoderzhaviye*, in which a feudal lord ruled the country with the help of his personal political police. Thus, he fell for the *"fantasy"* of another feudal aristocrat. Putin, he explained, inherited a ransacked and bewildered country, and he started to do whatever was possible for its restoration. That seems to be the drama of most Russians. Generations of them have kidded themselves about the glorious state of their country, and Putin makes them feel proud again.

Solzhenitsyn's contribution to the destruction of Soviet Communism, however, should not be shadowed by his misunderstanding of Western democracy. Dachau and Auschwitz became museums of freedom, to assure the world that the Holocaust would never be repeated. Solzhenitsyn's *The Gulag Archipelago* has become another museum of freedom. This dramatic eyewitness testimony demolished the moral standing of the Soviet Union, and it now motivates people around the world to prevent Kremlin-style political genocide from being repeated. Only giants could achieve such a gargantuan accomplishment, and Solzhenitsyn is indeed a giant.

FP: Thank you, Lt. Gen Pacepa. Solzhenitsyn was indeed a giant and deserves much praise and respect for his stand against the Soviet Empire.

But the stances he held toward Russia's authoritarian character and Western pluralism were quite sad. His attacks on pro-Western Russian dissidents were, in my view, mean-spirited, uncalled for and unfortunate. I know that my father, Yuri Glazov, a Russian dissident, very much valued Solzhenitsyn for his courage and work, and as a professor in the West, my dad taught Solzhenitsyn's texts to his students with a great admiration and passion. But he was very hurt by Solzhenitsyn's attacks on dissidents.

Dr. Natalia Sadomskaya, let me turn to you.

Your views of Solzhenitsyn and what our guests have had to say? What lingered behind, in your view, Solzh's attacks on his fellow dissidents?

Sadomskaya: As to the 'rapprochement' between Solzhenitsyn and Putin, the mystery is easily solved if one reads "The Letter to the Leaders" written in 1973 and published by 'Samizdat' in 1974. It was the same year that Solzhenitsyn was exiled from the USSR.

His views, which he brought with him to the West, were like these: addressing Brezhnev and the others, he emphasized his national homogeny with the Communist leaders, saying, "I am trying to say here the main thing: that I regard as salvation and good for our people, with whom all of us — both you and I surely belong by birth."

It's not a slip of tongue. His meaning was: "I wish well for all the nations, and the closer to us, the more dependent on us, the warmer the wish. Yet primarily I care for the good of namely the Russian and the Ukrainian peoples because of our incomparable sufferings."

Here is what he then wrote to the leaders about democracy:

"Here in Russia, due to a complete absence of habit, democracy had existed for only eight months, from February to October, 1917.

Groups of emigrants, former c-d & s-d, who are still living, are still proud of that democracy, stating it was wrecked by alien forces. In fact, though, that democracy was their disgrace: they had so ambitiously called out to it and promised it, but succeeded in establishing only something messy, a caricature of democracy; they proved first and foremost unprepared for it themselves, and Russia proved even more so. In the recent half a century Russia could have only become even less prepared for democracy, for a multi-party parliamentary system. A sudden introduction of democracy at present might come to be another sorry repetition of 1917. For a thousand years Russia had lived under an authoritarian regime and at the turn of the 20th century it still retained the people's physical and spiritual health.

Yet there was a very important condition fulfilled: that authoritarian regime had a strong moral base: Orthodoxy.

But the Russian intelligentsia that for over a century had been doing their best to fight the authoritarian regime, what have they achieved with their great losses for themselves and for the common people as well? The result was certainly contrary to the desired one. Then, probably, we should admit that the chosen way was wrong and premature? Probably, for the near future, whether we like it or not, whether we assign it so or not, an authoritarian regime is by all means predestined for Russia. Probably it is the only one Russia is mature for." *("Letter to the Leaders")*

Solzhenitsyn's negative attitude to the pre-revolutionary opposition intelligentsia very soon turned into irritation against dissident emigrants. He saw that in the West, having attained freedom, they supported those very forms of democracy and parliamentarism he considered premature and dangerous for Russia. And when the dissidents tried to talk to him politically, he accused them of Russophobia.

Solzhenitsyn's denial of the dissident intelligentsia was especially clearly expressed in 1982, in his article "Our Pluralists" (Collection of articles "On Return of Breath", Vagrius, Moscow, 2004). Though earlier he didn't like the Soviet intelligentsia very much either, calling its representatives 'obrazovantsy' - i.e. educated ignoramuses. (Article "Obrazovanshchina" in the collection "From Under Boulders" - 'Iz pod glyb').

Such were his spirits when, twenty years later, he came back to Russia. He was showered with favors and privileges. He was awarded the country's highest order. He was invited to appear on TV, to speak in the Duma. But he was displeased with Yeltsin, who had destroyed the Great Power, as well as with the democrats-westerners, and the orgy of multi-party politics. He refused to accept the award from Yeltsin.

Yet in Putin, Solzhenitsyn saw the ruler who could implement his program — and he was not mistaken. And he accepted the order.

They both did not like the democrats of the '90s. They had a common dislike of the flourishing Western democracies. Solzhenitsyn was not at all worried by the fact that only one 'united' party was now ruling the country. He never raised his voice against the closures of TV channels, or against demonstrations scattered, or in defense of pensioners debased. He kept silence.

Well, and what about the people?

During the two burial services for Solzhenitsyn, in the Academy of Sciences and in the Donskoy Monastery, there were no more than a thousand mourners present. But, as compensation, there were the president and the ex-president, and the mayor of Moscow.

Sharansky: When I was active in the Soviet dissident movement in the beginning of the 1970s, there were two clear camps. The first was led by Andrei Sakharov and was focused on fighting for universal human rights. The other, led by Solzhenitsyn, was fueled by a strong Russian identity. In a sense, this was a continuation of the classic divide among the Russian intelligentsia between "Westerners" and Slavophiles.

I was fully in the Sakharov camp. I was also part of the Soviet Jewry/Zionist movement, which had serious disagreements with

Solzhenitsyn. For instance, he was critical of the Jackson amendment, which was so important for our movement. Whereas Sakharov understood that any expansion of freedom inside the USSR was a victory for the human rights struggle and should therefore be embraced, Solzhenitsyn thought too much energy was being wasted on ensuring freedom of emigration when the entire regime had to go.

But while the differences between the camps were real and would later, as many of the previous writers correctly mentioned, result in profound disagreements, those differences paled in comparison to our common struggle against Soviet totalitarianism.

The main challenge for all dissidents — Democrats, Zionists, nationalists, etc.— was to convince the West that the Soviet regime was evil and that there was no place for appeasement. In this effort, Solzhenitsyn contributed more than anyone to unmasking that evil. His widely read books had a huge impact, and as a spokesman for the dissident movement, I can tell you that when I mentioned *The Gulag Archipelago*, everyone knew what I was talking about. By painting such a vivid and powerful picture of evil, he gave all dissidents an indispensable reference point for our struggle.

When the Iron Curtain fell, the differences between the camps came to the surface again. On one side were the democrats, heirs to the legacy of Sakharov. On the other was Solzhenitsyn, who put Russian identity first. Against the KGB, the forces of identity and freedom stood on the same side of the barricades. Today, unfortunately they often find themselves on different sides. And Solzhenitsyn was always a champion of identity more than a champion of freedom.

In a sense, Solzhenitsyn believed that one had to choose between being a man of his people and a man of the world. As I argue in my latest book, *Defending Identity*, this is a false choice. We can be both, as long as our commitment to our own unique history, people and faith is coupled with a firm commitment to freedom and democracy. For all his great insight, this was something that Solzhenitsyn never saw.

With Solzhenitsyn, one must also address the issue of anti-Semitism. In *The Gulag Archipelago*, he writes about some Jews as heads of the camps and in important KGB positions. While this is true, it is clear that he writes about Jewish (and other minority) support for the Soviet regime with a special bitterness and disdain. It is as if he wants his readers to understand that a kind of foreign element oppresses the Russian people.

In his book, *200 Years Together*, he analyzes the history of anti-Semitism in Russia and of Russian-Jewish relations. Sadly, his explanation of the many anti-Jewish laws and double standards applied towards Jews turns into understanding and even justification.

But to call him an anti-Semite would be unjust. His writing stems from a love of his own people rather than a hatred of others. He was more biased in favor of Russia than he was biased against Jews.

FP: Thank you, Natan Sharansky. Solzhenitsyn definitely was a hero, as you note, for contributing "more than anyone to unmasking evil." He exposed the Evil Empire and in so doing lent a major hand to its eventual destruction — and he must always be credited for that. But a critic can ask a legitimate question: How does it make sense that a person can write with "understanding and even justification" about the oppression of Jews and at the same time for it to be unfair to call that person an anti-Semite?

Pipes: Aleksander Solzhenitsyn strikes me as a remarkably contradictory personality. On the one hand, he stood up with great courage to the Soviet regime and paid for this courage a hard prize in the form of incarceration in the gulag and expulsion abroad. On the other hand, he recently agreed with Putin that the dissolution of the USSR was "the worst geopolitical tragedy of the twentieth century." What is one to make of this?

His knowledge of Russian and Western history was most superficial even though he talked about in an authoritative manner. He glamorized tsarism and, as in his Harvard Commencement speech, condemned the West for its excessive freedom and "legalism."

He is no spiritual guide for Russia. My impression is that the Russians pretty much ignored him on his return home and neither read his books nor listened to his TV program. I believe that in the long run, he will be little more than a blip in Russia's twentieth century history.

FP: Surely *The Gulag Archipelago* and the heroic figure who wrote it will never become a blip in Russia's twentieth century history? Well, perhaps if Soviet era-worshippers like Putin succeed in writing history books.

Recognizing Solzh's greatness in this context, of course, does not exonerate him from the dark elements that we have discussed here so far (i.e. regret over the collapse of the USSR, anti-Semitism, criticism of dissidents, opposition to liberal pluralism, etc.)

Yuri Yarim-Agaev, what do you make of the remarkably contradictory personality that Dr. Pipes refers to and that has been discussed so far in this discussion?

Yarim-Agaev: I would not call Solzhenitsyn controversial. The fact that I do not agree with a man does not in itself make him controversial. And though I disagree with Solzhenitsyn on many important issues, I must give him credit for the comprehensive and consistent position to which he adhered for most of his life. Accepting KGB officer Putin was not an inconsistency. There was no room for such confusion in a man who brilliantly defined Communist power by four letters: CKGB. That was a retreat from his position, the weakness of an old man who wanted to believe that he would see the light at the end of the tunnel before he died.

I feel it somehow wrong to start talking about one of the greatest men of the 20th century by discussing a rather inconsequential mistake of his old age. We should define first the broader context of his life and achievements. We should judge him first and foremost by his deeds, which had a great effect on our history and civilization, not by the quotes from his little known works, which had barely any influence. To me Solzhenitsyn's main legacy is the exposure of Communism with such precision and power that that totalitarian ideology could never recover from the heavy blow. *The Gulag Archipelago* influenced not only liberal-minded intellectuals, but the Soviet ruling elite as well.

Solzhenitsyn also had a great impact on Western intellectual life and politics. He may be considered the godfather of neo-conservatism, which played a decisive role in dismantling Soviet Communism and disarming that terrible ideology.

Now giving proper weight to his actions, let us consider in its totality possibly the strongest argument against Solzhenitsyn: his attitude toward Jews. His most zealous critics accused him of outright anti-Semitism, quoting writings known to a very limited audience, which hardly influenced any real events. What they forget is what a great effect Solzhenitsyn had on opening up the Soviet Union and Jewish emigration. His writings and actions helped thousand of Jews to emigrate and escape very real and tangible anti-Semitism.

Even in the very specific case of the Jackson-Vanik amendment, Solzhenitsyn's overall contribution was positive. He could have spoken against it, but that did not have any effect. The amendment was never repealed and is still in place. Yet, Solzhenitsyn's writings had a real effect on neoconservatives who were greatly responsible for initiating Jackson-Vanik amendment and getting it passed through Congress.

FP: Pavel Litvinov?

Litvinov: Alexander Solzhenitsyn's contribution to the fall of communism is tremendous, and we have to continue to be grateful to him. The fall of Communism in the Soviet Union brought about the end of the Russian empire, which, of course, was not intended by him. But, ironically, together with the explosive force of his great books, he revived a hopelessly outdated worldview and reactionary vision of Russian history. In the 19th century, Russian cultural life was dominated by an ideological fight between Slavophiles and Westernizers. Slavophiles, according to Solzhenitsyn, were right and Westernizers wrong. But somehow Westernizers deceived the Russian people and won, meanwhile showing their real face as Communists.

Today, the civilized world knows the true answer: the western way with market capitalism and respect for human rights is right, and Socialism and authoritarian nationalism is wrong. But the Slavophile's view, although outdated, still is capable of poisoning life in Russia. That view is inseparable today from anti-Semitism and xenophobia. There is a sad symbolism in the fact that the prisoner of the gulag, Alexander Solzhenitsyn, accepted the Russian state prize from unrepentant former KGB agent Vladimir Putin.

The central question today is how to transform today's world to make this intellectual victory into a real victory in Russia, in the Muslim world and everywhere. This is a problem in Russia as well as in the Muslim world and everywhere. And the ally in this fight is the other great Russian physicist, Andrei Sakharov, who consistently defended the democratic worldview and saw Russia as a part of the larger world — a view which still eludes many of his countrymen today. Today we know even better how insignificant are genetic differences between peoples, how in fact we are all indeed one family and we should relentlessly remind it to everybody and ourselves. At the same time, we must be ready to defend our civilization and its values. And that defense means using force when necessary. Dissident movements in the countries of the former Soviet Empire had a unique message to the Western World: you must believe in freedom and be ready to relentlessly take a stand in its defense.

Krotov: I guess I am the youngest among participants: born in 1957, my father was imprisoned on political grounds in 1958-1976 (18 years in Mordovia). I was charmed by Solzhenitsyn in my youth, but now I have few harsh words to say.

I don't think it is possible to speak about the downfall of Soviet communism. It is very much alive; it has only changed its face. It became less repressive, and due to this more sophisticated, versatile and powerful. This makes Russian despotism stronger than ever. The Kremlin said farewell to Communism, but Communist ideas never meant anything real in Bolshevistic reality. The "Soviets" never possessed real power; it was concentrated in the hands of the nomenclature.

Even in 1990-1992 it was a mistake to speak about the downfall of Communism, and many people after that paid with their lives for the optimistic proclamations of intellectuals and the practical political decisions of the West based on them.

So, in this context, what do we make of the claim that Solzhenitsyn made a monumental contribution to the destruction of this peculiar type of despotism, which was prevailing in Russia from 1918-1991? He is no hero. His naïve and straightforward self-appraisal depreciated even his real (quite moderate) contribution to political changes. And yes, certainly, Solzhenitsyn took risks, but many people risked much more.

His literary talent is very moderate. The Nobel Prize went to him and not to Shalamov.

Well, the Nobel Prize was given to Sienkiewicz when Tolstoy was still alive. Solzhenitsyn's only literary achievement is the style of *Archipelago*, but he never managed to repeat this success. He only made thing worse in his futile attempts to reproduce this piece of luck mechanically by reinforcing this style.

Solzhenitsyn is a complete analogue to a legion of petty-thinking imitators of counter-revolutionary Romanticism of De Maistre et al. Iyeremia Meschersky and not Dostoyevsky is his prototype. Dostoyevsky described Solzhenitsyn in detail as Foma Opiskin. The high estimation of Solzhenitsyn is a very bad sign, meaning that Russian despotism is rooted not only and not mainly in the nomenclature and in the Lubyanka, but in the intellectual milieu.

I cannot even rebuke Solzhenitsyn for being one of the makers of the modern modernized Russian despotism. He supported the evolution of a regime, but the regime is very self-confident and strong in itself and was not in need of his help. Although the Kremlin paid him.

In the end, Solzhenitsyn betrayed his own motto "to live without a lie." Did he live up to his own motto when he received from the nomenclature in the 1990s various gifts, which included a flat and a villa (previously held by Malenkov from the Politburo)? Did he live up to his own motto when he proclaimed a forgiveness of the KGB when he returned to Russia?

For most Russians born after 1970, Solzhenitsyn is and forever will be absent from cultural memory. His texts are dead and have been dead for many years. Only some political memories made some people his adherents.

FP: There are, without doubt, some very disappointing elements about Solzhenitsyn, as are being brought up here in terms of his relation to Putin and the KGB upon his return, in terms of his rejection of Western freedom, etc. But *The Gulag Archipelago* is not dead and it will never be dead. It will live on as a testament against the monstrosity of the Soviet experiment and of Socialism in practice everywhere. And Solzhenitsyn deserves credit for that. And if Russians who were born after 1970 do not know about Solzhenitsyn then that says something about them and not about Solzhenitsyn, and perhaps it explains why those who do not understand the past are bound to repeat it.

Dalrymple: It is true that one might see the present regime as a reconfiguration rather than a destruction of the old, but there is a very important difference, at least from the non-Russian's point of view: and that is that, whatever else one might say about Mr. Putin, no one in the rest of the world is likely to take him as an ideological inspiration or start a revolution in imitation of him and his ideas. In other words, all that Moscow-as-the-Third-Rome kind of stuff, with Marxism as its justification, is now dead, and for its death (a very good thing) I think Solzhentitsyn was in part responsible. His nationalism is unlikely to prove attractive to others, especially those coming from countries in contiguity with Russia, and so he helped to make Russia just one country among others and not the focus of world-wide dreaming.

I agree with Professor Pipes that he was a contradictory man. I am not sure how much of a criticism that is of him, however. Which of us is not contradictory? Who does not believe in the rule of law and yet rails against the law's delay? Who does not believe in popular sovereignty and yet is appalled when he sees it in action? We love freedom but are frequently appalled by the use to which freedom is put (by other people). True, we have to make a choice between the alternatives, and we choose what we think are the least bad ones; but Solzhenitsyn did point to real weaknesses in our culture, even if his proposed solutions were far worse than those weaknesses. It is not easy to be wholly consistent in one's pronouncements, especially if one pronounces a lot.

I think Solzhenitsyn wanted to save something from the utter wreckage of 20th Century Russian history. Of no country is it so easily possible to see history as a record of oppression, disaster and misery, punctuated by only a few cultural achievements. He wanted to think that there was some good essence in Russia, and it helped to contrast this with a bad essence elsewhere. This is dangerous, but it is human, all too human. And it did at least encourage him to examine seriously the part played by ideology in the disaster. When all is said and done, there was a difference in degree of evil between Tsarism and that of Leninism.

FP: Thank you, Dr. Dalrymple. As always, words of wisdom.

Yakov Krotov raised Varlam Shalamov. Thank you, Mr. Krotov, for I think this will help focus our discussion in the next round in some vital ways.

Shalamov was a Gulag survivor and author of the famous *The Kolyma Tales,* a description of Soviet hell.

Krotov raises the issue that Shalamov should have received the Nobel Prize in Literature instead of Solzhenitsyn. Or maybe along with Solzhenitsyn? So interesting question: Why didn't he? Is it because he was more or less unknown in the West? If so, why was he not well known?

What meaning is there in that one political dissident ended up in the West and then came back to receive privileges from the inheritors of the same system, while another remained in Russia, fighting to the end with dignity and without surrender, and ended up, with a broken body from the freezing gulag years, dying in an isolated ward in a mental house where the KGB placed him? (The details here of his final days are clouded by some mystery and up for debate)

Almost nothing is known about the polemics between Shalamov and Solzhenitsyn. These polemics are, undoubtedly, essential for our understanding of not only Solzhenitsyn and Shalamov, but also of the Soviet regime and, even more so, of the deepest philosophical questions relating to what it means to be human. Can our guests pinpoint the main argument in their polemics? What was their significance and consequence? We know that Solzhenitsyn saw potential redemption in suffering such as that which the gulag inflicts, while Shalamov saw such suffering as something that only demoralizes and breaks the human spirit and ultimately degrades man, making him sub-human.

I'd like the panel to touch on these themes.

Satter: I think Solzhenitsyn is far better known than Shalamov because he was much more political. *One Day in the Life of Ivan Denisovich* made him an international celebrity overnight. His novels and *The Archipelago Gulag* were all aimed at exposing the reality of the communist system. Shalamov depicted the depths of depravity and cruelty perhaps better than Solzhenitsyn but he was less concerned to convey a political message. As it happened, the message that Solzhenitsyn conveyed was very much in demand.

Natan Sharansky (who I last saw in Moscow moments before he was arrested) makes an interesting point about the relationship between identity and democracy. He writes that Solzhenitsyn did not understand that it is possible to be committed to one's own unique history and also to freedom and democracy. The general point is a good one but in the case of Russia, I'm not sure it's true. Russia's political culture, as it has existed traditionally, is not friendly to freedom and democracy. On the contrary, the emphasis in democracy on the value of the individual is missing in Russia. There is not a sense in Russia that the individual has irreducible value. On the contrary, he is seen as a means to an end, usually as defined by the state. I believe that to defend democracy in Russia, it is necessary to reject aspects of the Russian tradition. This is what Andrei Sakharov tried to do. It is what Solzhenitsyn refused to do and this refusal made his final embrace of Putin sadly logical.

Natan also talks about the book, *200 Years Together*, in which Solzhenitsyn politely suggests that Jews were always a foreign element in Russia and did not share his love for the country that persecuted them. Highlights of the book are the claims that Jews were over-represented among the Bolsheviks and the NKVD (true, at least for a while), that they found "soft" jobs in the gulag (did someone do a survey?) and that they spent their time during the Second World War away from the front (in fact, Jews had a higher percentage of "Heroes of the Soviet Union" than any other nationality). This is not the place to dwell on this book. But it is interesting for what it shows about Solzhenitsyn's attitude toward Russians. The tendency to blame Russia's misfortunes on Jews allows Russians to avoid looking at their own tradition. Without the Jews, the West and the other outsiders who ruined Russia, there is a real problem understanding where Russia's misfortunes come from. In light of the problems of present day Russia, people who share Solzhenitsyn's outlook would be better off to forget about the Jews and look for the sources of Russia's tragedy in aspects of themselves.

Pacepa: Our Symposium has blown up into an arresting cyclone. That is undoubtedly because Jamie has put together an outstanding panel, and because of Solzhenitsyn's impressive stature. But we should keep our feet on the ground. With all due respect, I disagree with Yuri Agayev's conclusion that Solzhenitsyn was "the godfather of neo-conservatism" and that he "played a decisive role in dismantling Communism."

Solzhenitsyn was not a conservative, and he went to great lengths to show that. He was not even a democrat. Solzhenitsyn did not believe in individual freedom — the collective well-being was what mattered to him. He described Western democracy as "a disaster" rooted in agnosticism and atheism. He despised the power of the law — the power of the ruler was all that counted for him. Nor was economic freedom a goal for Solzhenitsyn, who believed in a market, ruled by the state. No wonder he ended up endorsing Putin's "managed democracy."

In his 1978 commencement address at Harvard, Solzhenitsyn, speaking in Russian, accused American democracy of making "man the measure of all things on earth — the imperfect man, who is never free of pride, self-interest, envy, vanity and dozens of other defects." He blamed American democracy for being legalistic: "Wherever the tissue of life is woven of legalistic relations, there is an atmosphere of mediocrity, paralyzing man's noblest impulses." Solzhenitsyn never understood the American, or any other forms of Western democracy. Unfortunately, nor did he understand Soviet Communism, and he was never able to dig down to its roots.

Despite twenty years spent in the West, Solzhenitsyn remained a reformed Marxist. He blamed Europe for the evil of Soviet communism, but he was unwilling, or unable, to explain why Marxism had led to gulags only in Russia. He was also incapable of seeing that in Russia Communism devolved into the traditionally tsarist form of autocracy in which, behind a façade of Marxism, a feudal czar ruled the country with the help of his personal political police. When Professor Richard Pipes, one of the world's leading authorities on Russia, traced the Soviet terror to the Russian tradition of police state going back to the 16th century's Ivan the Terrible, Solzhenitsyn labeled Pipes's studies as either "a Polish" or a "Jewish version of Russian history," owing to the fact that the famous historian was born in Poland of Jewish heritage.

After Solzhenitsyn returned to Moscow and endorsed Putin, he fell into the KGB's anti-Semitic trap. In 2002, Solzhenitsyn published *Two Hundred Years Together*, a two-volume history of Russian-Jewish relations, in which he lays the blame for Soviet Communism on the Jews, and he "documents" that Zionism has historically been an enemy of Russia. This is a familiar theme to me from the years I spent at the top of the KGB's intelligence community.

In the 1970s I was given a tour of the infamous KGB interrogation complex Lefortovo, built in the shape of a K as a bizarre tribute to Catherine the Great. There I saw a large exhibit documenting the KGB's merciless intelligence war against Jewish traitors, which had started some two hundred years earlier and become an important chapter in the history of the Kremlin's *gosbezopasnost* (state security service). I was shown the torture chamber used to extort confessions from the "Jewish anarchists" seized by the *Okhrana* after Tsar

Alexander II was assassinated in 1882. I set foot in the office where Martyn Latsis — one of the deputies of *Cheka* founder Feliks Dzerzhinsky — signed the documents authorizing the *Cheka* to shoot tens of thousands of "bourgeois Jews" who were "sabotaging the people's revolution." I saw the cell where on March 12, 1938 the *Cheka*, by then upgraded to State Political Directorate, had forced the founder of the Third International, Nikolay Bukharin, to "voluntarily" write his "last confession" of the "dastardly crimes" he had committed on behalf of American Zionism. I also saw the cell where Swedish diplomat Raoul Wallenberg, who saved thousands of Jews from the gas chambers during World War II, had been secretly held after being kidnapped from Hungary in 1945.

Over the years, the Russian, Soviet and now again Russian political police has changed its name many times, from *Okhrana* to *Cheka,* to GPU, to OGPU, to NKVD, to NKGB, to MGB, to MVD, to KGB, to MSB, to MB, to FSK, to FSB, and the anagram game continues to this day. Lefortovo, however, has remained a monument to the unchanging hatred of Russia's political police for the Jews. It is unfortunate that, toward the end of his life, Solzhenitsyn became a port-parole of the KGB's anti-Semitism.

In the 1960s, when I first walked throughout Manhattan, I felt dwarfed by the majesty of its skyscrapers. Now they are part of my daily life. In 1964, when *One Day in the Life of Ivan Denisovich* was published in Russia, I felt dwarfed by Solzhenitsyn's courage. Now, when I know that Khrushchev allowed that book to be published in Russia because it served his purpose, and when I also know that Solzhenitsyn endorsed the KGB officers who are currently running Russia, he has ceased dwarfing me any longer. Solzhenitsyn may still be a skyscraper in Russia, but I agree with Professor Pipes that he will be little more than a blip in the history of the twentieth century.

Sadomskaya: Our discussion has fallen into two parts, one concerning the identity of Solzhenitsyn, and the other concerning Russian identity. I think these themes are to be regarded separately, as the two are not at all the same.

In Russia there have always existed at least two (if not more) trends for comprehending our own history. There used to be, and still exists, the trend towards openness, towards the Western model of democracy, and there also used to be, and still exists, the trend for isolationism, for rejection of the Western model of development.

Solzhenitsyn as a thinker tried to concentrate our attention on only one of these traditions, regarding only the latter to be "genuinely Russian". One shouldn't fall into this trap. Even the Slavophile, Kireevsky, published his magazine under the title "Evropeets" (The European'). The same refers to anti-Semitism. The Russian Okhranka, KGB, and even Solzhenitsyn with his *200 Years Together* are not the whole Russia. He chose the trend to suit his own nature or, maybe, that of his family.

As to Shalamov, he was surely much stronger as a writer than Solzhenitsyn, though he had no awards and died in poverty. And I agree with Mr. Satter: it was in a large part due to Solzhenitsyn being so politically-minded and headstrong that he succeeded to become so well-known. With all that, he was not just ambitious, he was lusting for glory, while the true artist Shalamov had never made an effort to push himself through to fame.

Solzhenitsyn saw the enemy outside and rather often was reduced to using psychological clichés; the subtle intellectual Shalamov presented a deep analysis of human nature in critical circumstances.

Solzhenitsyn's writings are a continuation of socialist realism. Shalamov's works follow A. Chekhov's tradition.

FP: Thank you, Natalia Sadamoskaya.

At the risk of repetition, I would like to reiterate a point about Solzhenitsyn. Many of the facts being raised here today reveal very non-redeeming aspects of Solzhenitsyn that cannot be denied, and they must be raised and discussed for the sake of truth and for the accuracy of the historical record. But in the context of these realities, I think we must always keep one thing in mind. A quote from Bernard-Henri Levy in his new book, *Left in Dark Times*, perhaps says it best:

"No other modern book has ever, as far as I know, unleashed an explosion like *The Gulag Archipelago*. It was a worldwide earthquake whose unexpected power I'd so much like the generations who didn't experience it to feel everything we knew without believing, or believed without seeing, or saw but didn't understand: by the millions, suddenly, by the tens of millions all across the world, we knew, believed, saw, and understood. . . The Communist dream dissolved in the furnace of a book." (p.58)

Sharansky: The quote above captures very well the significance of Solzhenitsyn's book. Something that was so critical in unmasking such a horrific evil will always be much more than a blip.

Reading the remarks of this distinguished panel, one might get the impression that the demise of the Soviet Union was inevitable. But few in the free world believed this at the time.

We dissidents knew that the regime was weak, that it could be toppled, but that it needed a West that believed in the power of its own ideals — a West that would abandon the course of appeasement, embrace moral clarity and confront the regime.

There were so many who wanted to understand, to sympathize, to find common ground, and there were so few who were really prepared to confront the regime.

If before it was politically correct to sympathize and draw a moral equivalence with the Soviet Union, *The Gulag Archipelago* made support for this regime something of an embarrassment. That was a critical stage in the struggle.

As to the argument that there were people like Shalamov who were both more talented and who suffered more, this is true. What differentiated Solzhenitsyn was not his towering literary talent or the extent of his suffering but the fact that he succeeded where so many others had fallen short. In secret, he meticulously collected and prepared material over many years and he became a voice for all those who dreamed to unmask the truth, who tried to unmask the truth, but who were unable to tell the world the true story of the horrors they were subject to. That is why his name will remain the symbol of the unmasking of Soviet evil, even though so many others contributed to it.

As to his book, *200 Years Together*, I agree with Yuri Yarim-Agaev, that this book will be forgotten. For anti-Semites, his critique lacks bite. For Jews, his arguments are nonsense. For the rest, it is simply boring.

As to David Satter's view that in Russia it is impossible to be committed to one's unique history and to be committed to democracy, I respectfully disagree. While David invokes Sakharov as evidence of this inherent incompatibility, in fact Sakahrov drew his inspiration in his struggle for democracy from the history of the noble spirit of Russia's intelligentsia.

With me in prison were many fervent Russian Orthodox Christians who were also staunch democrats. They were true to their Russian identity and firm believers in democracy.

Once people discover an identity or freedom that they have been denied, they often become zealous in safeguarding it. In Russia, people were deprived of both freedom and identity. That is why some of us who discovered both, cherished both. Part of the reason why Solzhenitsyn was such a skeptic or even critic of democracy may have been that his patience for its propensity for appeasement was very limited.

Yarim-Agaev: By the number of participants our panel looks more like a public opinion poll rather than a symposium. I can try to address only a few points made by others, and place them into the context of our discussion.

For almost a century Communism eliminated cultures, religions, and millions of people through the system of gulags, which it developed not only in Russia, but throughout the world wherever it came to power including Romania. This totalitarian ideology was the main threat to our entire civilization.

Fortunately, as a global ideology Communism collapsed by 1991 and cannot be resurrected. Communism still remains the ruling political system in China, North Korea, and Cuba — though not in Russia. Yet without ideological backing its days are numbered. In Russia we see only the remnants of Communist political structures, which without the context of political power and ideology are weak and will finally go away.

One may argue that the end of Communism was inevitable. It is more difficult to prove that its peaceful departure without destroying Russia and the rest of the world was predetermined as well. Such a departure required at some moment a critical combination of weakness on the part of the communist leadership and strength of the West. Dissidents deserve credit for contributing to both parts of that combination, and Solzhenitsyn's personal impact cannot be overestimated.

Here I rely on facts, not on my, or someone else's, feelings toward Solzhenitsyn or analysis of his philosophy, which are quite irrelevant. When I speak about Solzhenitsyn's influence on neo-conservatives, I follow the testimonies of the leaders of that movement, one of which was quoted at this symposium. Only they can say for a fact how Solzhenitsyn affected them, and they testify that his influence was positive and strong.

As for the bipolar model of Westerners and Slavophiles, I believe it was superficial even in the 18th century and is totally outdated now. Starting with the twentieth century, the main political struggle has shifted from nationalism vs. internationalism, to left vs. right. A more comprehensive analysis would consider at least three major political forces: Socialism, Democratic Capitalism, and Nationalism. To combine the first two into one, of Westerners, is to ignore political realities of the 20th century, when the second and third forces were united against the most extreme form of Socialism-Communism.

Solzhenitsyn's story merely confirms my point. The main opposition which he encountered upon arrival in the West came from the left, who rejected him, not for being a Russian nationalist, but for denouncing Socialism. Most American conservatives (Richard Pipes being among the few exceptions) were on Solzhenitsyn's side. They could hardly be considered less Western than their counterparts on the Left; they had little sympathy for Russian nationalism, and many Jews among neo-conservative leaders would hardly approve any form of anti-Semitism. Yet they realized that at that moment, the main focus was on the struggle of democracy against Communism, rather than of America against Russia.

The split in the dissident and human-rights community also started along the left-right line, long before the end of the Soviet Union. However artificial and superficial, that division took place in the 1980s upon the arrival of many dissidents in the West. I remember how I was told with apparent disgust, "Your Reagan," not "Your Ivan the Terrible." Only much later, around the late 1990s, did we see the second split on the right into western democrats and Russian nationalists.

My main concern, however, is not the order in which dissidents split, but that it happened too early. I do not agree that dissidents have been always divided in two camps of Westerners and Slavophiles. First, it would be difficult to assign to either of those camps Alexander Ginsburg, Tatyana Velikanova, and many other leading human rights activists who kept their loyalty and high respect to both Sakharov and Solzhenitsyn. Second, from my personal experience, being so closely associated with Sakharov, and the utmost Westerner, I still considered Solzhenitsyn as a close ally, rather than the one belonging to the opposite camp.

The camp opposite to me was Brezhnev and Andropov, as it was for most dissidents. Our differences were secondary to our unity against communist oppressors. And we should have kept that unity until the complete eradication of Communism. That could have helped to translate our intellectual victory into a political one.

We lost our focus, though, which was quite uncharacteristic for dissidents, but so typical for the intellectual community in general. This very panel shows how easy it is to drift from major issues to discussions on who was the better writer or who deserved the Nobel Prize. We are not a panel of literary critics but rather of political and human rights activists. With due appreciation for the refined taste and erudition of the panelists, shouldn't we focus more on political aspects, even when it concerns awards for literature?

From that standpoint, do we really regret that the Nobel Prize did not go to Shalamov? Have we really forgotten what a boost to our morale Solzhenitsyn's Nobel Prize was, what a sign of support by the democratic world to all dissidents, to all who opposed Communism? I doubt that that would have been the case had the prize gone to Shalamov. Wasn't that much more important than whose literary style was more refined?

I believe that Solzhenitsyn's Nobel Prize contributed to the earlier and harmless departure of communism. Aren't we forgetting that we were facing a real threat to our civilization? What was more important then: to take every step to save us from possible catastrophe or to sit on radioactive ashes reading the last copy of Shalamov's *Kolyma Tales* and enjoying the fact that he was properly awarded?

As to Solzhenitsyn's literary style, I would give it high marks only for the fact that millions of people managed to read through three volumes of *The Gulag Archipelago* and understood this quite complicated book. I hope that we will measure up to his style and that our readers will also be able to get to the end of this symposium.

Litvinov: Solzhenitsyn did not like democratic capitalism in the U.S. and did not want it for Russia. The opposite of Communism for him meant a paternalistic authoritarian state of a different kind based on Russian authoritarian tradition. For most of us, we take the opposite of Communism to mean a democratic capitalism.

We can argue forever if and when Russia will be on a genuinely democratic path or when it will inevitably fall back on its all too familiar police state matrix.

But I will never forget that by the mid-1960s all Russia read One Day of *Ivan Denisovich* and it became clear that the Stalinist labor camp regime had been really dead in the USSR no matter what else geriatric Soviet leaders could try to do to revive it.

In the 1970s, after the publication of *The Gulag Archipelago*, very few people in the West could keep alive any illusions about the possibility of humane state Socialism.

And for this we must be grateful to Alexander Solzhenitsyn.

Krotov: Solzhenitsyn's phenomenon says a lot about liberty and about humanism. Why did the West make an idol of the author of *The Gulag Archipelago*? Everything which was "collected" by Solzhenitsyn was well known in the West beforehand. The book didn't make any revolution in conscience. The revolution in Western conscience made an idol from this book. The date of this revolution was 1968. *Archipelago* can be compared with Webber's "Superstar". Webber didn't say anything new about Lord Jesus Christ; Solzhenitsyn didn't say anything unknown beforehand in the West about Communist atrocities. The West itself has changed its attitude towards religion and towards Communism. And this change marked some obvious progress in understanding humanity, a step from an anti-personalistic world-view to personalism and humanism.

Archipelago differs from "Jesus Christ superstar" as Gorbachev, Yeltsin or Putin differ from Jesus Christ. Archipelago said farewell to Communism only in order to replace Communism with a new, more subtle (and more dangerous) sort of imperialism. Despotism and suffering of the Russian people are not the essence of Russian Communism and, to speak more generally, of Russian slavery. Imperialism and militarism are the main issue. Soldiers can suffer from the stupidity of their generals, still, they are not victims; they are soldiers. Russia is still dangerous to the world, as we've been dangerous in the 16th century, and in 1913, because it is a unique case of a country with a highly militarized psychology which can begin an atomic world war, which can commit suicide — together with the whole planet.

Communism and its downfall are of a very small importance in this context. Moreover, Soviet Communism was less dangerous than modern Russian Imperialism. "Moscow-as-the-Third-Rome" is now alive with Russian Orthodoxy combined with Russian Nazism (in its

KGB version). This is much worse that Moscow-as-the-Third-Rome in Marxist skin.

Solzhenitsyn's name "will remain the symbol of the unmasking of Soviet evil" (as Mr. Scharansky said, and I admire Mr. Scharansky much more than Solzhenitsyn). But Solzhenitsyn's name will also remain the symbol of masking some evil which is much more dangerous and much more essential to Russian reality — the evil of anti-humanism, militarism, expansionism. Western support of Solzhenitsyn masked a sad fact: as a political entity, the West didn't oppose Russian Communism. Both Leftists and Rightists, Liberals and Conservatives of the West were too lazy, egoistic and blind. If Archipelago was as great a book as some participants of our discussion stated, then the West wouldn't betray Georgia (and Ukraine) as it did in 2008.

FP: I am not sure how wise it is to blame Solzhenitsyn for every dead sparrow that falls from the sky. The failure of *The Gulag Archipelago* is demonstrated by the West not going to war with Putin's Russia over Georgia? I am not sure how much legitimacy — or logic — there is to such a charge.

I am also not sure how much wisdom there is in diminishing the evil and threat of the Soviet regime in comparison to whatever has followed. And if everyone in the West knew about what Solzhenitsyn compiled in *The Gulag Archipelago*, then that masterpiece wouldn't have been the landmark watershed that it was and remains.

The sad, tragic and dark elements of Solzhenitsyn have been outlined in this discussion — as they should be. But they do not rob this great dissident of his bravery and of his monumental achievement in fuelling the shattering of a monstrous regime.

Final word goes to you, Dr. Dalrymple.

Dalrymple: Since I am the last to contribute, I shall try to be fair and judicious.

It seems to me that we have asked three fundamental questions:

i) What is the literary standing or status of Solzhenitsyn?

ii) What was his political effect in practice, in the Soviet Union and the West?

iii) Did or do his less attractive opinions detract from one or both of the above?

Let us take the first question first. Will anyone, other than specialists in Soviet and Russian history, read him in a hundred years' time, for what he tells us about the human condition *sub specie aeternitatis*? Here it seems to me that he will be in what Somerset Maugham called the first rank of the second-raters (where he put himself). I am reminded of Trigorin's self-proclaimed epitaph in *The Seagull*: He was a good writer, but not as good as Turgenev. But it seems unfair to criticize every writer because he is not as good as someone else. Which of us would ever put pen to paper if he were to be compared all the time with Shakespeare? But we wouldn't want there to be only Shakespeare.

It seems to me undeniable that he had a great effect in the Soviet Union and the West. It is possible of course that this tells us more about the West than about Solzhenitsyn. It seems to me also undeniably true that he told us nothing that we could, and should, have known before. But as Gide remarked, everything has been said before, but it has to be repeated. Solzhenitsyn confronted western intellectuals with evidence in such a way that they could not deny it any longer, and surely he deserves credit for that. The fact that some people suffered even more than he, does not make him any the less of a brave man, far braver than I, for example.

Finally, his undoubtedly unsavoury opinions on some subjects: Can he match Dostoyevsky for the viciousness and stupidity of his anti-Semitism, however? Surely not. But who thinks that Dostoyevsky's insights into human psychology and the real wellsprings of revolutionism are any the less valuable for that? Also, it seems to me that some charity is in order regarding Solzhenitsyn's age when he espoused Putinism. Not only is judgment sometimes impaired with age, but so too does the fight go out of some people, especially those who have suffered in their own flesh and blood.

In summary: Great as a man? Yes. Flawed? Yes. Of the first rank as a writer? Possibly not. Which of us on the panel equals him?

FP: True enough.

And lest we forget: Solzhenitsyn made sure that the royalties and sales income for *The Gulag Archipelago* were transferred to the Solzhenitsyn Foundation which, in turn and in secret, funneled it to aid gulag survivors and their families in the Soviet Union.

Before we go, I would like to thank my mother, and former Russian dissident, Marina Glazov, for providing many of the ideas, questions — and suggestions for guests — for this symposium.

Natan Sharansky, Pavel Litvinov, Dr. Natalia Sadomskaya, Richard Pipes, Yakov Krotov, Lt. Gen. Ion Mihai Pacepa, David Satter, Yuri Yarim Agaev and Dr. Theodore Dalrymple, thank you for joining this special Frontpage Symposium on Alexander Solzhenitsyn.

It was an honor to be amongst all of you.

Notes:

[1] Cathy Young, "Solzhenitsyn's tarnished legacy," *The Boston Globe*, August 6, 2008.

[Jamie Glazov, "Symposium: Remembering the Dissident," *Frontpagemag*, December 26, 2008.]

Part III: The End of a Superpower?

[6] American Economic and Military Decline?

Is America in economic and military decline? To discuss this question with us today, Frontpage Symposium has invited two distinguished guests:

Robert Lieber, Professor of Government and International Affairs at Georgetown University, where he has previously served as Chair of the Government Department and Interim Chair of Psychology. He is an authority on American foreign policy and U.S. relations with the Middle East and Europe. His most recent authored book is *The American Era: Power and Strategy for the 21st Century*. He is presently writing a book entitled, *The Future of the American Era*.

and

James Carafano, the Deputy Director of Davis Institute for International Study at the Heritage Foundation where he coordinates the foundation's research on foreign policy and national security. A 25-year veteran of the U.S. Army, Carafano is an accomplished historian and teacher as well as a prolific writer and researcher on a fundamental constitutional duty of the federal government: to provide for the common defense.

FP: James Carafano and Robert Lieber, welcome to Frontpage Symposium.

James Carafano, let's begin with you.

Let's start with the main question: Is America in decline?

Carafano: Rather than America in decline, it might be better to talk about the rest of the world ascending. Economists predict in the years ahead the world growth rate will be 4.4 percent. They say 3.3 of that will be in the emerging economies.

That said, I am not in the camp that thinks the U.S. will be swallowed up by China. Like the rise of Japan in the 1980s, China's economic reforms can only take it so far and then it will have to become a very different kind of country or else it won't be able to sustain its breath-taking trajectory.

On the other hand, it is painful to watch the U.S. squander the advantages of a free market, open society. I do worry about the U.S. ability to compete in the future and maintain a standard of living and civil society that is second to none.

I will sketch three areas of concern.

One is security. The notion that we have the world's finest military is increasingly at risk. True, we spend more than anyone else on defense, because we have far more to protect. In terms of GDP, however, U.S. defense spending is at near historic post-WWII lows. We have been under-funding modernization for decades and our defense industrial base is evaporating. That would be okay if the world was a less dangerous place. It is not.

The second concern is Science, Technology, Engineering, and Math education (STEM). America is falling behind. Some say that is not a crisis. There are lots of engineers. Sure, but that is only because the U.S. is losing its capacity as a builder and manufacturer.

Third, the traditional model of immigration and assimilation is under assault. Mostly what we do today is import poverty and generations are not assimilating as they did in the past. Their plight mirrors that of America's homegrown poor. Neither blacks nor Hispanics, as a whole, are capturing the American dream. They are not moving up the economic and education ladder. Immigration is an important part of the economy, our culture, and creativity. We are squandering this resource through a combination of bad immigration, poor border security, and devastating welfare programs that are growing, not shrinking, poverty and undermining the traditional American family structure.

FP: Thank you James Carafano.

Robert Lieber, what are your thoughts on America in decline and your take on Mr. Carafano's comments?

Lieber: I would rather respond to the main question of whether the U.S. is in decline. I do agree, though, that military modernization requires serious attention and that our immigration system has become badly dysfunctional.

Is the declinist proposition valid, that as a society, economy, and political power the country is in decline? Certainly the domestic situation is more difficult now than two decades ago. Yet while problems should not be minimized, they should not be overstated. Contrary to what many observers assume, the U.S. held its own in globalized economic competition and its strengths remain broad and deep. For the past several decades, our share of global output has been relatively constant at approximately one-fifth of world output — around 20% according to two recent reports.

Moreover, America benefits from a growing population and one that is aging more slowly than all its possible competitors except India. It continues to be a magnet for talented and ambitious immigrants (despite the immigration system). It is a world leader in science and in its system of higher education, and it has the advantage of continental scale and resources. In short, the U.S. remains the one country in the world that is both big and rich.

The American military remains unmatched and despite intense stress from nearly a decade of war in Afghanistan and Iraq it has not suffered the disarray that afflicted it in Vietnam. This is evident in indicators such as successful recruitment and performance of the volunteer force, the ongoing quality of the officer corps, and broad public support for the military, and in casualty tolerance.

Beyond material strengths, the society itself benefits from a durable political system, rule of law, vigorous free press and information media, and a competitive and adaptable economy, as well as strong traditions of entrepreneurship and innovation, leadership and critical mass in new technology, and a history of resilience and flexibility in overcoming adversity.

America does face a more competitive world, regional challenges, and some attrition of its relative degree of primacy. But because of the enormous margin of power the U.S. possessed after the end of the Cold War, it should be able to withstand a degree of erosion in its relative strength for some time without losing its predominant status.

However, given profound disagreements about policy, intense partisan rancor, growing social class division, distrust of government, and lingering divisions about foreign commitments, non-material factors could prove to be a greater impediment to our staying power than more commonly cited indicators of economic strength and military over-stretch. Can the American political system produce effective measures to cope with long term burdens of entitlement programs and national debt? Will cultural and generational differences about the uses and even legitimacy of American power lead to abandonment of a global leadership role? And are persistent foreign threats, especially from terrorism and nuclear proliferation, likely to sustain a domestic consensus or instead lead to intensified polarization and retrenchment? The U.S. retains the power and capacity to play a leading world role. The ultimate questions about America's future are more likely to be those of policy and will.

FP: James Carafano, what are some of the ways we can reverse the ride of some of the dangers you point to? And what is your take on Prof. Lieber's optimistic outlook that, despite the challenges he points to as well, America might not be in decline at all?

Carafano: Let's start with this proposition by Lieber:

"[t]he American military remains unmatched and despite intense stress from nearly a decade of war in Afghanistan and Iraq it has not suffered the disarray that afflicted it in Vietnam. This is evident in indicators such as successful recruitment and performance of the volunteer force, the ongoing quality of the officer corps, and broad public support for the military, and in casualty tolerance."

I would agree with all of it...but just add "past performance is no guarantee of future earnings."

The fact is US military superiority is indeed in doubt. While the American military turned the corner in Iraq and there are signs it is doing the same in Afghanistan-both of these were near run things...and I would argue largely because we under-invested in our military since the end of the Cold War. It is not that our enemies are devilishly clever, coming up with innovations such as improvised explosive devices (IEDs), it is just that since the Cold War ended, we never gave our armed forces sufficient resources to deal with emerging threats — because of this unfounded presumption that we had the world's finest military that could simply not be challenged.

Furthermore, not only have we struggled to keep up with new dangers from IEDs to WikiLeaks, we have been too complacent in preserving our conventional capabilities. We have been living off Reagan's "peace through strength" legacy for almost a quarter of a century. Well-guess what? We are on the verge of tapping out the bequest.

First, Congress stopped "modernizing" the military (buying new equipment to replace old systems before they wear-out or become outdated) at the end of the Cold War.

Second, Congress has allowed personnel costs (which accounts for more than half the Pentagon's budget) to sky-rocket out of control. According to the TechAmerica Foundation, military personnel costs have risen 32% since 9/11. Add to that the increased costs of operating and maintaining a war-time military — and it means there is even less money left to modernize the military.

Third, Congress keeps layering on new rules, new directives that make defense spending even less efficient. For example, the majority of the Army's research and development budget is directed through earmarks!

To make matters worse, as a recent TechAmerica Foundation study shows, the Pentagon could well get hit with a "double tsunami" — a drop in spending as the U.S. draws down in Iraq and Afghanistan (monies that were propping-up paying for manpower, as well as operations and maintenance) — coupled with calls to gut the defense budget to help deal with the deficit.

The first casualty of the double tsunami will be all the all-volunteer force. Sure everybody likes good pay and benefits — but young people mostly serve in the military both because of a sense of mission and because they believe the U.S. military is an effective institution. No one will want to join the armed forces if there is no money for training and readiness and if their equipment is falling apart. If Congress slashes the size of the military, no one will be interested in staying in the service if they have to constantly deploy without an opportunity to rest.

There are solutions to saving the all-volunteer force, reforms in personnel management, operations (like modernizing logistics that would save $35 billion), and procurement that can keep the all-volunteer force healthy and affordable. That would free up enough money to modernize the military and preserve the all-volunteer force. But, make no mistake if Washington becomes complacent about military prowess we will quickly lose our combat-edge.

FP: Prof. Lieber, your view on Mr. Carafano's warnings about America losing its combat-edge?

Lieber: I began my previous response by agreeing that military modernization requires serious attention. But note that James Carafano's alarm is based on predictions and a very pessimistic view of future decisions about the defense budget. Of course, hard choices will need to be made among priorities. Secretary of Defense Gates has targeted some $100 billion in possible cost savings that he would like to redirect to military modernization. Much will also depend on the pace of withdrawals from Iraq and on the progress of the surge in Afghanistan as well as on political developments there. As we do draw down, however, that will allow more scope for choices — both within the defense budget but also as a tempting target for budget cuts.

It is important to bear in mind that the U.S. has an experienced and battle-hardened military, with very capable leadership. The army has also demonstrated impressive learning capacity during the past decade and deploys the most experienced and effective counter-insurgency forces in the world. The base military budget, as a percentage of GDP, amounts to approximately 3.9%, with another 1% for the operational costs of Iraq and Afghanistan. Though the base figure is well below Cold War levels, it still represents a very large sum.

We live in a world in which there are real threats to U.S. security from both states and terrorist groups. My own sense of the future is that Congress, the public, and the executive branch will remain sufficiently concerned about these and will maintain an effective level of support for national defense. Isolationist sentiment remains very modest, and the political landscape does not (or at least not yet) seem to be one that would favor serious retrenchment.

Finally, bear in mind that American politics is an "invitation to struggle" (in the words of a prominent political scientist, Edward Corwin, a generation ago). Insuring America's defense preparedness is a necessary part of that process.

Carafano: Well, we agree that America has the capacity to address its ills. The real question is will it? I have not so much tried to offer a pessimistic outlook as lay out why it is vital for Americans not to be complacent about their future. There is no society so great that greatness cannot be lost in a single generation.

I would say first that America needs to re-establish its position as a free economy. Last year, for the first time in the history of the *Index of Economic Freedom*, the U.S. slipped from the ranks of "free economies" to a "mostly free" economy. That's alarming. High taxes, excessive regulation, and runaway government spending account for most of the problem.

Second, America is a federalist society. The continual shift of power from the states to the government is at the root of a number of our most troubling problems including education and welfare. More federal intrusion has not decreased poverty and improved the performance of students. It has, in fact, accelerated the race to the bottom. Federalism allows states to innovate, experiment, and adapt. Over-centralization is a threat to America moving forward.

Third, we cannot compromise on providing for the common defense.

If we start to under-invest in our military now, we will be right back in the state our armed forces were in 1973.

If the nation undertakes these three tasks, I have no doubts about what we could achieve.

I agree America's best should be ahead. That will largely be determined by what we as nation do to secure our own future.

Lieber: America's great strength lies in its flexibility and capacity to respond to crisis — though often only after the problem has become severe. There is no guarantee that the necessary steps will be taken, but the country has managed to overcome much worse in the past (Civil War, the Depression of the 1930s, World War II) and past history shows a remarkable capacity for renewal and response.

FP: James Carafano and Robert Lieber, thank you for joining Frontpage Symposium.

[Jamie Glazov, "Symposium: America in Decline?" *Frontpagemag.com*, December 24, 2010.]

Part IV: Islam: The Religion of Peace?

[7] Islam's War on Women's Pleasure

With "honor" killings on the rise worldwide and in the West especially, Frontpage Symposium has decided to explore the impulse that clearly lies behind this crime against women: the fear and hatred of women's sexuality. In this special Symposium edition, we have assembled a distinguished panel to approach this phenomenon from a specific angle that is almost always ignored in our media and culture at large. We ask: what are the toxic consequences to a culture in which males allow sexual satisfaction only to themselves? To discuss this issue with us today, our guests are:

Dr. Nicolai Sennels, a Danish psychologist who worked for several years with young criminal Muslims in a Copenhagen prison. He is the author of *Among Criminal Muslims. A Psychologist's Experience from the Copenhagen Municipality.* The book will be out in English later this year. He can be contacted at: *nicolaisennels@gmail.com.*

Dr. Joanie Lachkar, a licensed Marriage and Family therapist in private practice in Brentwood and Tarzana, California, who teaches psychoanalysis and is the author of *The Narcissistic/Borderline Couple: A Psychoanalytic Perspective on Marital Treatment* (1992); *The Many Faces of Abuse: Treating the Emotional Abuse of High-Functioning Women* (1998); *The V-Spot; How to Talk to a Narcissist* and a recent paper, "The Psychopathology of Terrorism" presented at the Rand Corporation and the International Psychohistorical Association. She is also an affiliate member for the New Center for Psychoanalysis.

Dr. David Gutmann, emeritus professor of Psychology and Behavioral Sciences at Northwestern University Medical School in Chicago.

and

Dr. Nancy Kobrin, a psychoanalyst with a Ph.D. in romance and semitic languages, specializing in Aljamía and Old Spanish in Arabic script. She is an expert on the Minnesota Somali diaspora and a graduate of the Human Terrain System program at Leavenworth

Kansas. Her new book is *The Banality of Suicide Terrorism: The Naked Truth About the Psychology of Islamic Suicide Bombing.*

FP: Dr. Nancy Kobrin, Dr. Joanie Lachkar, Dr. David Gutmann and Dr. Nicolai Sennels, welcome to Frontpage Symposium.

Dr. Sennels, let me begin with you.

As you referred to in our recent symposium, you are well aware - especially as a psychiatrist — of the vital role that bringing a woman sexual pleasure plays in a man's life. If a man's sexuality involves only bringing himself pleasure and satisfaction, and never involves bringing a woman pleasure, the consequences are not just devastating for the woman, but for the male himself. If this phenomenon occurs because the culture at large has shaped this disposition of males, and if this practice by males is therefore widespread and constitutes the norm, the effect on the male psyche in this culture, and on the culture at large, is perniciously harmful — to say the least. There are pathological and toxic results, which include not only the lust for terror against "the outsider," but also against oneself — suicide.

The Muslim culture and religion, and the roots of jihad, clearly come to mind here.

What are your thoughts to my introductory statement for our discussion here today?

Sennels: My findings are that growing up in the Muslim culture is psychologically unhealthy on numerous realms. The positive attitude towards anger and the narcissistic concept of honor prevents many Muslims from maturing as human beings. Together with the racist and aggressive attitude towards non-Muslims, a strong identification with the Muslim Umma and favoring of Middle Age religious dogmas at the expense of common sense, human rights and science, the Muslim mentality makes it impossible for most Muslims to integrate into our democratic, secular and civilized Western culture. Not only that: it makes Muslims into less happy and mentally healthy people. No wonder that the core of such a culture is based on the repression of sexuality and female qualities.

There is no doubt that Muslim men's negative view on women has a high price not only for the women but also for the men and Muslim culture in general. We men receive a long row of qualities when we open up to women: empathy, the ability to function in groups without creating hierarchies and more mature ways of experiencing and expressing our emotions - these are among the most important.

Besides several ancient nature religions and Eastern religions such as Hinduism, Taoism and Buddhism, Gustav Jung (1875-1961) was the first in the West to discover the importance of opening up to the opposite sex: men who suppress women never really grow up. Shy and nerd-like computer geeks and aggressive male chauvinists are the two most typical results. Both types are often lonesome, feel "empty," are sexually frustrated and in many cases perverse, easily depressed and socially incompetent. Since aggression is seen as positive in the warrior-like Muslim tribal culture, the latter is most often the result in Islamic societies. A recent study in Germany lead by the former German minister of Justice Christian Pfeiffer concluded that "Religious Muslim boys are more violent." According to this gigantic research project involving intense interviewing of 45.000 teenagers, Muslim culture cultivates an unhealthy and aggressive macho attitude among Muslim males.

Now Jamie, in terms of the specific issue of our discussion, when it comes to the male not bringing sexual pleasure to a woman, this has severe consequences not only on the woman, but also on the male and on the culture in general (if this is a standard cultural ethos, which is the case with Islam). The wish to bring happiness to one's partner — especially sexual happiness — is *fundamental for being able to experience and express love.* Men who do not have this wish will be cut off from the maturing experience of learning from the kind of wisdom and emotional life that only women express fully. This leaves men less mature and less happy. The point is that the more you give, the more you get - on all levels. Men who joyfully see themselves as a source of bliss, satisfaction and happiness to their female partner have found the key to their own human growth and a successful relationship. Since Islam and the Muslim culture prevents men and women from freely meeting as equal partners, Muslims are cut off from this important cause of happiness and maturity. The result is the childish fanaticism and immature ways of handling emotions that clearly characterize Muslim societies. The propagation of the Islamic scriptures and Muslim male suppression of women, their ignoring of female qualities and need for happiness, are the main course for the suffering and hate in Islamic societies. That terrorism arises is no surprise.

The suppression of women in Islam and Muslim culture is an effective tool in keeping its propagators aggressive and emotionally cold towards their infidel victims. If we manage to liberate the Muslim women, we have Islam cornered and removed its corner teeth. In Western societies, this can only be done by creating sufficient amounts of shelters for women fleeing from violent and suppressing husbands and installing strict laws on honor-related crimes. We already have around 40 shelters in Denmark. Seventy percent of the women contacting one of the biggest women shelters, Dannerhuset in Copenhagen, have Middle Eastern back ground. We also need to send female social workers into the immigrant homes to conduct regular interviews with the females to make sure that they feel safe and are free to use the many possibilities and rights that our countries allow them. If their male family members don't like it they are free to leave the country.

We do not want to see the suppressive and uncivilized Islamic view on women get a hold in our countries. Finally, our Western welfare societies should only give economic support to the first two or three children. This might prevent Muslim families from moving to our countries and have a lot of children that often become a burden to society.

It also leaves the immigrant women freer to integrate and use their Western standard freedoms.

The liberation of women in Muslim countries is mainly done by diminishing the amount of child births. Being pregnant five times or more and raising the same amount of children leaves poor and uneducated mothers no chance to empower themselves. They are bound to their homes and completely dependent on their often not so gallant husbands. The most effective way is to pay people in poor countries to have fewer children. Instead of giving economical aid to corrupt dictators it should be given directly to the women of the families, just like the Nobel Prize winning micro loans. The amount of money should be inversely to the amount of children. Also, no economic aid should be given to non-Western countries except if it is aimed at putting a lid on the over-population. This would leave the women stronger and freer to live the life they want. A pleasant bonus is that it will better the economy and general human conditions, thereby lessening the possibly for religious fanaticism and conflicts - which again will diminish the flow of refugees to our part of the World.

FP: Dr. Sennels thank you.

Nancy Kobrin, give us your thoughts on the topic and on Dr. Sennels' analysis.

Please touch on this in your answer: When Muslim males in their sexually repressive cultures get a glimpse, for one reason or another, of our female pop stars, let's say beautiful female stars such as Byonce, Rihanna or Mariah Carey, etc., it is unsurprising what ferocious dread and rage enters their psyches. It is crucial to explore how and why this happens. First, these females clearly represent female beauty and female sexual self-determination. So the Muslim male faces a great threat immediately. We know the many reasons why. But let me narrow in on one dynamic:

Let us suppose that a Muslim male is faced with one of these women — who are in charge of their own sexuality — in a possible sexual entanglement. In other words, let's picture the Muslim male here seeing these women and visualizing, even for a split second, the possibility of a sexual relationship with one of them. What is the thought process? We know that the Muslim male immediately faces, with terror, the reality of what would emerge in terms of a sexual encounter on an equal level of reciprocity. So, instead of just engaging in some kind of prison-like violent sexual aggression against a helpless, mutilated woman who has no rights of any kind, the Muslim male would have to try to function as a male to not only satisfy himself, *but to also satisfy the woman*. This means that, among other things, he would have to open himself up, not just for praise, but for possible judgment in terms of what kind of lover he is.

In other words, the woman afterwards will make a judgment and maybe, possibly, say something negative not only to him, but to someone else about him. She might even giggle about something she found insufficient and inadequate. She might even immediately dump him because of this — and might even laugh about it to her friends. This is what we call freedom, and one of the ingredients of the human condition that might surface within freedom.

One can just imagine the psychotic rage that results in the minds of many Muslim males in repressive Islamic cultures at the very notion and possibility of this reality. They would not only want to obliterate the woman for the reality of what she may think of their performance (and for what she may also say and do about it), but they would want to destroy the society that would allow this possibility. One of the products of this ferocious hatred of this ingredient of the human condition and its possibilities is, undoubtedly, jihad.

I would like you Dr, Kobrin, and the rest of the panel, to touch on this observation and how it applies to our discussion, thanks.

Kobrin: Pleasuring a woman — *which means helping her achieve orgasm* — is the key issue here. This sexual problem in the Middle East has not been fully appreciated by the West. It is not discussed in the Middle East because it is a subject of extreme shame that *the men are impotent.* Ironically we are dealing with shame-honor cultures who do not understand that the function of shame is *not* to willfully spill blood to cleanse honor. This is a cover-up for not having women who are truly free because of their own terrors and sense of vulnerability. This applies to Afghanistan and Somalia, as they are Muslim shame-honor cultures as well.

Jamie, you have hit the nail on the head, and I am not sure most of us are aware that we are dealing with psychotic thinking. This occurs when one is vilified and the other is devalued as the bad/hated or devalued object. This is a mechanism of defense known as splitting.

The Jihadi men can appear and present themselves as normal, but they are not normal.

Obviously, I do not want to sweepingly say that all Muslim males are stereotypically denying their females. However, given the fact that one does not hear moderate Muslim men discuss this issue of pleasuring women, we can tell that it is too sensitive of an issue. Even in the eye of the storm for moderate Muslim men, we could assume that this is not only a highly charged issue, but one that is extremely uncomfortable. Let alone think of how this could put them into a role of competing with other men, especially in democratic societies where domination and control of women are not a valued tradition. It has been said too that this is one of the reason white western men convert to Islam in significant numbers, because they are at a loss as to how to socially deal with western women.

Given that we are dealing with a shame-honor society, we might consider the following psychological defenses as playing a major role:

1. Splitting, that is, thinking in terms of black and white.
2. A highly enmeshed markedly paranoid family unit.
3. Boundary confusion.
4. Unspoken sexual abuse.
5. Terror reigns, hence we encounter governmental abuse and dictatorships.
6. Shame blame when the male is emasculated, the female is severely punished, nay obliterated - female genital mutilation, honor killing etc.

I agree with Dr. Sennels concerning the high rate of frequency of domestic violence which he describes in Denmark. The Centre for Social Cohesion in the UK did geo-mapping of where they found domestic violence and the jihadis. What a coincidence! There was tremendous overlap. Such violence is a shamefully revealing phenomenon that the ummah does not want to address in appropriate ways.

By contrast, look at the naked midriffs of young, free Israeli women, their tummies showing and expressing themselves dancing freely in this video. As you know, I have been working on this problem for years but it was when I was watching an Israel music video by one of the best funky jazz/r&b guitarists, Dudu Tassa in a song called "Zouzi" that I realized why the Saudis must really be peeved with the Israelis living so close by. It's not just because of the verses of hatred of the Jew in the Qur'an but also the freedom of its open society.

Clearly, Hamas and Hezbollah can't even remotely compete, that is why they resort to bonding through rage, hatred, roadside bombs, missiles and suicide bombers, etc.

Finally, I think that Dr. Sennels has a splendid idea about encouraging fewer children. However, it flies in the face of doing jihad through demographics. But from a child-rearing and maternal attachment point of view, Dr. Sennels has it right. Less is more and also better and healthier. Oddly, by denying women pleasure they deny themselves pleasure. Pain gets confused with pleasure and voila, you have sado-masochism.

FP: Very profound, Dr. Kobrin. John Racy, a psychiatrist with much experience in Arab societies, has touched on many of these themes. He has noted how the Islamic culture promotes a threatening sense of inadequacy in men (and therefore women) and that impotence (and related) problems among them are common phenomena.

In his classic work, *The Closed Circle,* David Pryce-Jones discusses these sexual pathologies in the Arab world and notes that it is therefore no surprise that the Arab male is obsessed with proving his sexual superiority. This obsession finds its expression by targeting the Western infidel with violence. Thus, it's not really that much of a mystery: by not veiling its own women and by giving them personal and sexual freedom and pleasure, the West enrages Islamists, leading them to unleash terror in a furious attempt to keep their own women enslaved, sexually unfulfilled, and their own personal sexual impotence hidden. (See Chapter 11, "The Seeds of Hate," in *United in Hate* for a further discussion.)

Lachkar: This topic borders on the broader picture: the violation of human rights that exists throughout the Middle East. The degradation of women in the Muslim world is one theme inextricably linked to not only the role of women and their functions, but to the power of their maternal capacities and sexualities.

As an example of such violations, it has been noted that in some Arab countries, as well as in other parts of the world, clitoridectomy, or female circumcision, is still practiced. It is most often performed on females between the ages of seven or eight (before menstruation). This is a practice whereby midwives and female family members grasp the girls legs apart to expose her genitals. Then a sharp razor is used to cut off the clitoris. According to Lloyd deMause, it is a harsh and perverse act, an enactment of one's frustration and aggression directed toward the innocent young victimized girls.

DeMause goes so far as to pronounce this act as the gateway to trauma and destruction not only for the child, but the society in general. Girls not only go through excruciating pain, but often faint from shock (no anesthetic), suffer from such after-effects as blood poisoning, childbirth complications, and unbearable pain during intercourse. Some report constant urinary tract infections, infertility, and sometimes die from hemorrhage.

It is important, by the way, to make a distinction with male circumcision. What is done to a boy is circumcision, while what is done to girl/woman is termed 'genital mutilation.'

In keeping with the theme of this discussion, the circumcision is designed to curtail a women's sexuality and keep her repressed. This can only leave us to speculate that if Muslim men are programmed to think of women as chattel or used as sex objects for their own pleasure, how do the women achieve sexual fulfillment?

How does a Muslim man rejoice in the woman's pleasure when he has been pre-scripted/pre-programmed to not only devalue her as a sexual object, but to deprive her of any pleasure? What seems to be most pervasive is not the sexual act in and of itself, but the idea that there is always a third bedfellow, a Qur'an that testifies that the way to avoid sin is to oppress women to maintain a shame/honor society. The woman can easily shame and dishonor her man by presenting herself as none less than the virgin the man will meet in Paradise, but until he gets there she must play and fit into the role of this perfect virginal paradigm. My fantasy is that as he lusts after her, he then repents by persecuting himself and maybe even abusing his wife for behaving as she did at the "scene of the crime." Although none of us are there to observe, as the Kafkian bug on the wall, we can only speculate as to what really goes on in the bedroom.

I believe these thoughts are in keeping with Dr. Kobrin's acknowledgement of an Arab-Muslim culture — a shame-honor culture. I might add how this differs from Judeo-Christian culture, which is based on sin and redemption, evoking guilt as opposed to shame. This difference is significant in that guilt tends to get turned inward against the self as self-punishment whereas shame is turned outward and needs to destroy the object/women who dishonored the male.

Dr. Kobrin rightfully refers to this as the psychological defense of splitting. The bad lustful "baby boy self" projects onto the devalued object, and therefore since he is fused with her he must destroy or humiliate her. Dr. Kobrin's new book, *The Banality of Suicide Terrorism,* details the toxic pathological attachment with the maternal object, where she not only parallels domestic violence to universal political terrorism as complimentary terrorism, but there is a synergistic and hence a power-terrorizing effect. There is no doubt that Muslim men's negative view of women has made them and their society pay a high price.

Dr. Sennels notes that the Muslim culture and religion, and the roots of jihad, are linked to man denying a woman pleasure. The point I would expand on is not the sexual act in and of itself, but the entire theme of a culture of deprivation and envy. I agree with Dr. Sennels that this practice by a male can lead to devastating effects not only on his sense of manhood but upon an entire culture heading toward death and terror. In response to Jamie's comment about "lust for terror against the outsider," and this can pave the way to suicide, that if the deprivation becomes more than the psyche can hold or contain, I would imagine there is no way out of this toxic inferno. Dr. Sennels also nails it when he calls our attention to the amount of childbirths. One might refer to the uterus used as a subversive act of terror.

Jamie presents an interesting scenario: how would a Muslim man (and it is clear we're referring to Muslim men who have internalized the misogynist Muslim culture) respond sexually in the face of a "normal" sexual uninhibited woman? My guess, he would act in one of two ways: display a false self or a persona to hide his shame, and go after her aggressively, or he would end up feeling grossly humiliated if she were to see through his masked self. Although Kobrin does not make reference to the false self, she does confirm that the "Jihadi men can appear and present themselves as norm, but they are not normal." Nevertheless, what is important is not how the jihadi male responds to the modern female, but how he defends an entire culture trained to repress such women so he can maintain his sense of control.

Gutmann: We all seem to be pretty much in agreement that the typical Muslim male's stance towards women is characterized by barely disguised anger and a need to control the woman's sexual response and pleasures. And these same neurotic tendencies are, in their turn, defenses against the man's fear of female sexuality (a fear that can lead to impotence) and against the shame which attends such fear.

The unexpurgated *Arabian Nights* dramatize these fears. In these lurid accounts, the woman is regularly presented as sexually insatiable, just waiting for the chance to copulate with any inferior man — a slave, a beggar, a leper — who's available, once her husband is out of the house. Her husband's honor is perpetually in pawn to an explosively sexual woman, who is perpetually looking for her chance to dishonor him with degraded men.

The Muslim male's fear of unchecked female sexuality is managed through legal as well as clinical means. Clinically, there is the widespread practice of clitoridectomy, which in effect surgically removes the orgasmic female "organ." And on the legal side we see the insistence, on the part of immigrant Muslim males, for host countries to allow the practice of Sharia law — the laws which for the most part limit female rights and freedoms, particularly in the sexual domain. The Muslim males want to enjoy their freedom from the restraints of the medieval societies that they have left, but they want to continue imposing, now in the free society, those same restrictions on their wives.

When these measures fail, there are, of course, honor killings.

On a larger scale, there is radical Islam's ambition to do away with Israel, that nest of liberated women in the heart of the Umma, and to impose the Caliphate on the non-Islamic world. The Muslim fears modernization because it leads inevitably to female liberation — including sexual liberation, and they have gone to war against that threat. Islam is the world's fastest growing religion — probably because so many infidels share the Muslim's fear of the sexually liberated woman.

For me, this question remains: why are Muslim males so intimidated by the full sexual response of the female? Does it represent the retaliatory rage of their oppressed women? Does it represent the bursting forth of their deeply hidden and shame-generating female identifications? (Perhaps the suicide bomber's fascination with death-dealing explosions reflects the Muslim male's fear of and fascination with explosive female sexuality?).

Perhaps our Psychoanalysts, Drs. Kobrin, Sennels and Lachkar, may have some answers.

Sennels: Though I would prefer to use the term narcissistic rage (instead of psychotic rage) I completely agree with Jamie. The repression and conscious ignoring of female sexuality in the Muslim world has a very simple and profound reason: Muslim men find it hard to handle the fact that women's sexuality is far superior to the men's. Most women can make love for longer time than men and many women can continue the sexual act after having orgasm. Some can even have more than one orgasm during sex.

The question is: Why are Muslim men so vulnerable? How did Muslim men end up on such a fragile pedestal? The answer is that Islam and Muslim culture depends on male aggression and needs to suppress female sensitivity. The reason for this is that this culture is aiming at conquering and domination. In such a culture, female softness and empathy would be distracting and a hurdle. In such a culture, men are simply worth more than women. This is the reason that Muslim boys are treated as kings from birth and therefore develop a fragile glass-like personality that is unable to handle defeat, inferiority and criticism.

I am sure that Dr. Kobrin and Dr. Gutmann are right about Israel: It is an unwelcome showcase in the Middle East that risks tempting the area's Muslim women by promoting gender equality, human rights and freedom. This, of course, provokes the insecure Muslim men and contributes to their hate and wish for destruction of Israel and Western civilization in general. The hate of women is, in this way, very closely connected with Islam's wish for destruction of the free world. Dr. Lachkar has a very interesting point: Muslim women, and their husbands are, no doubt, in a deep dilemma during the sexual act. On the one side the man wants the woman to display enjoyment to excite him and to confirm his abilities as a lover. On the other hand, she is expected not to enjoy it too much.   How can love grow in such a garden? How can a culture bring happiness to people when it does not allow the women to be happy and does not allow the men to rejoice in women's happiness? Islam does not care about such questions: As everybody who studies the Qur'an knows, love and happiness are not the goals of Islam.

Kobrin: Jamie, you make the observation of targeting the infidel. I would stress that within this mindset, the other is the female. It doesn't matter if you are male and other, you are still the female and a threat. The thinking is very simplistic because of the splitting — male vs. other = i.e. female. The splitting compensates for the inability to integrate self as a whole person and separate from one's mother psychologically. Everything gets split off and projected outwards but nothing is really resolved.

But why? Because the male identity is confused due to not being permitted to separate from the female who has no power. The male baby is misused by the mother as her narcissistic source of power. This in turn strips the male baby of ever feeling safe to trust, because he is so bound up in his mother's identity. The unhealthy dependency feeds into the erotics of Arab Muslim culture and other shame-honor cultures.

They are not just confused, they do not have a sense of their own healthy empowerment. If they did, they would not attack and destroy the female. I ascribe to what Dr. Gutmann says about the suicide bomber when he writes:

"Does it represent the bursting forth of their deeply hidden and shame-generating female identifications? (Perhaps the suicide bomber's fascination with death-dealing explosions reflects the Muslim male's fear of and fascination with explosive female sexuality?)"

I would add that this explosiveness is also entwined with the "explosiveness" and bloody nature of birth, hence life. Its opposite is death.

I won't quibble so much with Dr. Sennels about narcissistic rage. To me, there is always a hidden component of the psychotic because of this significant distortion about the female. A well encapsulated psychosis occurs in borderline and narcissistic pathology.

Dr. Lachkar raises the broader issue of human rights violations in the Middle East. This is key because the violations are tinged with the abuse of the female. We may surmise that this public behavior is extremely revealing because they have externalized rage-filled behavior against the other. We can hazard the guess that the public persona is emblematic of the private given the nature of cruelty. Most of life is psycho-sexual in nature, though many would probably deny that because it arouses too much in them and that is scary as it makes them feel "out of control."

The unspoken problem of not being able to pleasure women is really one of sadomasochism. Pain is confused with pleasure. What arouses one sexually is learned early in life; so if as Dr. Sennels says that this is a culture hostile to pleasure, this means that it is going to be very difficult to undo the sadomasochism of arousal. I would even suggest that this sadomasochism which infuses Arab Muslim culture is very

149

attractive to those on the Left in the West, as voyeurs. However, this is probably a subject for another symposium.

Lachkar: I remember attending a seminar about terrorism in the Middle East and during the question and answer period I mustered up the courage and blurted out a comment about how I felt the entire conflict to be linked to the role of women and their persecutors. The reaction was not only negative but they accused me of being rather "simplistic." After reviewing the comments of my colleagues in this symposium, I might take this view a step further and paraphrase the well known phrase: "Drive the Jews into the Sea" as a replacement to "Drive the Women into the Sea!" This is in accordance with Dr. Kobrin's dramatic view of free Israeli neighboring women cavorting around in skimpy bikinis!

Dr. Gutmann also offers justification, first when he states, "The Muslim fears that modernization leads inevitably to female liberation," and second his reference to clitoridectomy — the process which surgically removes the orgasmic female organ of pleasure. Nonie Darwish dramatically states how drastic and traumatic this is, and how the effort to reduce female orgasmic pleasure is in part to impose Sharia law throughout the world. Dr. Sennels also asks: why are men so vulnerable and agrees with Jamie that when it comes to sex, women are far more powerful and superior on several realms. This is a reality that the Muslim male cannot tolerate. Vulnerability has always meant something negative to the Muslim male, and he interprets it with weakness, impotence and smallness. Ironically, in clinical practice, to achieve vulnerability is the goal, especially with male abusers who think being a bully is a sign of strength and masculinity. So it makes sense for insecure men to destroy the power of the women and to diminish them into victims. In this way, fragile men think they are getting rid of the "weak" parts of themselves that they cannot tolerate. In psychoanalytic terms, this is referred to as projective identification.

Dr. Kobrin was on the verge of quibbling Dr. Sennels about narcissistic rage. Since she didn't, I would like to take on that challenge. I do not see anything narcissistic with the collective psyche of the terrorist. In fact, I would go so far as to say they share a more collective borderline disorder — or even a psychotic one. Narcissists use women as self objects, women who empower their grandiose omnipotent self. A self object is respected. For example, Mrs. Milosevic was an empowering, self-mirroring object for her husband. She gave him the okay to murder and slaughter thousands of Albanians. The Muslim male cannot make use of a powerful woman as a self object, because his culture and his forefathers have already diminished her existence. Second, narcissistic rage takes on an entirely different shape. The narcissist, when personally injured, will withdraw and go into isolation. The borderline, on the other hand, when injured, will spend the rest of his life retaliating, revenging and getting even. "We will not stop until we have destroyed every infidel through bombing, honor killings or whatever it takes."

Will Smith in *The Strong Horse: Power, Politics and The Clash of Arab Civilizations* (2010) reinforces two of the most perverse ways that the woman is viewed as powerful. First, her womb used as a weapon: "The womb of the Arab woman is her strongest weapon." Secondly, the veil used as a protection or shield, not to guard against man's lustful impulses, but rather to be used for her own protection. In other words, it is her choice to wear the veil as opposed to it being an object thrust upon her (Smith, 2010).

To conclude, I would like to end with a quote from Golda Meir, "We will have peace with the Arabs when they love their children more than they hate us."

Again thank you Jamie and everyone on this panel for your insightful contributions, and even where we differ, I hope this psychodynamic view of the conflict will open a new vision and way of thinking.

Gutmann: This time around I'm getting compelling answers to the question I raised in my first post, namely: why the excessive fear of female sexuality among Arab men?

Dr. Sennels suggests the possibility of "Vagina Envy" among Arab men, who feel shamed by a female sexual response stronger than their own. Dr. Kobrin refers to what men fear as a toxic identification with the mother, while Dr. Lachkar explores the ways in which Arab men use women as dumping grounds for denied aspects of the self. These insights pretty much cover the waterfront. However, in addition to these possibilities, Arab male homosexuality, hinted at by Drs Kobrin and Lachkar, should also be considered.

Phyllis Chesler recently reminded us that homosexuality and pedophilia are deeply established Arab traits, and clinical experience teaches us that, when the homosexual drive comes under repression, it can lead to precisely the kinds of paranoid fears of the sexual woman that we have been considering. As we know, the repressed homosexual identifies with the female sexual role, and, like the woman, wants to be penetrated by men. This wish, in the mind of the repressed homosexual, is intolerable, and is projected on to the spouse or girl friend: it is *she* who desires sex with other men. This projection leads to an associated fear of the female sexual response: the stronger that drive, the more likely that the woman will seek multiple partners to satisfy it. As a consequence, the female sexual appetite must be surgically blunted, and the sexually mature, unappeasable woman must be kept in *purdah* (out of sight), away from temptation.

When these measures fail, there is always the venerable practice of honor killing to fall back on.

Strange that the world is wracked by terrorism, women are kept in bondage, and we face nuclear war because of the quirks in the Islamic unconscious that this panel has explored. Psychoanalysis has gone out of fashion, but its methods and insights are needed more than ever.

FP: Dr. Nancy Kobrin, Dr. Joanie Lachkar, Dr. David Gutmann and Dr. Nicolai Sennels, thank you for joining Frontpage Symposium.

[Jamie Glazov, "Symposium: Islam's War on Women's Pleasure," *Frontpagemag.com*, August 6, 2010.]

[8] The Fear that Wilders is Right

In this special edition of Frontpage Symposium, we have assembled a distinguished panel to discuss the question: What psychological impulses and neuroses prevent people from objectively considering whether or not Islam is a religion of peace? In other words: Why the rigid disinclination *to even consider* the evidence that suggests that someone like Geert Wilders might be right?

Our guests today are:

Roger L. Simon, the author of ten novels, including the eight prize-winning Moses Wine detective novels, which have been published in many editions and translated in over a dozen languages. He is also a screenwriter and has written for all the major Hollywood studios, including *Bustin' Loose* with Richard Pryor, *Scenes from a Mall* with Woody Allen and the adaptation of his own *The Big Fix* with Richard Dreyfuss. Simon received an Academy Award nomination for his adaptation of Isaac Singer's *Enemies, A Love Story* in 1989. The author of *Blacklisting Myself: A Hollywood Apostate in an Age of Terror,* he is the co-founder and CEO of Pajamas Media.

Dr. Kenneth Levin, a clinical instructor of psychiatry at Harvard Medical School, a Princeton-trained historian, and a commentator on Israeli politics. He is the author of *The Oslo Syndrome: Delusions of a People Under Siege.*

and

Robert Spencer, a scholar of Islamic history, theology, and law and the director of Jihad Watch. He is the author of ten books, eleven monographs, and hundreds of articles about jihad and Islamic terrorism, including the New York Times Bestsellers *The Politically Incorrect Guide to Islam (and the Crusades)* and *The Truth About Muhammad.* His latest book, *The Complete Infidel's Guide to the Qur'an,* is available now from Regnery Publishing, and he is coauthor (with Pamela Geller) of the forthcoming book *The Post-American Presidency: The Obama Administration's War on America* (Simon and Schuster).

FP: Roger Simon, Robert Spencer and Kevin Levin, welcome to Frontpage Symposium.

Today we witness the blatant desperation in our culture and media for a "moderate Islam" — an Islam that many non-Muslims vehemently insist exists, but that mysteriously eludes them. This moderate Islam will make everything better, we are told, once the "extremists," who are the "minority" in Islam, are sedated. This sedation will be most easily achieved, the argument continues, when the Islamophobes stop blaming Islam after Islamic terrorists point to Islamic scriptures in explaining what inspired them to perpetrate their terrorist attacks.

Meanwhile, in terms of the planet that we happen to occupy, a "moderate Islam" is nowhere to be found; no school of Islamic jurisprudence exists that counsels Muslims to renounce the Qur'an's teachings on Islamic supremacism and the obligation of violent jihad. And yet, to suggest the truth of this reality in our culture gets one only the accusation of being a racist and an "Islamophobe."

Roger Simon, let me begin with you. What do you think of this phenomenon? You recently wrote a profound piece at Pajamas that touched on one of its crucial foundations. In analyzing why the likes of Glenn Beck and Charles Krauthammer have attacked Geert Wilders, you interpreted that these conservative individuals, from whom we might have expected something different on this score, are, when it all comes down to it, rejecting Wilders because they are afraid that *he might be right.*

Share your angle on this with us.

Simon: Although I have tremendous respect for my colleagues in this symposium, I can't imagine anything more depressing to write about or to discuss. The world is in a horrible Catch-22 and Geert Wilders is the ultimate "canary in a coal mine" for trying to tell the truth about it. Islam is an almost unsolvable conundrum. How do you deal with a religion with a billion adherents that is expansionist in ideology and threatens to kill its apostates? How do you get a reformation of that religion when its holy book, from which those dictums come, is reputed to be dictated verbatim by God and is therefore immutable?

Talk about "inconvenient truths," these are about as inconvenient as they get. No wonder they are buried from the discussion and ignored. We in the West live in a society that cannot even begin to wrap its mind around that. I know, it's hard for me.

So where does that leave Wilders? I believe that consciously or unconsciously those who brand him as excessive, or even racist, are living in fear that he may be right. They have to hate Wilders, because if he is correct, their whole world disintegrates. Who would want that? He and the small group like him have therefore morphed into our clearest contemporary examples of those poor Greek messengers to be killed for bringing the bad news. A salient recent example is Nicholas Kristof's unhinged attack on Ayaan Hirsi Ali in the New York Times Book Review — a supposed liberal going off on a woman who had a cliterodectomy for daring to dwell on how women were oppressed in the Islamic world. It's almost pathological. Another recent example is the similarly unhinged attacks on Israel over the Gaza flotilla incident while completely ignoring vastly more horrific acts occurring in the Muslim world on an almost daily basis. We dare not insult them lest they go mad.

It's almost as if the world has become a giant dysfunctional family, enabling their huge Muslim branch to remain besotted — or drugged out — on sub-Medieval ideology. And the situation is getting worse. The principle bastion of hope of reformation of the Islamic world, Turkey, made its turn back toward fundamentalism years ago now.

So again, where does that leave Wilders? One lonely canary. We have to support him, but I'm not optimistic. I hope my colleagues are.

FP: Thank you, Roger Simon.

Kenneth Levin, your thoughts? A species of the Oslo syndrome is involved in this phenomenon right?

Levin: I do see a form of the Oslo Syndrome operating here. In the Oslo agreements, Israel embraced Yasir Arafat and his PLO as its "peace partner" even as Arafat and those around him were making clear, in word and deed, that their goal remained Israel's annihilation. In looking at Israel's self-destructive Oslo policies, I discussed the phenomenon of segments within a minority population that is under siege — whether the situation be a minority marginalized, denigrated and otherwise attacked by the surrounding majority within a polity, or a small state under constant assault by larger neighbors, commonly embracing the indictments of their enemies, however bigoted or absurd or murderous those indictments. They delude themselves that by doing so, and promoting concomitant self-reform and concessions, their enemies will be appeased and grant them peace.

While most common among minorities at risk, the same phenomenon can be seen within large and powerful populations faced with new and dangerous external threats. This became obvious in the United States after 9/11.

The perpetrators of 9/11 and their myriad supporters quickly made clear their objective of imposing their Islamist rule worldwide and their comprehension of doing so as a religious duty. Yet many in America sought, and continue to seek, to recast the threat, to rationalize it, and to urge policies aimed at appeasing Islamist leaders and followers in the delusional hope of thereby extricating the nation from the dangers it faces.

Geert Wilders argues that Islamofascism derives directly from Islamic teachings, including Qur'anic exhortations. His movie, *Fitna,* advancing this argument, is unimpeachable in its citations of Islamic scripture and in its images of Islamofascism on the march. That those who oppose him are motivated in large part by a wish to appease the purveyors of the Islamist threat is indicated by the fact that the negative responses to Wilders have focused not on rebutting his arguments but on demonizing him and using anti-democratic means to silence him. As Roger Simon suggests, they are compelled to hate Wilders because they so want to cling to their delusional denial of the threat.

The ugly, perverse, self-destructive nature of the assault on Wilders, and the necessity to defend him, has been articulated by many. Particularly noteworthy is the stance of Daniel Pipes, in that Pipes disagrees with some of the substance of Wilders' arguments, believing in the possibility of a moderate Islam, but has forcefully supported Wilders and attacked the shoddy treatment to which he has been subjected, the anti-democratic efforts to silence him and punish him through the courts, and the broad movement, as illustrated in the indictments of Wilders, to quash free discussion of the nature of the Islamist war being waged against the West. Pipes has stated that Wilders' unique confronting of the Islamist challenge, pursued without the baggage of neo-Fascist, nativist, or conspiricist extremism that have characterized some others in Europe decrying Islamic inroads, has rendered him the most important European alive today. Beyond the unconscionable attempts to silence Wilders, there are other indications, both in Europe and America, that the hostility directed against him is motivated primarily by a wish to deny the threats we face and to appease its agents. Thus, in both Europe and the U.S., we have a huge chorus of officials insisting Islam is a religion of peace. They insist that Islamist forces pursuing a war of world conquest have "hijacked" the religion and that the vast majority of Muslims are peace-loving and tolerant. Yet these same officials give virtually no public support to those — too few — Muslims within their nations who at once declare themselves to be believing Muslims and do speak out forcefully against Islamofascism. On the contrary, such people are typically ignored and government outreach is almost invariably directed to individuals and groups linked to Islamist, hatred-promoting agendas.

In the U.S., for example, how much government attention or acknowledgement or support has been given to the likes of Zuhdi Jasser, an Arizona physician and believing Muslim who has dedicated himself to attacking the bigoted, hateful voices that have come to dominate Islamic institutions in America? Even if one is convinced that Jasser and like-minded individuals are pursuing a hopeless course because their interpretation of Islam is so starkly at odds with the religion's seminal texts and seminal message, one would still have to believe it makes sense for the nation to give such people all the support it can in advancing their perspectives. But in fact, Jasser and those like him have been essentially ignored by American officialdom and it is the allies of the Islamists who are courted and feted by officials at every level of government, including law enforcement agencies.

One can argue there is often a more venal motive behind this phenomenon. Saudi Arabia is the prime financier of Muslim extremism in the U.S., including of education in bigotry — particularly anti-Jewish and anti-Christian bigotry — in U.S. mosques and Islamic schools, and Saudi Arabia is pandered to because of its oil wealth and its readiness to use its prodigious financial resources to win official tolerance of its intolerant message. But if officials and others looked honestly at the existential threats we face from Islamofascism, the likelihood is they would be less inclined to politics as usual and to being swayed against defensive measures by Saudi blandishments. The impact of the Saudi role is a reflection of widespread official averting of eyes from the nature of the threat.

One can also argue that much of the Western accommodationist reaction to the Islamist threat, and desire to silence Wilders' message, are a product of Western leftist orthodoxy. The combination of hostility towards the West, moral relativism, and boosterism regarding virtually anything non-Western or anti-Western — all seminal doctrines of the contemporary leftist catechism — inevitably leads to denial of, or excuses for, or even defense of, the Islamist challenge.

But even among those whose ideological allegiances weigh against looking honestly at the nature of the threat, there were many individuals who responded to 9/11, and the additional terror that followed on the atrocities of that day, and the declarations of Islamofascism's leaders and minions, by re-evaluating their leftist ideology and abandoning their old verities for a saner comprehension of the realities we face. Those who continue day after day to cling to their delusions regarding the nature of the threat do so by persisting, day after day, out of a desperate desire to believe reality to be otherwise, to believe the threat can be wished away or rationalized away or appeased away, to continue averting their eyes from the nature of the challenge.

FP: Robert Spencer, your thoughts on the need to hate Wilders so one can cling to one's delusional denial of the threat we face. What do you think of Roger Simon's and Kenneth Levin's perspectives?

You bring a personal aspect to this as well, because your name can substitute Wilders in our own culture. You are very much hated for telling the truth that many people simply cannot accept, because the consequences are just too frightening and depressing. Share your thoughts with us on this phenomenon and also your personal experience with being a Wilders figure in our own society.

Spencer: Jamie, Roger Simon is quite right that those who call Wilders "excessive, or even racist...have to hate Wilders, because if he is correct, their whole world disintegrates." Although I am no Geert Wilders, I've encountered this phenomenon many times: people essentially admitting that they don't want to face up to the truths that Wilders and others enunciate because they believe the implications of those truths are simply too terrible to contemplate. I was told several years ago that the editorial board of a major American publication, when asked to do a profile on me and feature my writing, turned down the proposal because if what I was saying were true, "the U.S. would find itself at war with every Muslim country in the world."

I don't accept that as a natural outcome of what I say, but I find interesting the open avowal of the idea that what I say about Islam and jihad simply cannot be true, because if it were, the implications would be too disturbing to contemplate, and so therefore it must be false, or at least should be ignored! I encountered this again in a debate with a professor of Islamic studies at a significant American university, whose opening gambit in response to my initial presentation was to tell the audience that if what I said were true, it would be very depressing, as if that were sufficient to establish its falsity.

Contributing to the persistence of this unreality is something that Kenneth Levin alludes to. The fact that "the negative responses to Wilders have focused not on rebutting his arguments but on demonizing him and using anti-democratic means to silence him." That demonization is a tested and true weapon in the Islamic supremacist arsenal, as well as that of the Left (here is yet more evidence confirming your own thesis, Jamie, in your excellent book, *United in Hate*), and it is so frequently employed because it is so very effective. There are so many spineless conformists on the Right in America. They are very easily cowed by charges that someone is a "racist," or a "bigot," or even worse, an "Islamophobe," and maybe even a secret "neo-Nazi."

It doesn't matter if there is absolutely nothing to these charges (and in the case of Wilders and others thus charged and shunned, including my colleague and co-author Pamela Geller and myself, there isn't); for many prominent mainstream "conservatives," the charges themselves are enough. They will shun any contact or association with people who have been thus tarred. They are thoughtless and cowardly enough to run in the other direction at the mere suggestion of a taint, often without even investigating the case themselves. They don't seem to realize that by doing this they're playing the Leftist/Islamic supremacist game — effectively allowing the opposition to define the terms of the debate, choose the playing field, and make the rules. And that, it goes without saying, is a sure path to defeat.

FP: Thank you, Robert Spencer.

Roger Simon, our concluding round begins. What are the consequences we face with this mass psychosis and denial? What is the most effective thing we can try to do to put a crack in it?

Simon: To begin, I would like to thank my co-panelists for their excellent posts. I think the three of us substantially agree on this issue, which pushes us immediately to the most serious question: As Lenin put it, "What is to be done?"

Well, the answer to that is far from easy because, as a considerably better writer than Lenin, Charles Dickens put it best: these are "the best of times and the worst of times." By that I mean the very thing that could be our salvation, the unprecedented mass communication of the Internet, is the very thing that is most often used to perpetuate the Big Lie about the very problem we face. Unfortunately, the Internet often ratifies and amplifies the very societal hypnosis and self-hypnosis modern liberals undergo. This is as true for the trial of Geert Wilders as it is for anything else.

For make no mistake about it, we are engaged in a global psy-war. The question is how to win it when our side often seems uninterested in defending itself. Indeed, the current administration seems to want the reverse — to cede victory to our adversaries by refusing to name them, an extraordinary state of affairs. It reminds me of what my colleague Glenn Reynolds used to write about opponents of the Iraq War: "They're not anti-war. They're on the other side."

But back to "What is to be done?" Well, we must redouble our efforts in the psy-war and broaden our approach. That means not just preaching to the choir at venues like *Pajamas Media* and *Front Page*, but also finding ways to break through on their turf. The Great American Middle must be awakened and informed logically, not heatedly, about the Islamic threat. This is not about proving we are "right." This is about saving our civilization.

At this moment, the failures of the Obama administration, perceived now even by his supporters, may offer a window to reach out. We should seize it. Accusations of racism, like those habitually aimed at Wilders, also seem to be losing some of their punch — another signal it is time to go on the offensive. On top of that, the monumental Gulf oil spill — not Obama's fault, but further evidence of his incompetence, provides further opportunity.

So perhaps I am slightly more optimistic than I was on my first post. See what a little writing can do to make one feel better. Let's keep doing it. We'll be covering the Wilders trial closely at Pajamas Media and PJTV.

FP: Roger Simon, thank you. I would like to follow up with you for a moment. Can you briefly list what you deem to be some of the failures of the Obama administration? And also, in your view, what incompetence has Obama showed in dealing with the Gulf oil spill?

Simon: I can't think of anything I like about Obama, really, but his single most repellent act... or non-act... was his non-response to the

Iranian freedom movement at their moment of crisis, when revolution against the mullahs seemed possible. Obama's lack of emotional connection was stunning. It was almost as if he cared more about taking the credit for some mythical negotiation with Ahmadinejad than he did about the lives of the brave democracy demonstrators thronging the streets of Tehran. I can't recall an American president ever behaving worse in my lifetime, and that includes Watergate.

The rest of his foreign policy follows from that behavior. His treatment of Israel is beneath contempt and seems guided by his old friend Rashid Khalidi of the missing *LA Times* tape, but I'm sure the readers of *Front Page* know that.

As for the economy, he's been an obvious failure and is clearly out of his depth. I don't think he has a clue about what he is doing and any real discernible policy. He is also in a trap, because the only thing he does believe in (to the extent he believes is anything) is increased government spending and taxes, but the public knows, indeed many of his allies now know, that that is precisely the opposite of what the country and the world requires and is doomed to failure. The recession will only get worse.

The fortunate thing in all this is that whatever he does do domestically can probably be reversed (with great effort). But some of his foreign policies may be irreversible. The damage will be done.

Regarding the Gulf oil spill, as I have written elsewhere, this is the one area he is not really culpable, anymore than Bush was for Katrina, although, ironically, it is most likely to bring him down. That said, however, it is evident that Obama doesn't do empathy well. He couldn't be empathetic to the Iranian students and it took him ages to react to the people of the Gulf on a human level. Makes you nostalgic for Clinton (Bill, I mean). Anyway, Obama is up against it now. Things don't look good for him. As John Lennon once sang, "Instant karma's gonna get you. Gonna knock you right on the head."

Karma's catching up with Barack Obama.

FP: Thank you, Roger Simon.

Kenneth Levin, what is to be done? And I didn't mean to get us off track with Obama's failures, but in crystallizing them we can perhaps gauge, as Mr. Simon notes, how to seize the window of opportunity in terms of what to do in the context of our cultural denial.

Levin: The cultural denial of the threat we face will be overcome in one of two ways. Either it will be changed by the nation being subjected to sufficient additional carnage to force it awake or — obviously preferably — it will be abandoned in response to a sustained effort to saturate the public consciousness with images that effectively convey the threat. Convey it to the point where fewer and fewer are able to cling to their denial of reality.

Israel, to its misfortune, resisted the latter path to its waking from the delusions of Oslo. Pro-Oslo governments, and the nation's media, refused to address statements by Arafat and his associates, and by PA media, mosques and schools, that clearly demonstrated their goal remained Israel's annihilation. Nor did Israel's pro-Oslo leaders and media acknowledge the obvious implications of the Arafat-supported terror, unprecedented in its intensity, unleashed against Israelis during the early years of the Oslo process. It was only after Arafat, in September, 2000, rejected the offers of a comprehensive peace deal proposed by Israel and supported by President Clinton and instead unleashed his terror war, ultimately killing over a thousand Israeli civilians and horribly maiming thousands more, that Israelis in large numbers were shaken from their Oslo fantasies. For others, it required the Hezbollah terror that followed on Israel's full withdrawal from southern Lebanon, and the intensified Hamas rocket barrages that followed Israel's evacuation from Gaza in 2005, to disabuse them of their Oslo delusions.

The United States has, of course, experienced some additional carnage since 9/11 and numerous near misses. And many in America are open-eyed about the broader threat those incidents represent. Many were not only outraged by Nidal Malik Hasan's murder of 13 at Fort Hood. They were hardly less disturbed by the pathetic failure to stop Hasan when there were so many indications of the danger he posed, by the flacking for him in the military, by the refusal in both government and media circles to acknowledge his more than obvious motives and the significance of his beliefs and his actions.

Much of the public reacted similarly to the government's handling of the would-be Christmas bomber: the failure to use available intelligence to stop his attempted mass murder; the rapid granting to him of Miranda rights; the reluctance to acknowledge his Jihadist agenda; the unsupported assertions that he acted alone; the claims that his failure to destroy his plane demonstrated "the system worked." So too did the public react to the equally ludicrous, similar, and similarly dangerous, initial government and media responses to the Times Square bomber — the initial reluctance to associate the act or its perpetrator with any broader threat, the absurd grasping for alternative explanations of his motives, again the claims that his attempted mass murder failed because "the system worked," the ongoing refusal to name the actual threat.

But clearly public concern has not reached the level of effectively pressuring the government to abandon its prevarications and its apologetics and indeed its sympathies vis-a-vis the enemy. It is only to be wished that it won't require a disaster on the scale of 9/11 to rouse the public to that greater determination to bring about a change in government policy.

One element of promoting that determination is not only to speak to the public about the nature of the threat but to demonstrate vividly the threat. This can be advanced by disseminating to broader audiences such works as *Fitna*, the documentary *Obsession*, and other films that offer footage both of Islamist leaders explicating their murderous agenda and Islamist cadres acting on that agenda.

Roger Simon notes that the Internet, which could be an effective tool for getting out the truth about the Islamist threat despite mainstream media silence and obfuscation, has actually largely cut the other way by being used to promote the Big Lie about the threat, the denying it and rationalizing it and prettifying it. The Internet is also used by the Islamist enemy to recruit to its cause. But the new media could be used to expose more effectively the Big Lie, with images. I agree with Roger Simon on the repellent non-response of Obama to last June's mobilization of the freedom movement in Iran. The snapshots and film images captured on cell phones of the popular uprising and the regime's brutal response were seen around the world, and brought home to many the nature of the Iranian branch of the enemy and the moral bankruptcy of Obama's response.

Images of events in Darfur can also be mustered to convey the counter-message to the Big Lie. The people of Darfur, like those in the streets in Iran, are Muslims, but their tormentors, the rulers of the Sudan, are closely allied with the Iranian branch of the Islamist threat, it's chief boosters are drawn from Iran, Hamas and Hezbollah. Sudan's rulers enjoy as well the unanimous backing of the Arab League, the friendship of Erdogan's Islamic government in Turkey, and the support of additional non-state backers such as Al-Qaeda. Many on this roster, including the Sudanese government, are the object of Obama Administration blandishments and outreach and offerings of carrots, even as the slaughter in Darfur, and indeed in other minority areas in Sudan, goes on unabated. Images, in photos and film, of what is actually happening there can help promote public eye-opening to the broader threat and impatience with our government's fecklessness.

Those who speak the truth, or convey it in photos and video, will be demonized, as Robert Spencer says. That is, indeed, the Islamist way, and leftist way. But one can challenge the censors. If their counterparts in Europe, including the indicters of Wilders, are largely able to escape serious challenge, we're not obliged to give the censors a free pass here.

Material demonstrating the threat — in the words and deeds of the Islamists themselves — can be offered, in universities and elsewhere, as material to be discussed and debated. If it contains errors, let the critics demonstrate it. Those who refuse to allow the discussion, in whatever venue, should be called out for violating the norms of a free society, whether they are motivated by fears of the physical retaliation supporters of the Islamist threat so widely employ, or by fears of being labeled "racist" or "anti-Muslim," or, as the anecdotes cited by Robert Spencer effectively convey, by refusal to recognize the nature of the threat because it is too daunting and upsetting.

During the late thirties, Churchill was censored. He was virtually blackballed by the BBC and demonized by other major media. They were afraid to have his message aired, afraid of its implications. When Chamberlain brought "peace in our time" back from Munich, Churchill was denounced as a warmonger for criticizing Chamberlain's capitulation to the Nazi threat.

But we do have tools to circumvent the censorship of the appeasers, and only through those tools can we hope to break the dominant self-delusion by means that will spare the nation a ruder awakening via future 9/11's.

FP: Thank you, Kenneth Levin. Robert Spencer, final thoughts?

Spencer: It is indeed, as Roger Simon, a global psy-war, and it is by no means over. We have the truth on our side, and as Kenneth Levin ably adumbrates, we have the alternate media — which is still very small compared to the mainstream media, but it is growing apace as the frustration of people who realize they're being lied to increases. The biggest challenge we face is that all too many people who no longer buy the lies of the Left still allow themselves to be cowed by this psychological manipulation, such that they're afraid to speak out for the truth themselves, or afraid to venture outside the bounds of what the Left has delineated as acceptable discourse. The hardest obstacles to clear away are not the Left's control of the mainstream media, but our own mind-forged manacles.

As for Obama, no one should be surprised by what is happening. As Pamela Geller and I show in our book *The Post-American Presidency: The Obama Administration's War On America*, he is not only presiding over America's decline, but is in a very real sense the apostle of that decline. The course he is taking as President could have been predicted by anyone who knew the activities and associations of his earlier career, as we outline in the book. And so it is no surprise that the list of his anti-Israel and even anti-Semitic appointees and associates just keeps growing: not just Reverend Wright, but also Samantha Power, Robert Malley, Rosa Brooks, Chuck Hagel, Zbigniew Brzezinski, and more. Likewise also, his appointees who wish to give international law precedence over American law: Harold

Koh, Sonia Sotomayor, Elena Kagan, John Holdren, Carol Browner - on and on.

In light of all this and more, the situation is very serious, and the time for appeasement, and what Levin terms "the censorship of the appeasers," is over. William Jennings Bryan said it in 1896 in a vastly different context, but every word applies to conservatives today:

We do not come as aggressors. Our war is not a war of conquest; we are fighting in the defense of our homes, our families, and posterity. We have petitioned, and our petitions have been scorned; we have entreated, and our entreaties have been disregarded; we have begged, and they have mocked when our calamity came. We beg no longer; we entreat no more; we petition no more. We defy them!

We beg no more. We entreat no more. We petition no more. We defy them. We are not the aggressors. We are not haters. We are not racists. We are not bigots. We are not neofascists. Those who claim otherwise are knowingly or unknowingly abetting a monstrous evil. We withdraw our sanction from them. We must no longer treat journalists as if they were objective reporters when they are ideologues and propagandists. We must constantly call them out on their game. And refuse to play it ourselves.

FP: Roger Simon, Robert Spencer and Kevin Levin, thank you for joining Frontpage Symposium.

[Jamie Glazov, "Symposium: The Fear that Wilders is Right," *Frontpagemag.com*, July 9th, 2010.]

[9] When Does a Religion Become an Ideology?

In this special edition of Frontpage Symposium, we have invited two distinguished guests to discuss the question: When does a religion become an ideology? Our guests today are:

Tawfik Hamid, an Islamic thinker and reformer who is the author of *Inside Jihad: Understanding and Confronting Radical Islam.* A one-time Islamic extremist from Egypt, he was a member of *Jemaah Islamiya,* a terrorist Islamic organization, with Dr. Ayman Al-Zawahiri, who later became the second in command of al-Qaeda. He is currently a senior fellow and chairman of the study of Islamic radicalism at the Potomac Institute for Policy Studies.

and

David Satter, a senior fellow of the Hudson Institute and a visiting scholar at the Johns Hopkins University Nitze School of Advanced International Studies (SAIS). He was Moscow correspondent of the *Financial Times* of London from 1976 to 1982, during the height of the Soviet totalitarian period and he is the author of *Age of Delirium: the Decline and Fall of the Soviet Union,* which is being made into a documentary film. His most recent work is *Darkness at Dawn: The Rise of the Russian Criminal State.*

FP: Tawfik Hamid and David Satter, welcome to Frontpage Symposium.

Mr. Hamid, let us begin with you. Make an introductory statement for us to get our discussion started: When does a religion become an ideology?

Hamid: A religion becomes an ideology when the followers of this religion cannot tolerate the existence of those who have different views or beliefs, and when they understand their religious text literally and refuse to accept any way of understanding the religion other than their own way of understanding.

FP: Thank you.

Dr. Satter, how would you now build on Mr. Hamid's statement?

Satter: I think another way of putting it is that a religion becomes an ideology when man-made dogma is treated as infallible truth.

Although there are adherents of all three major monotheistic faiths who believe that every word of the sacred texts is to be taken literally, for the post-Enlightenment rationalist mind, there is a distinction between transcendent moral truths, exemplified in the case of Judaism and Christianity in the Golden Rule and the Ten Commandments and the dogmatic contents of the religions expressed in their historical accounts and ritual requirements.

This distinction is important to bear in mind because transcendent moral truths are never the content of an ideology. An ideology contains an assertion about society that is treated as ultimate truth and applied indiscriminately to explain all aspects of political reality. Since transcendent moral truths owe their character to the fact that they are "over and above" society, they cannot contribute to the content of an ideology. In fact, the effect of an ideology is always to destroy true moral transcendence.

The ritual requirements or dogmatic assertions about the history of a religion, however, are perfectly suitable for the construction of an ideology. The obligation in Islam to wage jihad, properly interpreted, can be made the basis of an ideology which treats waging war on unbelievers as the highest obligation of a Moslem and evaluates all actions in terms of the extent to which they support this sacred obligation. Other religions too have aspects that could become the material of an ideology. One example is the doctrine of the Jews as the "Chosen People." Although this doctrine has never been used to justify the oppression of others, it could be.

A religion becomes an ideology when its man-made elements become an *idée fixe* and are seized upon as an idea that can be imposed on all political and social institutions in the interests of power. The temptation was explained best in Dostoevsky's tale of the Grand Inquisitor where the inquisitor explains to Jesus the essence of an ideology's appeal:

Instead of the strict ancient law, man had in future to decide for himself with a free heart what is good and what is evil, having only your image before him for guidance. But did it never occur to you that he would at last reject and call in question even your image and your truth, if he were weighed down by as fearful a burden as freedom of choice.

Laying down that burden may be easiest of all if the mental prison thereby created is constructed with the materials of supposedly sacred religious teachings.

Hamid: In general, I agree with many of the above views. I would like to add that, based on David's analysis, I see that having an ideology is not by itself the problem. For example, the ideology of the chosen people — as he mentioned — was not used to oppress others. It is the part of ideology that is used to oppress others, such as 'violent Jihad' in Islam that is actually causing the problem.

A good distinction that David made was the distinction between true moral transcendence and ideology. It is important to mention that one of the main problems in traditional Islam is that the pillars of the religion [to say No God other than Allah, Mohamed is the prophet of Allah, the 5 prayers, the obligatory tax (Zakkat), the fasting of Ramadan and the pilgrimage (Haj)] are rituals rather than moral values. In other words, based on the traditional views within Islam, Bin Laden can be a good Muslim because he follows the 5 pillars of Islam. On the contrary, if the pillars of Islam include 'you shall not commit murder' or other moral values, Muslims would not have seen people like Bin Laden and the terrorists as real Muslims. The ideology and the religious dogma of the 5 pillars made many Muslims unable to use the transcendent moral truth to judge people like Bin Laden.

Regarding the view that 'man had in future to decide for himself with a free heart what is good and what is evil,' I agree with this but I will add that the inspired moral values from religion such as 'you shall not commit murder and 'you shall not steal' should remain as the back bone for future moral values. We may change some practical applications for these values but the pillars for such values will remain

170

— at least in the view of many — as inspired values via the creator (i.e. not man-made).

Regarding the statement that "Laying down that burden may be easiest of all if the mental prison thereby created is constructed with the materials of supposedly sacred religious teachings." I have seen the practical application for this in our Islamic society when many in the Muslim world adopt Islam as an ideology as a reaction to the moral relativism concepts that flourished in the Muslim world in the 1950s and 60s partially due to the work of liberal movements. The Islamic societies could not tolerate the lack of clear borders or 'prison' for their mind and it was much easier for many in these societies to follow an 'ideology' with clear borders rather than having the burden of freedom of choice.

Satter: Muslims, of course, are not the only ones who seek "clear borders." Very few people have the confidence to identify their fundamental moral values and apply them to the myriad of complicated situations with which life confronts us. Even the most educated people fall back on mental borders that are the product of past habit and unchallenged assumptions. The problem becomes much greater when the mental borders are ubiquitous and the product of a false universal theory — as in Nazism or Communism — or the dogmatic contents of a religion as in the case of radical Islam.

We are also confronted with the problem of group dynamics. Ethical judgment is the property of an individual. Dogmatic rules guide the behavior of a group. They eliminate differences and mobilize people for common action. So to the difficulty of thinking for oneself is added in an ideological situation the emotional trauma of confronting the group. Under the circumstances, it is small wonder that fanaticism in power has such terrible force. It operates on the difficulty that people have, when challenged, of defending what is truly human in each of them, their ultimate moral sense.

So what can reinforce the moral sense of the individual in the face of religious or secular fanaticism? If I understand him correctly, Tawfik provides the answer with his reference to the five pillars of Islam, none of which deal with ethical values. I think we need to be very clear in distinguishing between dogma and genuinely transcendent values. In the case of Nazism and Communism, the task was easier because there were no transcendent values. Communism prided itself on its rejection of metaphysics. But in the case of radical Islam, the fanatics can draw on an authoritative religious tradition. Every word of the Qur'an is treated as divine truth and the authoritative interpretation of the Qur'an is or, at least, can be seen as being implicitly terroristic.

It seems to me that, under these circumstances, we must insist on our ability to define terms. To be truly religious, values must be transcendent. They cannot be derived from a political objective, for example, creating a classless society or a restored Caliphate. They can't be based on the hatred of outsiders whether capitalists or infidels because the tensions that these hatreds reflect owe their origin to society which higher values necessarily transcend. Where the measure of right or wrong is the interests of a group, whether the proletariat, Aryans or the ummah, we are dealing with man-made dogma regardless of any pretended religious justification. Its absolutization creates an ideology not a religion and it should be treated as an ideology and not granted the legitimacy of a religion with which it actually shares nothing. In the case of Islam, this does not mean an attack on Islamic practices as such but only their use in the service of terror under which circumstances, the issue of transcendence becomes relevant. To search for meaning is only human but it can lead to barbaric conclusions if it proceeds without ethical guidance. In a nuclear world, we need to defend the distinction between higher values and dogma as a matter of fundamental self-defense.

Hamid: I agree with the points that David mentioned and would like to add more applied points that relate to radical Islam.

David raised the point of "Difficulty to think for oneself." This is exactly what happened to me and to many members in the radical organizations. We felt that we are like sheep that just need to follow the leader. Individual thinking was lost, especially when the radical leaders discouraged us from 'thinking'.

David considered the ummah concept as "a man made dogma regardless of any pretended religious justification". This could be true.

However, Muslims see the ummah concept as a religious based one. It is vital to understand how Muslims see such a concept in order to be able to approach the problem and deal with it correctly. In this regard, it is also important to emphasize that Communism and Nazism were seen by most of their followers as man-made ideology. In Islam, the situation is completely different as most Muslims see the ideological component as a religious revelation from Allah. In the former situation (i.e. man-made ideology) it is much easier to change the ideology as you can prove it wrong. When the ideology, as in case of Islam, is processed at the subconscious and emotional levels of the brain (as a religion) rather than the high cortical levels (as the case of Communism and Nazism), it is much more difficult to change it.

I completely agree with David about the need to have a clear distinction between religion and ideology. Islam that only works inside a mosque as a form of individual worship can be considered a religion. However, Islam that is used as a political power and a controlling system for the society must be treated as an ideology. The West needs to be clear about this issue, as giving the ideological part of Islam (that promotes violence and control of others) the protection and privileges that are given to a religion can be catastrophic. This ideological part of Islam has to be fought as the case with fighting Communism and Nazism. If we failed to make such a separation between Islam as personal type of worship and Islam (or its interpretations) as a political and driving force to dominate others, we will not be able to control radical Islamic ideology in the future. In fact we may be actually giving support to the radical ideology if we gave it the advantages of a religion. Allowing the ideological part of Islam to flourish under the banner of religious freedom weakens the spiritual part of the religion itself and makes things more complicated.

Satter: Politics dominates our lives and there is always a temptation to make a religion out of politics. If a political objective has divine significance, it is worth dying for and, of course, worth killing for. Those obsessed with a political mission are fearless and resourceful. Relieved of the need to exercise individual moral judgment, they become ruthless spies, talented strategists and remorseless killers. This is why it is so important to show a political ideology in all its man-made artificiality. Only in this way can an ideological movement be discredited. One hopes that it will be harder to organize mass crimes on behalf of a system that has been shown to be not divinely inspired but man-made. In any case, the effort offers some hope for the future.

FP: Tawfik Hamid and David Satter, thank you for joining Frontpage Symposium.

[Jamie Glazov, "Symposium: When Does a Religion Become an Ideology?" *Frontpagemag.com*, June 4, 2010.]

[10] The World's Most Wanted: A "Moderate Islam"

In this special edition of Frontpage Symposium, we have invited four istinguished guests to discuss the question: Is there a moderate Islam? Our guests today are:

Timothy Furnish, a former U.S. Army Arabic interrogator, he is a consultant and author with a Ph.D. in Islamic History. He is currently working on a book on modern Muslim plans to resurrect the caliphate. His website, dedicated to Islamic eschatology, is www.mahdiwatch.org.

Tawfik Hamid, an Islamic thinker and reformer who is the author of *Inside Jihad: Understanding and Confronting Radical Islam*. A one-time Islamic extremist from Egypt, he was a member of *Jemaah Islamiya,* a terrorist Islamic organization, with Dr. Ayman Al-Zawahiri, who later became the second in command of al-Qaeda. He is currently a senior fellow and chairman of the study of Islamic radicalism at the Potomac Institute for Policy Studies.

M. Zuhdi Jasser, M.D. is the President and Founder of the American Islamic Forum for Democracy (AIFD). A devout Muslim, he served 11 years as a Lieutenant Commander in the United States Navy. He is a nationally recognized expert in the contest of ideas against political Islam, American Islamist organizations, and the Muslim Brotherhood. He regularly briefs members of the House and Senate congressional anti-terror caucuses and has served as a guest lecturer on Islam to deploying officers at the Joint Forces Staff College. Dr. Jasser was presented with the 2007 Director's Community Leadership Award by the Phoenix office of the FBI and was recognized as a "Defender of the Home Front" by the Center for Security Policy. He recently narrated the documentary *The Third Jihad*, produced by PublicScope Films. His chapter, *Americanism vs. Islamism* is featured in the recently released book, *The Other Muslims* (Palgrave-Macmillan), edited by Zeyno Baran.

and

Robert Spencer, a scholar of Islamic history, theology, and law and the director of Jihad Watch. He is the author of ten books, eleven monographs, and hundreds of articles about jihad and Islamic terrorism, including the New York Times Bestsellers *The Politically Incorrect Guide to Islam (and the Crusades)* and *The Truth About Muhammad*. His latest book, *The Complete Infidel's Guide to the Qur'an*, is available now from Regnery Publishing, and he is coauthor (with Pamela Geller) of the forthcoming book *The Post-American Presidency: The Obama Administration's War on America* (Simon and Schuster).

FP: Timothy Furnish, Tawfik Hamid, Dr. M. Zuhdi Jasser and Robert Spencer, welcome to Frontpage Symposium.

Dr. Furnish, let me begin with you. Robert Spencer recently entered a debate at *NewsReal Blog* where he argued that there is no moderate Islam. What is your perspective on his argument?

Furnish: I find myself in the curious (and somewhat uncomfortable) position of disagreeing with my friend Robert Spencer, for whom I have the utmost respect and with whom I almost always totally agree. However, on this issue of whether moderate Islam exists, I think Robert may be missing something.

He is exactly right that Sunni Islam — whence comes directly Salafism, Wahhabism and jihadism — promotes violence against non-Muslims in order to make Islam paramount over the entire planet. I have no quarrel with that stance. But I would argue that this is largely because within this majority branch of Islam the only acceptable exegetical paradigm regarding the Qur'an is a literalist one: and of course when passages such as "behead the unbeliever" [Suras 47:3 and 8:12] are read literally the good Muslim had better reach for his sword-or be rightly accused of infidelity to Allah's Word.

However, perhaps because Robert is so well-versed in the theology of Islam, as opposed to the historical record of how that religious theory has been acted out on the stage of history, he seems to overlook the key fact on the ground that certain minorities within Islam have developed a non-literalist, even allegorical, approach to reading the

Qur'an. Foremost among these moderates are the Isma`ilis, the Sevener Shi`is, whose global head is the philanthropical Aga Khan. Isma'ilis may number only in the tens of millions (out of the total Muslim community of some 1.3 billion, second only to Christianity's 2+ billion), but they do exist and they define, for example, jihad not as killing or conquering unbelievers, but as economic development and charity work.

In general, all branches of Shi`ism (which makes up perhaps 15% of the world's Muslims), including the Twelvers of Iran, Iraq and Lebanon, allow the practice of ijtihad, "independent theological-legal judgment"— which is decidedly not the case for Sunnism. And while this has allowed for the ayatollahs to come up with negative novelties such as vilayet-i faqih (Khomeini's "rule of the jurisconsult"), it also leaves the door open to non-literal exegesis of the anachronistic passages of the Qur'an.

Even within Sunnism, many of the Sufi (Islamic mystic) orders are more akin to the Shi`i than the woodenly literalist Sunnis in their exegesis. (Yet I would not go as far as Stephen Schwartz, who in his book *The Other Islam: Sufism and the Road to Global Harmony* thinks Sufis are basically "Quakers with beards" and sees them as the antidote to jihadists. This rosy view overlooks the historical facts of the many jihads led by Sufi shaykhs and fought by Sufi adherents over the centuries.)

Today, many Sufis are non-literalists and focus on the batini, "inner" or "esoteric" meaning of the Qur'anic verses rather than on the zahiri, "outward" or "exoteric"— i.e., literal-meaning as Bin Laden and his ilk do. Another sect of Islam that is rather moderate in its approach to the Qur'an is the Barelwi (or Barelvi) one in India and the UK.

In fact, the recent 600-page "anti-terrorism" fatwa that received much media adoration was written by Muhammad Tahir al-Qadri, a Barelwi. As I observe in the "*Washington Times*" article, al-Qadri's adherence to what is essentially a sect of Islam makes it very problematic that his fatwa will have any major effect on the jihadists in the short term-but, over time, if enough sectarian Muslims keep condemning the purely literalist approach to Islam's holy book, perhaps Islam might enter into its own much needed Enlightenment, or at least Reformation. But it's clear from these examples that moderate Islam, not just moderate Muslims, truly does exist — even if often in a minority, often persecuted, status."

Spencer: In all this my friend Timothy Furnish, whose work I admire, is entirely correct. That is why I am always careful to say that there is no "mainstream" sect of Islam, or one that is generally recognized as orthodox by Muslim sects in general, that does not teach the necessity to make war against and subjugate unbelievers. But I am not sure that the existence of Muslims who are generally considered heretics and persecuted for their heresy, which often consists precisely of their rejection or reconstitution of the jihad doctrine, constitutes the existence of a "moderate Islam" upon which Westerners should place any hope. The likelihood that these groups are going to stop being persecuted minorities and eventually attain mainstream status without abjuring exactly the elements of their beliefs that make them appealing to Westerners is slim at best.

FP: Dr. Jasser?

Jasser: Jamie. Thank you for including me. Let me start by addressing the premise of your initial question to Dr. Furnish regarding his opinion on Robert Spencer's assertion that, "there is no moderate Islam."

In my experience, there is a significant distinction globally between "Islam" as a personal spiritual faith (a personal *submission* to God, if you will), and the "House of Islam" which more broadly includes the entire human corpus of Islamic scholarship, knowledge (ilm) and jurisprudence (shar'iah) as espoused by leading global Islamic jurists and thought leaders (a *'submission'* to the House of Islam if you will). As a devout Muslim, I believe in the former in my personal relationship with God, but as an anti-Islamist I reject any "submission" to the latter which is human. Certainly, academe is central to understanding and effectively reforming Islamic thought against salafism. But my identification with the Islamic faith as a Muslim in no way obligates me or any Muslim to drink the Kool-aid of the Islamists even if they do control most Muslim institutions globally.

For those trying to pigeon-hole my Islamic philosophy, I am a devout Muslim raised in my youth in a conservative, orthodox, Sunni Muslim family in a small town in Wisconsin. I am neither an ideological mutation nor was I born in a vacuum. My parents escaped the despotic fascist regime of Syria in the mid-1960's, seeking the liberty and freedom of America. My grandparents were also conservative Muslims who raised their children to have a strong moral character and ethical upbringing free of corruption and grounded in Islam but not political Islam. Those values as a force for good, under God, were transmitted down our familial generations. While the specifics of our faith arose out of the Sunni tradition, the overarching ideas included some diverse Islamic influences ranging from Sufi to orthodox to Quranist to name a few. Significant diversity existed within our family, as it did among many other intellectuals from Syria. But there was also agreement on core moral principles and liberty. These modernists, moderates, and liberals have been lost in the intellectual wasteland of the battle between the likes of the secular thugs of the Assads of the world and the radical Islamists of the Ikhwan.

To pigeon-hole many Muslims into one theological construct is misleading given the lack of any Islamic mandate for a "church" which communicates or excommunicates Sunni members. Many of the sects Tim describes have this type of regimented circumscribed Islam with fealty to their leaders that gives the sect's thought-leaders better control on the central message. However, most Sunnis I know (non- Islamists) do not have such a fealty to any specific imam or school and are profoundly decentralized.

Now certainly the Wahhabis and Salafists of the world practice takfir (defining who is and who is not Muslim) in an effort to control "membership" and ideology in the faith community. However, we, as anti-Islamists, reject takfir and will not give up the domain of Islam to Islamists.

The reasons for the pre-Enlightenment fossilization of thought in Muslim majority countries are many. They include a need for deep generational reform of theology (Islamist foundations of Islam), education (illiteracy and lack of western influence), economics (the lack of free markets), politics (the absence of democratic principles of real liberty with control by monarchs, theocrats, and autocrats), and culture (an endemic, suffocating tribalism).

Many devout Muslims, like most youth, establish our moral compass of life under God within our superego long before we had the knowledge or the skill to investigate scriptural Qur'anic or Hadith exegesis. Thus, the moral lens through which we interpret our scripture is long established before we could ever fall prey to the fascist radical Islamic interpretations. But many are not immune to the supremacism of Islamism. There is a dire need for moderates to reinterpret the Qur'an and Hadith and dismiss ideas or sira not commensurate with modernity. (See Part I, Part II, Part III and Part IV)

I use the same non-political, anti-Islamist construct of Islam I learned from my parents to teach my own children about our faith while preserving conservative values not in conflict with American law or loyalty. That ultimately was why we formed our American Islamic Forum for Democracy in 2003 dedicated to defeating the root cause of terrorism- political Islam.

Tim and Robert and others may view this as heresy or marginal thought in Islam. I would disagree, but also admit that it is not predominant among the thought-leaders of Sunni Islam. So the crux of the question is who and what defines Islam — all Muslims or only the subset of Muslims who are clerics? I do believe that it is a majority if not a significant plurality of Muslims that reject political Islam. We do obviously have a lot of work to prove this assertion. Our ideas are harder to find than those of the Islamists — so yes, 'Houston, we do have a problem.'

But, our anti-Islamist reform can only happen against political Islam from a bottom up (lay to cleric) approach rather than the top down (cleric to lay) approach which Tim and Robert appear to be seeking. History shows that other reformation movements in Europe occurred that way when combined with a political liberty movement. Again, attempting to pigeon-hole the Muhammad Al-Qadri's of the world as a 'sect' does not help their movements and rather makes their fate sealed as marginal within the 'House of Islam'.

180

The majority of the ulemaa (scholars) of the "House of Islam" are controlled by Islamists who use an authoritative shar'iah which is incompatible with the ideas of liberty and the separation of mosque and state. This is especially true for the hubs of central influence in Sunni thought in Saudi Arabia and at Al-Azhar in Egypt. Anti-Islamist Muslims do know and understand our faith. But we are in dire need of developing new platforms to get our voices heard.

An intellectual civil war within the House of Islam will be the only way to figure out which Islam and whose Islam will ultimately prevail. To dismiss all of "Islam" as immoderate leaves without a platform your greatest allies for freedom — devotional anti-Islamist Muslims who worship God. We are the only ones, I believe, with a tangible viable solution that will achieve the defeat of supremacist, radical Islamism. We are the only ones with a viable treatment to the ideological disease.

Hamid: Thanks, Jamie, for organizing this symposium.

If we defined Islam in terms of what is being taught and promoted in mainstream Islamic books such the Tafseers and Fiqh, then Robert Spencer is absolutely correct is saying that moderate Islam does not exist. The problem is that this form of Islamic teaching is not counterbalanced by a theologically-based peaceful interpretation of the religion. Until today, all main schools of jurisprudence in Islam accept violence in some way or another.

Dr. Jasser is correct in stating that many of these interpretations and jurisprudence books or Sharia are man-made. However, the reality is that this man-made version of the understanding of Islam is currently the most dominant one in the Muslim world. I agree with Dr. Jasser that there is a need for a reformation, but I disagree with him that the reformation needs to occur from the bottom-up. Based on my experience within Islam, waiting for this "bottom-up" approach is likely to fail, as any small group of Muslims that starts to think differently will be considered by the majority and by leading authorities in the Muslim world as non-Muslims.

This is simply because denying some traditional ways of teachings is considered denying "Maaloom Mina AldeenBildarora' (a fundamental belief in the faith) which makes a Muslim an apostate (non-Muslim) for denying it. The change in my view needs to occur "Up-Bottom," not the other way around. This can occur by exerting more pressure and criticism for the violent teachings that exist in mainstream theological Islam. Dr. Jasser's view to have Islam without these authorities is very revolutionary and difficult or impractical to achieve. I agree with Dr. Furnish that there are some elements of reform that already exist in the Muslim world. However, these elements of reform do not have a complete theological interpretation or jurisprudence that can stand against the current and dominant Salafi teaching within Islam.

My main point is that, what people generally mean as Islam (Tafseer, Hadith, Sira, Jurisprudence, Sharia) is certainly not peaceful. However, peaceful understanding of the religion is possible. Moderate Muslims such as Jasser and others do exist because they do not practice the traditional dominant theology and alternatively they have developed their own personal interpretations for the religion. *Until these personal interpretations become the mainstream type of teaching within Islam, I have to agree with Robert Spencer that moderate Islam does not exist.* I will only change his phrase to be "moderate Islam does not *currently* exist."

Furnish: Robert Spencer makes a good point that many Muslim sectarians are considered "heretics," but he paints with an overbroad brush. Not all Islamic sects are persecuted minorities: the Ibadis run Oman and constitute 70% of its population; the Alawis, while a minority, still run Syria; the Isma'ili minorities are certainly not persecuted in India, Tanzania or Britain (although they are in Saudi Arabia — but who isn't, besides Wahhabis?); and Sufis, while often at loggerheads with Wahhabis and Salafis, are popular and powerful in places like Senegal, Sudan and Indonesia. And while the Islamic sects *in toto* are certainly a minority, somewhere around 7-8% of the world's Muslim population, that still amounts to perhaps 100 million people — twice that many if the Twelver Shi`is are included. Luther certainly started with far fewer Christians, and yet he sparked a Reformation.

While I admire Dr. Jasser's personal revival of Mu`tazilism (a rationalist Islamic ideology that was snuffed out in the 10th century AD), I fear his views are idiosyncratic within Sunni Islam — and my own research indicates that the closest analogs to what he preaches are found in those very sects whose degree of regimentation and cult-like devotion he somewhat overstates. But even in those cases where a sect is at least partially predicated on charismatic leadership (the Isma'ilis; the Turkish Gülen movement; etc.), I would say that as long as the leader is telling his followers that jihad does NOT mean holy war— then that's infinitely preferable to the "current and dominant Salafi teaching," as Dr. Hamid so aptly puts it.

I agree with Dr. Hamid, regretfully, that Dr. Jasser's hope for a grass-roots Islamic reformation from within Sunnism is very unlikely — another reason I favor putting our hope for such in sects. Dr. Jasser seems to forget that the Enlightenment could only take place after the Protestant Reformation had broken the monopoly of the Catholic hierarchy in Europe — and that the reformation of Christendom was in fact led by clerics (Luther, Calvin, Tyndale), NOT by layman. What Islam really needs right now are such reform-minded clerics, and these are found for the most part today among Islam's sects, not its Sunni majority.

Spencer: There is a certain dancing-on-the-precipice feel to this entire symposium. Dr. Jasser rejects the contention that his views amount to "heresy or marginal thought in Islam," but acknowledges that they are "not predominant among the thought-leaders of Sunni Islam." You can say that again, and I would doubt that he would be able to name even one among the "thought-leaders of Sunni Islam" who would accept that there is, as Dr. Jasser puts it, any "significant distinction globally between 'Islam' as a personal spiritual faith (a personal *submission* to God, if you will), and the 'House of Islam' which more broadly includes the entire human corpus of Islamic scholarship, knowledge (ilm) and jurisprudence (shar'iah) as espoused by leading global Islamic jurists and thought leaders (a *'submission'* to the House of Islam if you will)." Indeed, he would be hard-pressed to find even one among those "thought-leaders of Sunni Islam" who would not classify this as a heresy.

Dr. Hamid, in contrast to Dr. Jasser himself, notes correctly that interpretations of Islam such as Dr. Jasser's are personal, idiosyncratic, and non-traditional — a fact that is all too often glossed over by his enthusiastic and well-heeled non-Muslim backers, who would prefer to pretend that he represents the dominant mainstream. Dr. Hamid is also quite correct that "*Until these personal interpretations become the mainstream type of teaching within Islam, I have to agree with Robert Spencer that moderate Islam does not exist.*" He remains optimistic, however, maintaining that "peaceful understanding of the religion is possible" and changing my phrase "moderate Islam does not exist" to "moderate Islam does not *currently* exist."

I don't claim to know the future, and history is full of events that would have been dismissed as impossible by people of previous centuries. I have never ruled out the possibility that some form of Islam could one day arise that teaches that Muslims must live together with non-Muslims as equals on an indefinite basis in a state that does not establish a religion. I have simply tried to be realistic about the prospects of such an entity.

As Dr. Hamid notes, denying certain Islamic teachings makes one an apostate in the eyes of nearly every mainstream Islamic authority around the world today, and apostasy can bring a sentence of death. It was only after the prospect of such a death sentence was removed in Reformation Europe that Luther, Calvin, Tyndale and the rest were able to gain large followings and influence. But the theological foundations for such a death sentence are much stronger in Islam than they ever were in Christianity. Will it, then, one day become possible for genuine and sincere Islamic reformers to try to win over Muslims to their point of view without fear of violent reprisal? Perhaps it is already happening in the West — witness Dr. Jasser's health and prosperity, although I daresay his influence is far larger among non-Muslims seeking reassurance than it is among his co-religionists. In any case, the murder of Rashad Khalifa in Tucson, Arizona, in the early 1990s stands as a cautionary notice that the execution of those deemed heretics and apostates can and does happen even here.

Dr. Furnish, meanwhile, makes the leap from the numerical dominance of various Islamic sects in various areas to the idea that they will become the vanguard of a Luther-like Reformation. His demographic data is undeniable; however, the idea that these groups will become the leaders of a movement to create a truly peaceful theological and legal construction of Islam is belied by his willingness to include the Twelver Shias among them. Twelver Shi'ism is, of course, the official religion of the Islamic Republic of Iran — and yet the mullahs of Tehran are hardly paragons of Islamic moderation. His inclusion of the Turkish Gulen movement is also troubling: Fethullah Gulen may not wish to lead a violent jihad, but does he want to impose Sharia upon Turkey? That is undeniable. And Sharia, with its draconian punishments and institutionalized denial of rights to women and non-Muslims, is hardly "moderate."

In any case, while I hope that truly reform-minded clerics do gain wide influence, I am afraid that the more influence they gain, and the more genuine reform they advocate, the more likely it will become that they will be labeled heretics and persecuted. I would be glad to be proven wrong in this. But I don't think I will be.

Jasser: While I reserve disagreement on a number of the historical analogies and pigeon-holing made here about Muslims and Islam, let me address in the space I have how I believe Muslims can move forward. Let me emphasize *forward*. One of the differences often between historians (agents of the past) and innovators (agents of change) is that innovators use the tools and lessons of history to think out of the box and create and promote a new and often unpopular paradigm. Often new paradigms that spend years floundering can all of a sudden propel into dominance. Some of the lessons of history are essential, but innovators *refuse* to pattern themselves after any previous human mindset. Today's Islam needs innovators.

Groundbreaking innovation starts with a meme which leads to a *tipping point* that creates a new platform for those that share revolutionary ideas. My own lifetime has been filled with experiences with thousands of pietistic Muslims from almost every sect of Islam who reject political Islam. But obviously key elements necessary for a palpable Muslim liberty movement to counter Islamism are missing.

To look toward any one sect and pigeon-hole any single moderate Muslim's modernism as a product of only that particular sect belies the diversity needed for a successful global movement against political Islam. Each sect will always have its own internecine biases about the other sect. That is not the obstacle. Looking *forward* we must find some overriding memes necessary to defeat pervasive Islamist collectivism. Sectarianism is always trumped by Islamism. So, looking forward, a meme of liberty can rise above political Islam and sectarianism for Muslims.

My bulwark against political Islam has always been my belief in our inalienable rights: freedom of speech, the Establishment clause, classical liberalism, and especially the separation of mosque and state. Once devotional Muslim youth believe in this, many will take these foundational ideas and mature into theologians who transform Islam away from political Islam.

Hamid misunderstands me. I agree, Islam will always certainly need to be grounded in its own sound theological scholarship, but that is a late stage not the first phase in modernization and reform.

Religious teachings of today are molded by the environment. It took Christendom 1789 years until a government led by Christians had a document which was protected by an Establishment Clause and the separation of Church and State. And even that brilliantly codified Constitution and Bill of Rights took centuries, a Civil War, and a civil rights movement to effectuate its core principles in a way that truly respected the human rights of all its citizens as the founding fathers intended.

At this time, modernization of Islamic theology can become viral. But sadly so can the scourge of pan-Islamism. A top-down change would surely fail, as it has, because there is little popular respect for innovation, individualism, or liberty among most of the products of oppressive Muslim run institutions around the world.

In fact, Tim's reference to the ruling Alawite minority in Syria as somehow exemplifying the hope for the rights of Muslim minorities is very concerning. It disregards the toxic environment which has put political Islam into overdrive. The Assad regimes have been some of the most despotic barbaric regimes of the last century. The only example Hafez and his son Bashar Assad provide is how to systematically and generationally destroy a nation and its people. No modern anything can come from that environment let alone an enlightened Islam. Thugs like Assad, Saddam, Qaddafi, Mubarak and others use religion as a tool for oppression. They fuel political Islam when it suits them while murdering Islamists when they threaten them. The moderates are lost in the middle between the secular fascists and theocratic fascists. This battle has created an untenable foundation of corruption, tribalism, ignorance, and fear.

Look at the Green revolution of Iran or the Cedars Revolution of Lebanon — all millions strong. It is easier to find a desire for reformist, anti-Islamist movements in many Muslim majority nations like Egypt, Lebanon, and Iran where the population knows what happens when the Islamists get control. Yet their environment is missing the empowering sustenance of western liberty.

The solution forward must come from America's safer laboratory. Many American Muslims understand how a nation can be free and pious without theological coercion from government. The seeds of change forward can be found in some scholars who are looking to the West for innovation within Islam. Just look at some of the recent work on secularism by Abdullahi Al-Na'im, Muhammad al-Ashmawy, Alija Izetbegovic, or also many of the Sufi imams mentioned already like Al-Qadri's recent work. This is not a blanket endorsement of any one of them. But much of their writings do point *forward*, not backward. In this wired viral planet, no longer is an ideology like political Islam hermetically sealed in its own history and aquarium. While Robert, Tim, and Hamid look into the aquarium of "an Islam" for the Muslims they study, they ignore a broad swath of westernized Muslims who read their Qur'an, pray, fast, give charity, and supplicate devotionally to God in a purpose-driven patriotic life dedicated to liberty and Americanism who hold another Islam.

The obstacles to the predominance of modern Islam over political Islam are many — frequent death threats, blind corruptive tribalism, societal and financial power of Islamists and Muslim illiteracy. This is not to mention the facilitation by western media and government of Islamists due to political correctness.

Change cannot be imposed upon a rotten foundation. Lasting modernization will be generational and must be built on the ground first with Muslim institutions based in a liberal education, free markets, and universal human rights.

Hamid: I agree with Dr. Furnish that Luther started with far fewer Christians, and yet he sparked a Reformation. The dynamics, however, of reformation are different between Islam and Christianity. The concept of killing apostates is not an integral part of the Gospel of Jesus. On the contrary, Redda Law that allows killing apostates is a fundamental part of the Hadith of prophet Mohamed. For reformation to happen in Islam, Muslims need first to abandon some of the Sahih (accurate) hadith. The dilemma is that while Muslims can stop Redda Law as it is not part of the Quran, denying a Sahih hadith makes a person an apostate according to the traditional teachings in Islam. The Muslims need to stop this catch 22 situation to allow for reformation to occur.

Separating the mosque from the state in Islam, as Dr. Jasser suggests, is certainly considered a form of heresy according to the standard Islamic theology, as refusing to implement some Islamic laws and replacing them with secular laws is considered "Kufr" (act that makes a person an Infidel) according to traditional understanding of this Qur'anic verse (Al-Ma'idah [5:44]). Reinterpretation of this verse is needed first to allow for Jasser's view to work. This is certainly possible since the verse was talking about the Jews who refused to apply the Torah.

I agree with Robert Spencer that the current situation in the Muslim world and the historical and theological depth of the problem in Islamic teaching should not make any person very "optimistic." However, the use of the Internet and the speed of communications that we witness today give me some hope that a change in the Muslim world can happen.

I can see the view of Dr. Jasser that the theological stage should not be the first phase in modernization and reform, but I have a completely different view about this issue. Any trial for modernity in Islam will always face resistance because of the current theology. For example, you cannot teach equality of women while the teaching in Islam teaches that women are half of a man as a witness or that men can beat their women. Removing the obstacle first is fundamental for making the change or in other words changing the theology is pivotal to facilitate the process of modernity itself.

I also disagree with Jasser's view that "A top-down change would surely fail". Generally speaking, Muslims feel much more comfortable to accept a change in religious theology when it is approved by the leading Islamic authorities such as Al-Azhar University. Accordingly, "A top-down change" is, in my view, imperative for a reformation in Islam to occur. Some elements of reformation can still happen at the grass root level but their impact and effect will be minimal compared to the top-down change.

FP: Ok, last round and final thoughts, gentlemen.

Furnish: Again, I agree with Mr. Spencer regarding the inherent violent strain of mainstream, historical Sunni Islam (which, I must stress, stems from a literal reading of the violent passages of the Qur'an) regarding not just apostates but non-Muslims in general; however, to equate "mainstream" with existence *per se* is ahistorical. And of course sometimes, even today, Islam's apostates and heretics are executed — the plight of Ahmadis in Pakistan and Indonesia is a case in point. But such persecution has not even come close to wiping out that group, and they stand as a living rebuke to those who would employ Qur'anic teachings to do so.

Mr. Spencer finds ironic (if not contradictory) my adducing of the Twelver Shi`is as reform-minded, based on the neo-fundamentalism fervor regnant in Tehran since 1979. However, *vilayet-i faqih*, the "rule of the [Shi`i] jurisprudent" devised by Khomeini, is by no means universally accepted even within Twelver Shi`ism; in fact, the modern world's two most prominent Shi`i ayatollahs—Iran's recently-deceased Montazeri, and Iraq's al-Sistani—both are on record as opposing the Khomeinist system and regime. The salient point is that Shi`ism, unlike Sunnism, allows for *ijtihad* — and thus contains at least the seeds of new approaches to the Qur'an and Hadith. And Robert and I simply disagree about Gülen and his movement — I think his neo- Sufism is truly moderate, not a *shari`ah* Trojan Horse.

I will reiterate my respect and support for Dr. Jasser in his efforts to drag the Islamic world kicking and screaming into the 21st — or at least the 16th century. But I simply disagree that "sectarianism is always trumped by Islamism." That may largely be true for parts of the Arab world, but it's certainly not the case in Africa, where sects and Sufi orders are often more respected and more legitimate than the Wahhabis, Salafis and jihadists. As to my adducing of the Alawis of Syria: I was not referring to the undeniably brutal, repressive al-Assad family regime that runs the country, but to the theological beliefs of the neo-Shi`i sect that truly is Alawism, the syncretistic (and borderline Christian) teachings of which are far afield from strict, *shari`ah*-based Sunnism. Just as the Khomeinist regime does not represent the totality of Twelver Shi`i thought, neither does the Alawi clique in Damascus speak for all Alawis.

I totally agree with my friend Zuhdi that "change cannot be imposed upon a rotten foundation." Yet many Muslims, Sunni and sectarian, blanch at rebuilding Islam upon a Western, especially American, foundation — which is why I propose that working with, and drawing ideas from, the Shi`is (Zaydis and Isma'ilis, as well as Twelvers), the Sufis, the Barelwis, et al., might very well provide a sounder, Islamic foundation, after which the rest of the revamped Islamic domicile could be built with more Western materials.

Dr. Hamid is entirely correct (as was Robert) that the New Testament does not promote killing apostates, and that this made a Christian Reformation markedly easier than would be the case in Islam, wherein Hadiths considered Muhammadan sanction such killing. And in fact, I don't think Dr. Hamid goes far enough — not just the traditions of Islam, but the Qur'an itself, justifies and indeed mandates killing of "unbelievers, as most famously in Sura al-Tawbah [IX]:5: "when the sacred months have passed, kill the unbelievers/idolaters wherever you find them…capture, besiege, ambush them…." But, at the risk of redundancy, the problem here is reading the text literally, as mandated in Sunnism — and as NOT adhered to by, for a prominent example, the Isma'ilis.

Finally, I agree with Dr. Hamid, *contra* Dr. Jasser, that a top-down reforming of Islamic teachings could possibly work better than a grass-roots one. Yet I disagree, based on a close reading of Islamic history, that this imposed (new) paradigm should be a Westernized, desacralized, frankly idiosyncratic "Sunnism Lite"— which would not only taste bad to most Muslims outside America, but would certainly be less filling than reformist ideas with legitimate Islamic ingredients, as is certainly the case with the Isma'ilis, Barelwis, Ibadis and Haqqani Sufis.

Spencer: I find the disagreements among the panel interesting. Dr. Jasser thinks "a top-down change would surely fail," while Dr. Hamid believes that a "top-down change" is "imperative for a reformation in Islam."

Dr. Jasser finds "concerning" Dr. Furnish's "reference to the ruling Alawite minority in Syria as somehow exemplifying the hope for the rights of Muslim minorities." Dr. Furnish defends his including the Twelver Shia as among the "reform-minded" in Islam, pointing to their acceptance of the concept of ijtihad, as opposed to the Sunnis who generally reject it. But the Twelver Shia, like the other sects mentioned in the course of this discussion, have been around for over a thousand years and yet with all that time to practice ijtihad they have not managed to come up with a version of Islam that is not supremacist and does not teach that unbelievers must be subjugated as inferiors under the rule of Islamic law.

This is not to say that nothing can happen except what has happened before. Islamic reform certainly could happen, and Dr. Hamid's point about modern communications media making it more likely than ever before is well taken. But the disagreements among the most optimistic of the present panelists shows that Islamic reform circa 2010 remains largely an abstraction, a postulate, an intellectual construct. No one has ever actually seen it, and so everyone imagines it in a different way. Islam has been around for 1,400 years, and yet there is still no mainstream sect or school of jurisprudence that teaches the separation of mosque and state, the equality of rights of women with men, the freedom of speech, the freedom of conscience, or the equality of rights of unbelievers with believers.

Will such an Islam ultimately appear? I would never say that something could not happen; history is full of too many surprises for that. But so much of American foreign and domestic policy is based on the assumption that such an Islam not only will appear, but already exists, and is the Islam of the broad majority of Muslims. The consequences of investing so much in this erroneous assumption grow more apparent with every Nidal Hasan and Faisal Shahzad.

Dr. Jasser points optimistically to "a broad swath of westernized Muslims who read their Qur'an, pray, fast, give charity, and supplicate devotionally to God in a purpose-driven patriotic life dedicated to liberty and Americanism." Great — but insofar as such Muslims actually reject the material in the Qur'an and Sunnah that forms the basis for political, supremacist, and violent Islam, they will find themselves under threat. It was again Dr. Jasser himself who summed this up: "The obstacles to the predominance of modern Islam over political Islam are many — frequent death threats, blind corruptive tribalism, societal and financial power of Islamists and Muslim illiteracy."

I wish that weren't the case. I hope that some genuine Islamic reform ultimately succeeds. But let's not kid ourselves as to its prospects, or about how much non-Muslims can or should actually depend upon it.

Jasser: In the end, Robert Spencer here seems to agree with me regarding the major obstacles I listed to genuine reform. Yet, he concludes a bit dismissively, "let's not kid ourselves as to its prospects, or about how much non-Muslims can or should actually depend on it." I can somewhat understand the sense of frustration, since that is my daily battle against the forces of political Islam. However, without a coordinated strategy to overcoming those obstacles to genuine Islamic reform, then what are we left to do as a nation? How do we, *moving forward,* sustain security against the growing militant Islamist threat? Is that not the purpose of this discourse? These discussions matter little in the absence of a strategy. I do certainly part with Robert on many of his ideas (not covered in this symposium) with regards to accounts of the morality of the Prophet Muhammad and many conclusions about the faith, the Qur'an, and spiritual path of Islam I and my family have chosen to embrace. However, ultimately, my deeper more relevant quarrel is with my own coreligionists — and some of their ubiquitous Muslim sources that provide supremacist Islamist narratives.

I do believe as most Americans do, that all of us agree on the *goal* which is the intellectual neutralization of the supremacist agenda of Islamists and their political Islam. Simple kinetic neutralization alone against militants will never be enough. My strategy, our strategy, at the American Islamic Forum for Democracy (AIFD) is transparent and built upon a need forward for a liberty movement by devotional Muslims within Islam against Islamism. We must have a positive outlook for the victory of liberty rather than a pessimistic one basically based in a narrative of an impending global clash between Muslims and non-Muslims.

Even pessimists need to have a strategy. Disagreements on history matter a lot less than a discussion on strategy and where we think our nation and counter-radicalization work should head. In fact, there are strong indications that the pessimistic narrative is fodder for radical Islamists and helps Islamists attract impressionable youth who want to believe that America is at war with Islam and Muslims. Rather, I believe the ideologies we promote at AIFD to be the type that ultimately can drive Muslim youth away from Islamism toward a modern Islam rooted in American nationalism and Constitutionalism toward a victory for freedom.

We will also need to breakdown walls of deep denial in the west rooted in political correctness if Muslims are going to get the long overdue major nudges toward modernity and reform. But then what? Does Tim Furnish want us to believe that some of the more modernized minority sects or those more amenable to modernization will win out in the war of ideas? How would that happen and from which sect or sects? Does Dr. Hamid want us to be confident that there will be a post-modern imam or scholar who will arise to marginalize political Islam? How will that transpire in the current environment?

I do hope readers leave here, however, understanding that not only does the solution need to come from devout Muslims within the "House of Islam", but we all desperately need to develop a coherent, coordinated, and constructive domestic and international strategy to defeat political Islam — no different than we did in the Cold War against the global spread of Communism. Therefore, it stands to reason that all intellectuals in the West should do whatever they can to facilitate the authentic and moderate Muslim allies of the United States who are working tirelessly to break down those obstacles.

That makes a lot more sense than sitting back and watching, like a car accident, the marginalization or demise of genuine, credible, and devotional Muslim reformists. Dr. Hamid and I agree on some but do disagree as to whether the reform will begin from the top or the grass roots. I have no faith at all in those "leading" inherently corrupt institutions like Al-Azhar University in Cairo or the Kingdom of Saudi Arabia ever completely purging themselves of their deep rooted intellectual and economic foundations in political Islam and Salafism. The only solution I see lies in building new honest Muslim institutions founded in genuine classically liberal academics, free markets, and morally sound Islamic teachings. This reform will only be authentic if it remains separated from government and integration into national legal systems (shar'iah). Thus, the primary protection for Muslims against Islamist supremacism is a belief and enforcement of the same ideas that created the Establishment Clause of our Constitution. This new paradigm or meme — the separation of mosque and state — will need generational change just as the Muslim Brotherhood has spread its ideas in the last century. It is time for the ideas of liberty to take the offense! And we can do this neither alone, nor with those who firmly believe that there can be no modern Islam.

I and my family and many other Muslims have lived and believe in an Islam and modernization of the message of the Prophet Muhammad that is not in conflict with our oath to the U.S. Constitution. I believe that the only winning strategy is to develop those ideas of liberty within an Islamic consciousness through the separation of mosque and state — our *Muslim Liberty Project*. This project is the Muslim counter-narrative, the offensive for the ideas of liberty and against the ideas of the Brotherhood Project. While I may be proven wrong, and I have absorbed significant critique of my own lifetime of understanding of Islamic history, I do not believe I have heard here any other convincing alternative winning strategies in the long term against political Islam. After the critique of my vision or anyone's vision, how do we move forward? That's what we are doing every day. How are you providing alternative visions that can neutralize the ideas that threaten our security?

Hamid: It is good that Furnish mentioned the Ahmadeia example as the situation of Ahmadeia in the Muslim world illustrates the fact that one of the major problems that the Muslim world faces is that it cannot tolerate any new or different interpretations of its religious texts. This represents a major obstacle for reformation. Teaching the Muslim world the concept of tolerance to other views is vital to assist the reformation of Islam.

The verse that Furnish used to indicate that the Quran supports killing Apostates is not traditionally used to justify killing apostates. In most approved Tafseers and Interpretations the rule of killing apostates is based on the Hadith rather than the Qur'an. Recently, some Salafists tried to use this verse to justify killing apostates mainly to prove that the Qur'anic groups — who disagree with killing the apostates — are wrong. Traditionally, Redda Law is based only on the Sunna.

I may only partially agree with Furnish that in some areas in Africa, Sufi orders are often more respected and more legitimate than the Wahhabis, Salafis and jihadists. However, we have to admit that Salafies are gaining ground, e.g. in Somalia and Sharia-controlled parts of Nigeria. This is partially due to the lack of strong theological foundations for many of the Sufi practices and the tremendous support of Salafism by the wealthy Wahhabists.

I support the view of Mr. Spencer rather than Furnish that the Twelver Shi`is are not truly reform-minded, as their belief system still accepts the violent edicts of Sharia. However, I can say that this particular group has more potential to reform than Sunnis as they still allow Ijtihad.

I also agree with Mr. Spencer that the current situation of Islam is not very promising. Removing the obstacles to reformation such as lack of the separation of mosque and state, inequality of rights of women with men, religiously based suppression on the freedom of speech, lack of the equality of rights of unbelievers with believers may mean for some the end of Islam. Despite this I still see hope that non-literal teaching of Islam can make a real reformation within Islam.

The efforts of Dr. Jasser in American Islamic Forum for Democracy (AIFD) to promote a liberty movement by devotional Muslims within Islam against Islamism must be saluted. The concept is great and I will add only that giving a strong theological base to the views of this organization will be very helpful. Asking Muslims to separate between mosque and state and to adopt secularism, while traditional Islamic text teaches the opposite, is a major obstacle to the progress of these secular views. Giving a theological base for secularism within Islam is needed.

FP: Timothy Furnish, Tawfik Hamid, Dr. M. Zuhdi Jasser and Robert Spencer, thank you for joining Frontpage Symposium.

[Jamie Glazov, "The World's Most Wanted: A 'Moderate Islam'," *Frontpagemag.com*, May 27, 2010.]

[11] A Psychiatric Conference on Truthful Girl

As most of us are by now aware, Jumanah Imad Albahri, the infamous Muslim student at the University of California at San Diego, recently endorsed a new genocide of Jews during the question-and-answer period after David Horowitz's talk at UCSD. When Horowitz asked her a direct question, if she was for or against Hezbollah's goal of putting all the Jews in one place (Israel) so it would be easier to exterminate all of them, she answered confidently: "For it." (Look up on YouTube: "David Horowitz at UCSD 5/10/2010. Hosted by Young Americans for Freedom and DHFC.")

Shortly after, Truthful Girl engaged in some curious and mind-boggling denials regarding her initial statement, which, to say the least, were not very effective in negating her yearning for another Final Solution. Robert Spencer has written a good synopsis of this saga in "Lies of a Truthful Girl."

Today, four distinguished experts on human psychology join Frontpage Symposium to analyze Truthful Girl's behavior. What explains her yearnings for another Holocaust and her bizarre and failed attempts to cover her tracks — after being verbally honest about her yearnings?

Our guests today are:

Dr. Nancy Kobrin, a psychoanalyst with a Ph.D. in romance and semitic languages, specializing in Aljamía and Old Spanish in Arabic script. She is an expert on the Minnesota Somali diaspora and a graduate of the Human Terrain System program at Leavenworth Kansas. Her new book is *The Banality of Suicide Terrorism: The Naked Truth About the Psychology of Islamic Suicide Bombing.*

Dr. Kenneth Levin, a clinical instructor of psychiatry at Harvard Medical School, a Princeton-trained historian, and a commentator on Israeli politics. He is the author of *The Oslo Syndrome: Delusions of a People Under Siege.*

Dr. Joanie Lachkar, a licensed Marriage and Family therapist in private practice in Brentwood and Tarzana, California, who teaches psychoanalysis and is the author of *The Narcissistic/Borderline Couple: A Psychoanalytic Perspective on Marital Treatment* (1992, *The Many Faces of Abuse: Treating the Emotional Abuse of High - Functioning Women* (1998), *The V-Spot, How to Talk to a Narcissist* and a recent paper, "The Psychopathology of Terrorism" presented at the Rand Corporation and the International Psychohistorical Association. She is also an affiliate member for the New Center for Psychoanalysis.

and

Dr. Nicolai Sennels, a Danish psychologist who worked for several years with young, criminal Muslims in a Copenhagen prison. He is the author of *Among Criminal Muslims. A Psychologist's Experience from the Copenhagen Municipality*. The book will be out in English later this year. He can be contact at: nicolaisennels@gmail.com.

FP: Dr. Nancy Kobrin, Kenneth Levin, Dr. Joanie Lachkar and Dr. Nicolai Sennels, welcome to Frontpage Symposium.

Dr. Kobrin, let me begin with you. What do you make of Truthful Girl's statement and then her "denials/explanations" afterwards?

Kobrin: Jamie, first, David Horowitz is to be applauded for how he confronted, set boundaries and contained Jumanah Imad Albahri's rage. He didn't take the bait of her provocative statements, which she attempted to mask through a juvenile cutesy female demeanor. It is very difficult and exhausting to do what he does, so easy to get "sucked into" the vortex of genocidal paranoia. Paranoiacs are not going to change their mindset easily, if at all. They think, in part, like this:

If there is a blank sheet of white paper on the table and you were to point to it and say, the paper is white, these kinds of people will say, no it is black. They have to be oppositional because that is how they support their fragile personalities. The hatred is their bond to the other.

They do not know how to live without hatred. It's not fun being the object of such hatred when they seek to kill you.

Strikingly, Albahri tried to play the victim card by invoking the sacred image of Christ on the Cross. Jesus dies alone. Joan of Arc dies alone. But in the perverse "Third Reich-ish" world of Islamic suicide terrorism, they don't die alone — they have to take you out in the killing. That shows their weakness. They are delusional; yet within their world they really do believe that they are martyrs.

She admitted that she couldn't contain her rage. This shows who has the problem. Second, Robert Spencer also gets kudos for parsing the layers of denial in its verbiage. Denial is the psychological shield Albahri throws up to protect her shame-filled self from being found out as to the fraud she really is. Why? Because she comes from Arab tribal culture and Islam, which completely devalues the female. She lacks a stable healthy sense of self. Her need to hate the Jew is really her own "anti-Semite" self-hatred projected onto the Jew. She attacks because she is envious of the Jew and the fact that Islam is deeply indebted to Judaism but could never really acknowledge that debt. Having been brainwashed from a young age by being fed a steady diet of garbage about Jews, she moves to annihilate them — and me.

Albahri embodies the quintessential Arabic saying: "S(H)e hits me and cries and races to me to complain." David Horowitz picked up on the nonverbal dress — the neckerchief of Islamic terrorism.

As I was re-reading and watching the video clip I thought of "The Albahri Syndrome." While she does not wear a suicide bomb vest *yet*, she throws herself at Horowitz trying to take him out, but fails. As a willing executioner, she is just as much a *predator* as the Hamas terrorist mastermind, its charismatic leaders, engineer bomb makers, handlers and suicide bombers.

FP: Thank you Dr. Kobrin, you have sparked my curiosity about something I would like to follow up on. You say: "They have to be oppositional because that is how they support their fragile personalities."

This is not to get away from our main theme, as it will help clarify our discussion, but can you expand a bit on this theme of oppositional people in general? I have run into a few individuals along the course of my life who have baffled me in the context of their toxic pathological yearning to say "no." No matter what I would say to them, their instinct is to disagree immediately. Often, they do so even on an issue where it is completely apparent, *even to them*, that they are wrong. But they cannot help themselves because their need to disagree is stronger.

Can you shed light on this pathology? How does being oppositional support a fragile personality (in the minds of those doing the opposing)? In answering my question, help define Truthful Girl some more in the process.

Kobrin: A fragile personality needs to be oppositional because it is the extreme way in which they try to find their sense of identity. Something went awry during maternal attachment. Something did not get put down on the motherboard of their mind. They must define themselves in opposition to you. It is as if you are a fence or a wall and you provide definition of where they begin and end. Psychologically, they are like a blob. So if you say white, then they know to say black. They reject what you say, even if it is undeniable reality, because they need to assert their skewed world view, no matter what, in order to make themselves feel more secure that they have an identity. It is very desperate, but they will cling to it nonetheless.

As for Albahri, she has written a script in her mind that explains her existence as different from the Jew. The Jew to her becomes her "wall" and garbage pail for her bad, yucky feelings. She must expel these intolerable feelings on to me, the Jew, because she wants to remain pure, perfect, in control and defined against whom she considers impure, toxic. This goes back to the female who gives birth to them but who is considered devalued and contaminated. They are perfect and of course all powerful.

FP: Thank you, Dr. Kobrin.

Dr. Sennels, what do you make of Truthful Girl and Nancy Kobrin's analysis?

Sennels: Thanks Jamie.

Albahri expresses the very common lack of personal responsibility and victim mentality that I have found among my 150 Muslim clients. Both during her confrontation with David Horowitz and in her following excuses and explanations for defending Hamas' "Endlösung" — their Hitler-inspired solution of their "Jew problem" by simply transforming Israel into a huge concentration camp and killing all Jews — she shows a prime example of the Muslim culture's relationship to responsibility concerning both one's actions and feelings.

My finding is that one of the main psychological differences between Westerners and Muslims concerns what is sometimes called the "locus of control." I have written extensively on the subject in my article "Muslims and Westerners: The Psychological Differences," in the *New English Review* and discussed it in my interview at Frontpage, "Among Criminal Muslims." The locus of control is a psychological term that describes whether an individual feels his or her life controlled by outer or inner factors. From a psychological point of view, it is clear that Muslims mainly feel their lives influenced by outer factors and that Westerners look inwardly when trying to understand their life and reactions. Our Western view is that our own point of view, our own feelings, thoughts, choices, etc. define to a high degree the way we experience the world and our lives. We also believe in free will and thus see the ability to take responsibility for our own actions as an expression of human maturity, while blaming others for our own disturbing feelings or negative behavior is seen as less mature.

Western therapy and pedagogics are all aimed at making people aware of how they create their own lives and thus empowering children, clients and people in general to solve their problems and take responsibility for their own happiness. Our kiosks, book stores and libraries are full of magazines and books describing how to look inside to find peace, get control of our thoughts and emotions, make the right choices, etc. The Muslim world has none of these things — and the little they have is imported from the West. This is because people in the Muslim culture are mainly told to follow outer guidelines set by their Allah, the laws and regulations expounded by their prophet in the Qur'an and the Hadiths, imams preaching the correct Islamic relationship to everything from sexuality, integration, child raising and politics every Friday in their mosques, etc. For a Muslim, the rules are clear and the consequences for breaking them are severe, both now and in the afterlife.

Muslim culture is extremely authoritative and the consequence is that the focus on self-reflection in Muslim upbringing is close to absent. Thus, it is no surprise at all that a devout Muslim girl such as Albahri follows this pattern: She blames Horowitz for making her so angry that she loses her capability to hear and as a consequence she also blames Horowitz for her supporting genocide.

Another important point is also brought up by Kobrin: Insecure individuals and groups have a tendency to strengthen their feeling of self-confidence and righteousness by imagining unjust outer enemies. Islam and Muslim culture is a prime example of how to create an almost unbeatable unity in this way. This Islamic unity is called the "Umma" and includes all Muslims. The incitement to hate is, first, fueled by the Qur'an, where one finds the word "infidel" (non-Muslim) 347 times. In the eyes of the Muslims' God, his prophet and their holy scriptures, we infidels are inferior, dangerous, treacherous, unclean and to be avoided, hated, suppressed and killed. Thus, the term "innocent" is in no way reassuring when Muslims like Jumanah Imad Albahri say that they condemn the killing of the "innocent." According to the Qur'an, non-Muslims are not innocent — quite the contrary.

Having an outer enemy does not constitute the only "glue" in the Umma. Leaving the Umma — meaning converting to a non-Islamic religion or acting as a non-Muslim (this especially counts for Muslim women) — has severe consequences. Many ex-Muslims live with constant death threats over their heads and are most often expelled by their families and Muslim societies. Such expulsions are especially hard on the Muslim women since they have often not been allowed to educate themselves and create a social network, making them able to live without the support of their relatives. On top of this comes of course the special clothing, food and complicated religious behavior and taboos ordered by Islam which all contributes to making it difficult for Muslims to function in non-Muslim environments and engage unhindered in non-Muslim social groups and societies.

This is a great part of the reason that only 14 percent of Muslims living in France feel themselves to be more French than Muslim (*Le Figaro*, 29. October 2008 "L'Islam de France bien intégré") In Germany, the share is 12 percent (The German Ministry of the interior, 2007, "Muslims in Germany"). In Denmark, it is 14 percent ("Democratic Muslims," Newsletter 3). My own experience in working with Muslims follows the same pattern: Only a handful of the clients, even though very few were actually practicing Islam, felt themselves as more Danish than Muslim.

The Umma and its strong religious and social glue contribute immensely to the mentality disclosed in our study case of Jumanah Imad Albahri. It also makes us able to answer the question: How can a person have the wish to completely annihilate a group of several million people? The Qur'an and the Muslim culture with their view on "infidels" and especially Jews is obviously the catalyst: As in all kinds of war, the fighters are incited to see their enemies as inferior beings, unjust and strange to one's own values. Such propaganda is an important element for every individual, group, culture or religion seeking victory at the expense of others.

The more we are able to demonize our self-chosen enemies the easier it is to inflict pain on them, and Muslims and their Umma receive immense help for this via their holy scriptures. If somebody should think that Muslims do not take these scriptures seriously, I would suggest that they read the above mentioned report from Germany and The Gallup Coexist Index 2009: A Global Study of Interfaith Relations. The German research shows that 80 percent of Muslims living in Germany "completely agree" that the Qur'an is Allah's true words. It also shows that 87 percent of Muslims in Germany feel themselves "religious" or "very religious". The Gallup report shows that more than 90 percent of the population in 12 different Muslim countries answer that "religion is an important part of my life."

A recent study conducted at the University of Bologna, Italy, puts the Islamic hatred toward non-Muslims in perspective: The more signs of racial prejudice a person shows, the less empathy they are likely to have with other races' pain. The new evidence shows how racism feeds on itself. The lack of empathy causing greater dehumanizing of others which in turn leads to more racism. A culture or religion that includes hostility towards non-members thus lessens the members' empathy towards non-members. An important point of the study is that such tendencies are not congenital, but learned. In further studies, the researchers tested individuals' responses to pain inflicted on models. Under those circumstances, participants' empathetic responses were restored. Professor Salvatore Aglioti, of the University of Rome, said that the second result showed that racism was not inherent but learned. When we had no prejudice, we were more likely to empathize.

This is quite important because it suggests that humans tend to empathize by default unless prejudice is at play.

While Western society is acutely aware of sensitizing its members to the equality of all human races, religions, nationalities etc., Islam and the Muslim culture aims at making its adherents feeling separated and different from non-Muslims. This might be the reason that while 75 percent of all violence in Denmark is committed by mainly Muslim immigrants, 75 percent of the victims are ethnic Danes. It might also explain why people who are from birth told that they belong to a special group that their God perceives as better and cleaner than the unclean and unequal individuals not belonging to that group, can suggest and support such racist and hateful as propagated by Hamas and Jumanah Imad Albahrij.

Lachkar: I thank you, Jamie, and appreciate you giving us the opportunity to do a psychiatric diagnosis of Truthful Girl, Jumanah Imad Albahri. First, I go along with Dr. Kobrin, applauding David Horowitz for catching her in her startling words and lies on tape regarding her threat for genocide. Spot on.

I will start with two approaches. First, Albahri, an individual I observed using the criterion of the psychiatric mental status evaluation, and second, my observations from a cultural perspective. This armchair diagnosis is based on solely what I observed in terms of her affect, appearance, tone of voice, impulse control, body language, facial expression and ego deficits. Overall, I agree with Dr. Kobrin's observation how she could not control her own personal rage. To this I might add a lack of impulse control, and the inability to think realistically of what the consequences would be for her words and actions.

Spencer says it quite well when he refers to her "high-sounding words but empty ones," or as Wilfred Bion would say, "a thought without a thinker." She apologizes, yet with no reference to Israeli civilians as being the main audience for her apology. So when she states that killing civilians is one of the highest crimes in the eyes of God and is morally abhorrent, one does not have to be a therapist to see the transparency and the lack of logical sequence of thought. She reminds me of many oral aggressive borderline patients who come into treatment and immediately begin a fight with the therapist: aggressive, attacking, blaming and shaming. Through this oral aggression the feeling is as though the patient has eaten you up. It was noteworthy that Albahri was quite overweight.

This leads us to the second point. How much is pathology and how much is cultural? In a previous article, *The Psychopathology of Terrorism*, and in my recently published book, *How to Talk to a Borderline*, I suggest that terrorists share a collective borderline personality disorder. This "diagnosis" takes into account the following aspects:

(1)   child-rearing practices, ideology, mythology, and
(2)   psychodynamics such as shame, guilt, envy, jealousy, control/domination, dependency, victimization and how they are qualitatively and culturally experienced.

It is astonishing to see how they seem to share many of the same traits, states and characteristics as the clinical borderline personality (splitting, projection, projective identification, magical thinking, shame/blame, envy, paranoia, victimization and an obsessive idealization of God.

Clearly, Albhari is a product of, as Kobrin states, an Arab tribal culture where Islam completely disavows the female. She is also a product of the radicalization of our universities; she reflects the voice of robotic automatons, in sing-along mantra style, "Death to all Jews!" I might mention that she may truly believe that she is bringing honor to her religion and culture. Indeed, what honor means to a Muslim takes on complete different meaning to a Westerner. To a Muslim, honor means peace and when all infidels are obliterated from the earth then there shall be "peace."

So from a cultural perspective, I might speculate that David Horowitz represented three things:

(1)   Her anger and rage toward men,
(2)   Horowitz as a Jew and as the infidel,
and
(3)   Horowitz as the projected external enemy that invades and intrudes into the Arab plight to kill all Arabs.

Henceforth, she must "eat him up," devour him with her oral aggression. He may also very well represent a soft-spoken benevolent father figure, as an open invitation to her repressed urge of self-expression.

Dr. Sennels expands on the point above in terms of the victimization mentality. She also calls our attention to how Westerners and Muslims "think" or don't think. It is clear that the Western mind is prescripted with the 'I" and "Me" mentality whereas the Eastern mind is empowered by the group mind "We." Westerners are encouraged to think and, as Dr. Sennels states, to take responsibility for their own personal lives and to problem solve, whereas the Islamic mind is dominated by the group and if an individual strays from the group's collective beliefs, myths and ideology, he is immediately shamed, ridiculed or humiliated, let alone stoned to death. Ummah in Arabic depicts the meaning of community, a community of believers all bonded together in unison and synchronicity.

I agree that Albahri is typical of one who dares not question Allah's true words. So in my analysis, Horowitz is seen as a target to project all her rage, envy, and repressed sexuality onto — as she follows the verses which have been prescripted and programmed for her to follow. Only when she feared her crucifixion on the cross did she have a moment of "truth."

Levin: First, I'd like to join the others in commending David Horowitz on his responses to Albahri.

However we construe the nature of Albahri's particular pathology as indicated in her exchange with David Horowitz and in her attempts at self-exculpation cited by Robert Spencer, her performance brings to mind a number of key attributes of the current Islamofascist assault.

Islamofascist indoctrination is focused on cultivated hatred of the "other," particularly — but hardly exclusively — the Jews. In advancing this hatred, it plays upon whatever elements in the host culture predispose its members to looking outward for the source of all woes, and it channels this into construing all difficulties as emanating from the "other." As Dr. Sennels notes, there is much in Arab and broader Islamic culture, including its Qur'anic sources, that lends itself to this comprehension of reality.

In addition, the message of Islamofascist indoctrination will be particularly appealing to those who are psychologically vulnerable. Dr. Kobrin discusses what she detects as paranoid elements in Albahri's performance and speaks of the paranoid individual's predilection to hatred as a projection of his or her own "shame-filled" sense of self and concomitant self-loathing. As she notes, the traditional devaluation and abuse of women in Arab and other Muslim societies add a further layer to this negative sense of self and to the allure of negative projection. Dr. Lachkar notes characteristics of borderline personality in Albahri's verbal and non-verbal responses and rightly observes that defining an object of hatred is a virtually ubiquitous element in such individuals' organizing of their world. As Dr. Kobrin had said of those suffering from paranoid disorders, borderline personality disorder as well hatred of another is used to create boundaries for one's self to buttress what is experienced as a painfully, existentially threatening, amorphous self.

One could add other forms of psychopathology and cultural contributions to, or amplifications of, such pathology, that make for particularly ripe responders to the Islamofascist catechism of hate.

But not only do the purveyors of such hate find ready recipients among the psychologically compromised, they also seek out such compromised individuals in their recruitment of, for example, suicide bombers, as well as other agents of their murderous agenda. Those whose social integration has been impaired by their psychological difficulties, as well as those who are ostracized for somehow transgressing the rigid cultural strictures of their societies, are offered not only acceptance but recognition, honor and glory in exchange for embracing the hatred purveyed by their Islamofascist mentors and martyring themselves in the service of that hatred.

Dr. Sennels points out that while, in Western societies, a premium is placed on the individual perceiving himself or herself as largely in control of his or her destiny and responsible for his or her life. Muslim societies commonly foster a predilection to see one's situation in life as shaped by external forces and so predispose their members to be receptive to any targeting of the "other" as responsible for the problems in one's life. There is, no doubt, much truth to this point. But Western totalitarian movements, such as Nazism and Soviet-style Communism, have also been very successful in getting their target populations to perceive their own and their society's woes as due to external enemies and in mustering popular hatred of those "enemies."

Also, Western totalitarian movements, like Islamofascism, have been particularly attractive to the psychologically compromised, those whose personal psychopathology has led them to be particularly drawn to absolutist ideologies with defined objects of hatred. And, again like Islamofascism, Western totalitarianisms have widely made use of the psychologically damaged in their searching out of agents for their murderous agendas.

Of course, one way that those in the West with totalitarian agendas have sought to undercut and redirect the Western valuing of individual acceptance of responsibility for his or her decisions and the direction of his or her life has been through "education." By seeking control of education systems and shifting their mission from education proper to indoctrination, those promoting totalitarian goals have striven to inculcate in students a vision of their lives as beset by demonic external forces against whom they must wage wars of annihilation if they are to survive and prosper.

There is a sense in which many college students — far beyond the numbers of those suffering from what is formally recognized as psychopathology — share some of the characteristics of the psychologically compromised. In particular, they are typically at an age and position in life when what has until then been a very structured and directed existence is about to end and they are going to be launched into a world in which their place, their status, the possibilities opened to them, are much more amorphous, undetermined, undefined; and many respond to this with trepidation and are receptive to indoctrination into ideologies that provide definition and direction for them. That offer them, as totalitarian ideologies do, clear-cut identification of what is good and what they should hate and how they should embrace the one and attack the other. All that is required are ideologue-educators, such as those of the far Left who dominate so much of Western university pedagogy today, particularly in the humanities and social sciences, and who are very often sympathetic to Islamofascism as sharing with themselves common enemies — to make our university campuses less places of education than places of hate-indoctrination, proffering their toxic messages to readily receptive audiences.

This phenomenon has been a virtual constant in the history of totalitarian creeds. Whether Nazi brown or Communist red or Islamist green, university students have always been in the lead in donning the fashionable totalitarian colors of the day.

So it is hardly surprising that David Horowitz's efforts to fight totalitarianism in whatever form takes him particularly to university campuses, and that it is particularly there that he encounters the likes of Albahri.

Kobrin: The infiltration of the universities has had devastating consequences for fostering the Islamofacist doctrine, as Dr. Levin stresses. Developmentally, college students go through another adolescent "growth" spurt and hence are particularly predisposed to becoming extremists, especially if they already come from cultures of hatred and if they lack a healthy psychological "infrastructure." For many, the university is the first time they separate from their families. Like the jail, the university provides fertile soil for recruitment to jihad, to borrow the title of Patrick Dunleavy's forthcoming book on prison recruitment in New York.

As for Albahri, Drs. Lachkar and Sennels have correctly cited — locus of control, thoughts without a thinker, childrearing practices and psychodynamics of a cult. But I would be remiss if I didn't encourage all of us to remember to "read" such incitement to violence functionally — that is by expanding the context and to include current events such as the Gaza Flotilla. Why? Because it is the chronic, accumulative daily effect of hate speech which facilitates a recalcitrant identification with the aggressor. To take one small example, Albahri's condoning of genocide makes it more "acceptable" within this bizarre universe of Islamofascism to call the Israelis pirates, as Spanish MEP María Muñiz De Urquiza of the socialist group described the Israeli raid as an act of "piracy," for instance, and called for an end to the Israeli naval blockade of Gaza.

Having grown up under a death threat, Albahri merely turns the tables to decree a death threat. She has identified with her aggressors by becoming one. She is a willing executioner in this tsunami of genocidal hatred.

FP: Yes, thank you, Dr. Kobrin. So, devalued as a female in her own culture and religion, and facing barbaric punishments for certain threatening ways that, if she dares, she may exercise her own self-determination (i.e. the sexual realm), Albahri identifies with the tyrants who would abuse and kill her by demonizing and working for the genocide of her oppressors' scapegoated "enemy."

Dr. Sennels, aside from your other thoughts, in your concluding thoughts on this discussion, kindly touch on this theme, thank you.

Sennels: Several of my colleagues in this panel discussion have touched on sexuality and suppression. The mechanism that lets suppressed and abused individuals end up as abusers has been known since Freud. Albahri seems to be no exception. As the vast majority of Muslim woman, Albahrij does not have such basic human rights such as the right to choose her own clothing, sexual partner, life style, religion etc. The Somali writer Ayaan Hirsi Ali has described the resulting emotional immaturity among Muslim women in several of her books: insecurity, lack of individual responsibility, increased aggression and the crude experience of the world as being black and white, us and them, good and bad, and the need to project one's undesirable emotions on outer enemies, becomes dominant.

Islam and Muslim culture are to a wide extent centered around sexuality. I have written extensively about this issue in my article "Sexual abuse widespread among Muslims." The direct consequences of the Islamic view on women's sexuality are visible and known to all. Besides the psychological consequences mentioned above, veils, genital mutilation and extreme limitations of personal freedoms are the reality of most of the world's 700 million Muslim women. Such facts should leave no honorable woman or man passive. But I would like to draw the reader's attention to the fact that the Islamic distortion of the relationship between the sexes also has severe consequences to Muslim men.

Homosexuality in itself is not considered a perversity according to Western psychology — as long as it is not a result of unhealthy psychological circumstances. An American military report recently disclosed that it is completely common among Afghan men to "have sex with other men, admire other men physically, have sexual relationships with boys and shun women both socially and sexually." A recent study in Pakistan shows that "At least 95 percent of truck drivers in Pakistan consider indulging in sexual activities" with young boys. Other studies show that there is a clear connection "between people who were followers of theocracy and Islamic fundamentalism, and their use of child porn." Google seems to confirm that the interest in the most perverted and traumatizing kinds of sex is largest in the Muslim world. Google Trends allows you to see in which countries and languages a certain word is most frequently searched for. If you write "children sex" in Google Trends, Muslim countries take up four out of five places on the top-five. The languages, in which "children sex" is most often searched for are Indonesian and Arabic. If you search for "rape sex," Muslim countries take up three out of four on the top-four. And again Indonesian and Arabic are the languages in which this type of sex is most frequently searched for. As an experiment, I tried searching for "donkey sex" and again it turned out that Muslim countries take up four out of five places on the top-five. Being told that women are impure and reinforcing this impression for oneself by treating women badly leaves male sexuality in a disturbed state: Almost all women and men have a sex drive but if your culture prevents you from having a natural meeting with the opposite sex, the sexual drive will find other, and often less constructive, ways of expressing itself. All cultures have their ways of allowing the individual to express his or her suppressed sexuality, and as we see the Islamic is no exception. The ability to fully enjoy sex while at the same time to enjoy bringing one's partner as much bliss as possible is both the necessary basis and pleasant result of a healthy mind. Through its view on sex and the relationship between the sexes, no culture prevents emotional maturity more than the Muslim.

Seen from the psychological point of view, freeing Muslim women and Muslim sexuality is a main tool in fighting Islamofacism. Setting up countless refuge homes for Muslim women in both the Muslim world and the West is crucial. The same goes for sex education of both genders. The banning of the suppressive Muslim veils and hard punishment on families that do not allow their women to leave their homes, learn our Western languages and join our work markets are necessary. We have to make it standard that authorities in the West visit Muslim homes to interview the women and check if they are allowed the same freedoms as everybody else.

The question is of course: What is left of Islam and its aggressive, intolerant and non-empathetic culture, if we take away their control of women and sexuality? And would Albahri condone genocide if she had not been taught that women are less worthy than men, if she had been allowed to dress sexy and join sports to enjoy her body and look better? Would she be so insecure, aggressive and non-empathic if she had had the same maturing experiences with love, sexuality and freedom as her non-Muslim sisters? I am sure: no.

Lachkar: I am pleased to receive the validation from Dr. Kobrin and Dr. Levin noting characteristics of borderline personality embedded in Abahri's verbal and non-verbal responses as she represents the embodiment of many collective group Islamic fantasies. This is so fitting with the borderline's defenses of shame/blame, attack/paranoid society. Levin explains how Islamics shape their life, making the "other" responsible for all the wrongdoings in life. He mentions that those who have been psychologically compromised make them particularly susceptible to rebellion or Islamofascism. He seems to address the puzzling dilemma why students in the West who seek out an education suddenly shift to taking over the system. Students who are vulnerable will suddenly defend against their feelings of impotence and suddenly lash out to defend a cause whereby the cause becomes more pervasive than life itself or even their education.

"Rebellion Uber Alles!!" or "Islamofascism Uber Alles!" In psychological terms this is referred to as omnipotent fantasies. It is like the little boy who tries on daddy's shoes but then realizes he can't walk in them because they are too big. I believe this is what happened to Albari when she tried to stand up to Horowitz and found herself in deep waters.

Islam and the West are in a clash of civilizations. The dysfunctional Muslim family displays this contrast, the "Muslim mind of jihad". To this point I am adding here a fantasy analysis of what it would be like for a Western therapist to treat someone like Albahri:

Th: Hi, Albahri.
A: I really don't want to be here.
Th: Then why are you here?
A: Because I don't want to go to jail.
Th: But I thought in your culture you will do anything and everything to fight for your cause.

213

A: I would go to jail in that case, but I didn't do anything wrong.

Th: Threatening Jews is doing nothing wrong?

A: I am angry.

Th: You are not angry; you are enraged and full of hatred (expression of Islamofascism).

A: I have a right to be enraged and to hate. All I do now is eat (symptom of repressed society/deprivation).

Th: Eating takes the place of other needs that are not being met.

A: I do get my needs met. I fight for my country and my cause. Those are my needs (clash of civilizations).

Th: Your needs are not healthy. Look at the trouble you got yourself into.

A: How dare you say my needs are not healthy. Look at you (attack/blame). All you care about in your society is money, wealth, materialism (envy).

In this armchair fantasy analysis we see how this cultural clash is contrasted to the contaminated "Muslim woman's mind". This is quite fitting with Dr. Sennel's comments on sexuality and suppression, how suppressed and abused individuals end up as the abusers. He reinforces the theme of deprivation noting how Albahri does not have the same basic rights to choose her own clothes, sexual partner and life style.

I thank you Jamie for giving me the psychological liberty to incorporate these concepts from my psychological couch.

FP: Dr. Levin, last word goes to you, sir.

Levin: My co-panelists have all elaborated in very insightful ways on the cultural factors and concomitant psychological scars that make individuals within Arab and much of broader Islamic society particularly ripe for indoctrination to genocide. As Dr. Kobrin points out, the denigration and abuse of women in that society almost inevitably leads to manifestations of "identification with the aggressor," in which female victims embrace the biases and hatreds of their society in order to feel closer to it, a part of it, and not merely its victim.

Dr. Sennels discusses the link between the devaluation and sequestration of women in Arab and many other Muslim societies, the associated suppression of women's sexuality in those societies, and the high prevalence of homosexuality and pederasty in them. Where women are at once denigrated and sexually secluded, men are more likely to find other males not only more available but also more fitting as partners in intimacy. To the degree that this involves pederasty, which, along with the physical abuse of male children, is widespread in those societies, the culture generates another large sub-population predisposed to "identification with the aggressor" and thus to embrace the culture's hatreds of others as a vehicle to such identification.

Dr. Lachkar's imagined therapeutic exchange with Albahri effectively highlights the playing out of dynamics that figure in her embrace of Islamofascism's genocidal hatred.

Dr. Sennels poses the question of whether Albahri would still support genocide if she had not been subjected to the abuse of women, including suppression of their sexuality that pervades her culture. He answers in the negative. I'm less sanguine.

Certainly we all regard the psychosexual scars that are almost invariably products of growing up in societies such as Albahri's as providing fertile ground for indoctrination to genocidal hatred. But groups such as Hamas and Hezbollah, which explicitly, openly, advertise their genocidal intent, have won many supporters and sympathizers among people with Western backgrounds, people who — whatever the vagaries of their individual experience — were reared in societies dramatically different, less systemically abusive and demeaning, than Albahri's.

Again, hate indoctrination will invariably find particularly fertile ground among people subjected to early, and perhaps ongoing, abuse. But the histories of totalitarian ideologies such as Islamofascism and their promotion of genocidal hatred strongly suggest that they are able to find a receptive audience beyond those with backgrounds of growing up under abusive and repressive conditions.

Whatever can be done to lessen the systematic denigration and sexual suppression of women and abuse of boys will be, of course, all to the good; not least because it will decrease the production of moral monsters. But recruiters for monstrous causes will still find willing followers, especially when their cause seems to be in the ascent and when those who ought to know better seek to close their eyes to the threat, or to appease it, or in other ways to shrink from opposing it.

FP: Dr. Nancy Kobrin, Kenneth Levin, Dr. Joanie Lachkar and Nicolai Sennels, thank you for joining Frontpage Symposium.

[Jamie Glazov, "A Psychiatric Conference on Truthful Girl," *Frontpagemag.com*, June 21, 2010.]

Part V: Leaving the Faith

[12] Radical Son: The Ten Year Anniversary

The year 1997 marked the tenth anniversary of the publication of David Horowtiz's autobiography *Radical Son*. Upon its publication, the memoir was immediately recognized as the most important literary memoir by anyone from the 60s generation. *Radical Son* has earned a place among the best in the genre of ex-revolutionary literature, a company that includes Chambers' *Witness*, Arthur Koestler's *Darkness at Noon* and George Orwell's *Animal Farm*. The author's achievement prompted George Gilder to call Horowitz's book "the first great American autobiography of his generation."

With the year of the tenth anniversary *of Radical Son's* publication having just passed, Frontpage Symposium has assembled a distinguished panel to discuss the meaning of the memoir. Today we ask: what explains Gilder's comment about the memoir? And has *Radical Son* stood the test of time?

Our guests today are:

Paul Hollander, an expert on anti-Americanism and the author of two masterpiece works on the psychology of the Left: *Political Pilgrims and Anti-Americanism*. He has gathered together an unprecedented volume consisting of more than forty personal memoirs of Communist repression from dissidents across the world in the new book *From the Gulag to the Killing Fields: Personal Accounts of Political Violence and Repression in Communist States*. His latest book is *The End of Commitment: Intellectuals, Revolutionaries, and Political Morality in the Twentieth Century*.

Philip Terzian, the Literary Editor at *The Weekly Standard*.

Douglas Murray, a bestselling author and commentator based in the UK. His most recent book is the critically acclaimed *Neoconservatism: Why We Need It*. He appears regularly on the television and radio across Europe and America. He is a trustee of the newly founded European Freedom Fund and a member of the Advisory Board of the European Institute for the Study of Contemporary Antisemitism. He is the Director of the Centre for Social Cohesion in Westminster, London.

and

Claudia Anderson, the managing editor of *The Weekly Standard*.

FP: Paul Hollander, Philip Terzian, Douglas Murray and Claudia Anderson, welcome to Frontpage Symposium.

Paul Hollander, let me begin with you.

Your view on Gilder's description of *Radical Son*? And do you think the memoir has stood the test of time?

Hollander: I do think that it stood the test of time very well and has very few counterparts. Actually, it is an exceptional document because most other members of David Horowitz's generation refrained from similar soul searching, refusing to confront their youthful illusions and delusions. Thus it is quite unrepresentative (but not uninformative) of his generation.

Presumably, Gilder called it a great autobiography of his generation because of its authenticity and the light it shed on the subculture and ethos of the radical activists and true believers of the period. Moreover it helps to grasp both the differences and (the more often ignored) similarities between the new and old Left. It also is enormously informative of other important figures, fellow radicals and their mindset; not only a credible and often moving autobiography and memoir but a rich social history.

FP: Thank you Prof. Hollander. Let me follow up for a moment: in the introduction. Horowitz noted that the people who could benefit most from it — young leftists like himself — would never read it. Was he right?

Hollander: It is of course very hard to know who read a particular book and who did not but it is very likely that many of his contemporaries and fellow radicals would refuse to read such a book.

And in the unlikely event if they read it, they would reject it or scorn it. I suspect that most left-of-center publications (e.g. Nation, Village Voice, NYR of Books) did not review it or if they did, managed to dismiss it. People avoid the kind of information that conflicts with their deeply held beliefs.

FP: To be sure, the Left ignored *Radical Son* or instead completely castigated it without considering its main themes and arguments. Yes, people avoid the kind of information that conflicts with their deeply held beliefs. But the Left has a special talent in subordinating reality to utopian dreams.

Philip Terzian?

Terzian: I'm reluctant to join George Gilder in claiming 'RS' as the 'first great autobiography' of that generation (I'm not too much younger than DH) only because I'm generally hesitant about superlatives: It's a little too early, in my view, to judge either the epoch in question or the merits of those personal accounts that have thus far appeared.

That said, 'RS' certainly captures the milieu in which DH subsisted— the romance, intrigue, irrationality and violence of the 1960s/early 70s — and best of all, is intellectually honest, a claim few political memoirs can make.

As for the critical cold shoulder, there is no greater villain on the left than the apostate — traitor, turncoat, call him what you will — but this puts DH in good company: I well remember the contempt my parents had for Whittaker Chambers.

FP: Let me follow up with you for a moment, Mr. Terzian.

Why do you think that the Left cannot digest a dissenter?

Can you also tell us a bit about why your parents had so much contempt for Whittaker Chambers? Who were they? And what similarities differences do you see between Chambers' and Horowitz's memoirs?

Terzian: I can't say with any certainty, except that the Left operatesunder certain moral presumptions which seem firmly fixed. That is, anyone who moves from Right to Left has found enlightenment, or at least seen the error of their ways; while anyone who moves from Left to Right has sold their soul, been seduced by power, chosen to betray their comrades for personal gain — whatever metaphor you prefer.

My parents were both professional people in the Washington area — my father (b. 1908) was a research scientist, my mother (b. 1912) a lawyer — and classic anti-anti-Communists of their time, although uninvolved (so far as I know) in serious Left politics. (My mother was, in fact, a very active Democrat — an appointed judge in Maryland.) They believed that the Cold War was a product of American belligerence, that the U.S. military was far more dangerous than the Soviet Union, that it was Moscow's forbearance in the face of American provocation that kept the peace. They were relieved by the 1968 Soviet invasion of Czechoslovakia, fearing that the West Germans had their eyes on Czech munitions works. They looked upon Alger Hiss as a kindred spirit — a progressive-minded public servant with impeccable credentials and familiar associations — who got caught up in the McCarthy purges while Chambers was a right-wing opportunist who purged his personal demons by profiting from wild accusations against an innocent bystander (Hiss).

Both WC and DH, in effect, caught a glimpse of the nature of the hard Left, and recoiled — although, in both cases, it was not so easy to move away from their formative political allegiance. I would say that the primary difference between 'Witness' and 'Radical Son,' as memoirs, is that Chambers' leftism was almost wholly theoretical while Horowitz's had a basic emotional content, and their respective tones reflect that.

Murray: People always ask of early apostates "How many followers do they have?" The truth is, and this is certainly the case with the effect of *Radical Son,* that the knowledge that there is a route out emboldens countless people. What Horowitz says about the people who won't read the book is true to an extent. But many such people will at least have become aware that a work was out there, and that the case for the prosecution was being made. This is the vital difference. It

221

is the difference between thinking your totalitarian ideology is impregnable, and even conceiving that it might be fallible. The seed of doubt, or stick of dynamite, at the root of the movement does glorious damage.

Toeing the line, not breaking the picket-line is one of the traits of the Left. It has, in its focus on human solidarity, noble origins. But it becomes deeply totalitarian. Both *Radical Son* and the reaction to the book show this. I did a panel last week in George Galloway's constituency in East London where one of the other panelists (all of whom were leftists) decried Trevor Phillips, the former head of the Commission for Racial Equality for voicing concerns over multiculturalism. Suddenly everyone tumbled in on how despicable he was for saying such things. It became clear that nobody had an argument against, and indeed some agreed that parts of what he said were true. What they despised was that he had broken the line. The Left's fear of this is one of their greatest weaknesses and one which it is a pleasure to exploit. Their response may be silence, but it is a seething silence.

FP: Thank you, Douglas Murray, let me come back to you for a moment.

As noted earlier, George Gilder called *Radical Son* the first great autobiography of that generation. What you think of Gilder's view of the memoir?

Also, overall, what makes this book stand out in your mind? What are its particular strengths? For instance, Horowitz's melding of his intensely personal story in his own political odyssey is quite powerfully done, and this is quite unusual, especially in regards to the memoirs of former members of the political faith.

Murray: I agree with Philip Terzian that the emotional content is what distinguishes *Radical Son* from similar works. Other members of his generation have written as affectingly since, but none I think before.

A book I like to equate *Radical Son* with is Roger Scruton's equally moving and brilliant autobiography, *Gentle Regrets*. Scruton was of course always on the right of centre, and his book written much later, but he, and many others, have followed Horowitz's lead in being unafraid to put themselves into the story of their time.

When discussing political history and political upheaval there is a great temptation to be academic and solemn — writing as though events are not something which you yourself went through, with personal consequences. Things can go, and I think recently have gone, in political memoirs too far the other way into the *What was happening in the world while I was alive?* school of memoir-ing. But *Radical Son* is the first memoir of its generation that I know of which so perfectly justifies telling a personal story about those times.

People of my generation (born 1979) are often under the misapprehension that the upheavals of the 60s were somehow harmless — a bit of student fun. Horowitz is right to be personal in response to this, and in response to the self-justifying narrative offered up by the Left. What is especially important is showing, as Paul Berman has more recently showed in *Power and the Idealists*, that the radical Left was not and is not some pacifist, anti-totalitarian, liberating care-group, but something which, at its radical fringes and disconcertingly further in, becomes what it claims to abjure. To show this, and do so from personal testimony, is, apart from anything else, a great service to future generations.

Anderson: Like Douglas Murray, I see *Radical Son* as an exceptionally valuable record of the sixties in America. No young person can read it and retain intact an idealized vision of that angry, violent decade. It was, after all, a murder that catalyzed the realizations that finally freed DH from the false ideas he'd been reared with. And not just one murder. His investigation of the disappearance of his friend Betty Van Patter ultimately led DH to conclude that the Panthers — true to their slogan "Off the Pig" — had killed not only her but something like a dozen people. The willingness of leftist intellectuals and celebrity apologists to look the other way was part of the signature corruption of that time and place.

223

But I'd also like to emphasize that Radical Son is much more than an account of a particular generation. One thing that lifts it to a higher plane is the qualities of mind and character the author displays — notably, the passion for truth. I don't mean just philosophical Truth, but concrete, confirmable fact as opposed to fabrication, deception, lies. After his years of high-flown theorizing about "the system," it is humble, fact-based journalism and research for a string of biographies that becomes DH's lifeline: the Ariadne's threat that leads him out of the labyrinth of leftist ideology and toward a truer world view.

Then there is the integrity of certain key relationships: the respect, not to say reverence, with which Horowitz writes of his first marriage; the commitment to his children; the refusal to walk away from difficult relationships with his parents but instead the struggle to honor and love them; and the long professional partnership and cherished friendship with Peter Collier. This is, to be sure, "A Generational Odyssey," as the subtitle has it, but it is also the testimony of an individual gifted with unusual courage and sensitivity. (And nobody's paying me to say this.)

FP: Dr. Hollander, your thoughts on the comments of the panel?

Hollander: The comments amplified my own positive feelings about the book, especially because it is one of so few that revealingly chronicles disillusionment with 60s radicalism (whereas there have been a considerable number of writings probing disenchantment with the old, pro-Soviet left).

As I have suggested before, the greater reluctance of the more recent generation of the disillusioned (or the more limited disillusionment among them) is probably the result of the fact that the 60s left behind a huge subculture of mutually supportive people. Rather than interested in political soul searching, they have been determined to salvage or eulogize their youthful idealism.

There is a further, broader issue *Radical Son* raises, namely: why is it so difficult for most people (of similar experience, intelligence, social background etc) to change their minds about important political-philosophical matters? Why do people have such different moral

224

sensibilities, or thresholds of moral indignation? Why have some been perfectly willing and able to rationalize, say, the thuggish behavior of the Black Panthers, or the perverse and destructive fanaticism of the Weathermen, while a handful of others (like David Horowitz and Ronald Radosh) became repelled and have been willing to say so in public? (These are matters I discussed at some length in my 2006 book, *The End of Commitment*) I suppose I am raising here the rather large question of why human beings are different. Among its other virtues, *Radical Son* makes one think about this ancient question.

FP: Philip Terzian, your angle on the themes raised by the others? Kindly also give us your views on what Dr. Hollander has touched on: what do you think was the fertile soil inside David Horowitz (and some others) that allowed second thoughts to grow, whereas in most leftists that soil is non-existent?

Terzian: I suppose what struck me as a near contemporary of DH's was not so much his ultimate apostasy as his commitment to radical leftism for so long a period of time. To have been in any way involved with the Black Panthers as late as the middle 1970s — indeed, to be involved with the Panthers at all — is astonishing to me. Perhaps my reactionary, not to say tory, inclinations were closer to the surface and, as I have said before, my family left background was almost exclusively conversational.

Anyway, my own political activities in the late 1960s were very soft Left — occasional anti-war gestures, the Eugene McCarthy campaign, an internship and speechwriting job at the Democratic National Committee — and my peripheral experience of the radical left was so unpleasant, and so thoroughly inimical to anything I believed, that the whole phenomenon — from the Weather Underground to the Greenwich Village bomb factory, even unto the Baader Meinhof gang in West Germany — struck me as a kind of social psychosis. I use the term advisedly. Which brings me to my own, probably sui generis, response to Paul Hollander: That is to say, it occurred to me at the time that commitment to radical leftism, involving as it did infatuation with violence and a genuine hatred of one's own culture and society, constituted a mental, rather than political, syndrome, explained better by psychiatry than philosophy.

I would guess that while the genetic tendency toward leftism was clearly present in DH, it was not accompanied by the kind of nihilist disposition that perverted so many of our contemporaries. Confronted by evidence, his principled response was to break ranks rather than rationalize the indefensible; and given the human tendency to conform, it is no surprise that DH's 'second thoughts' are the exception on the left not the rule.

Incidentally, Douglas Murray makes a very important point, to which Claudia Anderson alludes: Namely, the popular perception that radical leftism in the 1965-75 period was largely harmless, undergraduate folly. While I don't want to exaggerate the influence of the radical Left in that period (or its residual influence) this is a dangerous and false perception. Those were scarifying years, and seemed so at the time.

FP: This largely harmless, undergraduate folly helped, if not caused, the communist victory in Southeast Asia after 1975 and engendered the mass bloodbath there.

Douglas Murray, go ahead.

Murray: The mass-killings in Southeast Asia and the multiple other crimes which have been committed over the years in the name of the left, at the behest of the left, and with the complicity of the left have still not been laid at the feet of the left. To find out about these things now a young person must educate themselves, because they will not learn much of this in the classroom. But this is to return us to the fundamental question raised by Paul Hollander, which David Horowitz's book so powerfully recalls. It is the question: why do some people wake up and others not? Why do some people 'get it' from the start, others 'get it' at some point and others defiantly not 'get it' at all?

The question is as current now as it was in the 60s. I was reminded about this in quick succession by passages on pages 74 and 78 of *Radical Son*. The former describes the Robeson/Feffer story, reminding us that for some people, preserving a political-religious falsehood is more important than protecting human life. The latter describes the Leninist duty to lie in order to further the cause. I'm sure

I don't need to expand on the current manifestations of these tendencies.

Radical Son reminds us that no truck whatsoever should be given to those who seek to be excused for perpetual wrong-headedness. Very few individuals have the strength to lead the way out of radical movements, but that does not mean that those who fail to do so should be exculpated. It is not enough to say 'I didn't know' or 'I didn't work it out.' To cite just two examples in recent years of individuals who have found their own way out of radical movements through strength of mind and independent inquiry I would cite Ayaan Hirsi Ali and the former member of the IRA Sean O'Callaghan. People like this are very rare, but they are also our hope. Through examples like them countless others become aware not necessarily of the *way* out of the cave, but of *the fact that there is a way out*. Examples are few, but their followers can become legion. They show that the human spirit is capable of wrenching itself out from the most enveloping quagmires of lies and pull its way upwards.

Anderson: Why do some people wake up and not others? What makes people different? How does a person find his way out of an intellectual blind alley into which his formative experiences have led him? What Paul Hollander calls "ancient questions" of individual destiny and psychology are what give DH's book its deepest lasting interest. *Radical Son* belongs in the literature of conversion — which goes all the way back to Augustine — even more than the literature of political disillusionment. I am second to none in my admiration of *Homage to Catalonia*, for example, but that is a work far more modest in scope and subject matter than *Radical Son*. Orwell's firsthand experiences in Spain over a period of months caused him to revise his view of the Soviet Union's role there, with appropriate ripple effects through his whole understanding of Marxism-Leninism and democratic Socialism. DH's encounter with the Panthers triggers not just a rejection of the radical Left, but an inner revolution that dismantles the entire world view he was raised with and educated into, all the way down to the foundations: all the way to the unforgettable moment when DH realizes that original sin is true and that man, far from being perfectible by politics, is by nature bent toward self-deception.

David Murray's invocation of Ayaan Hirsi Ali is apt. Though her memoir *Infidel* rarely achieves the white heat of *Radical Son*, it too describes a comprehensive inner change and a painful, circuitous journey of escape. Both books illuminate a political moment, but they move us because they are the soul-baring stories of individuals, in all their particularity, struggling toward the light.

FP: Paul Hollander, your thoughts on the previous round?

Let me also bring up, and revisit, this theme:

One significant phenomenon is that *Radical Son* is *not* part of the curriculum, the canon. This reflects the deliberate suppression that is practiced by the 60s radicals and their disciples who make up the tenured Left. Indeed, books on the Panthers, the Weathermen and the 60s appear with almost no reference to Horowitz's work or to the work he has done on the decade with Peter Collier. This is not much different from Chambers who did not get a biography until 40 years after his death, even though he was obviously a major figure of the era.

Also, as we all know, the author has been caricatured as a rightwing McCarthyite. Paul Berman, in reviewing *Radical Son*, called Horowitz a "demented lunatic."

What do you make of this suppression of thought as well as slander that is perpetrated by the Left?

Hollander: I think that the exclusion or overlooking the important writings of DH (esp. *Radical Son*) cannot be explained purely by matters political. E.g. Paul Berman's views on many issues (esp. Islamic terror) are not so different from his. There must also be more idiosyncratic, personal elements involved. I think a lot of people dislike his style (confrontational) more than the substance of his ideas. Also, of some importance that DH retains access to television, i.e. his exclusion from the realm of public communication is far from complete.

It is interesting to compare David's case with that of Christopher Hitchens who has also vocally and publicly renounced his leftist beliefs, supported the war in Iraq, resigned from the *Nation*, engages in public polemics, and yet he is all over the liberal media. I don't think that it is the case because of his residual sympathy for Trotsky, or his atheism.

I am not sure that I have an explanation; perhaps being a foreigner (English) makes a slight difference, it might incline his critics or potential critics to be slightly more tolerant. I have the same theory about the *relative* tolerance of my own politically incorrect views in academia; I felt sometimes that people made allowances on account of my foreign, 56-Hungarian background, that they would have been far nastier had I been a native-born American). But all this is speculation. As to my thoughts about the previous round, we did not get to the bottom of the question of why human beings are different. (Won't happen soon.) But as to the far greater preference for hanging on to old beliefs (esp. if acquired in youth) that is not difficult to understand: discarding them requires considerable intellectual and emotional exertions, it is far more convenient to retain them, esp. when there is sub-cultural or group support for doing so.

FP: Thank you, Dr. Hollander, perhaps I will contribute something to our discussion at this point.

There is something like 600 academic courses on the 60s nationally. Our researchers have been unable to locate a single one that assigns texts by Horowitz, Collier, Radosh, Hollander or any critic of the 60s who is not himself a leftist. Surely there is a political edge here, no?

You're correct that there is a personal issue in Berman's case. Berman's remark was an expression of his outrage that Horowitz quoted Berman's praise for Horowitz's role as a 60s radical in an advertisement for *Radical Son*. In other words, his outrage was that anyone should think he was endorsing the author of *Radical Son*. Ten years before the publication of *Radical Son*, Berman denounced Horowitz as a "renegade" for turning against the Left. So his ire is really political. For his part, Horowitz has praised Berman's work on Islamic terrorism both in Frontpage and in his book *Unholy Alliance.* Hitchens is an interesting case of an incomplete apostate. He has published a book calling Henry Kissinger a War Criminal and taking what is basically a New Left view of the Vietnam War and the Cold War. Hitchens' soft spot for Isaac Deutscher and Trotsky and thus for a version of totalitarian Marxism is also telling — as is his fond eulogy for the late Edward Said. Hitchens also chose the occasion of Ronald Reagan's death to call him an idiot. None of these gestures were uncalculated. It is hardly surprising that there is a degree of acceptance for Hitchens on the moderate Left that is denied to people like Horowitz.

Horowitz has made a *complete* break with the socialist faith. That is his cardinal sin.

Dr. Hollander, you state, "I think a lot of people dislike his style (confrontational) more than the substance of his ideas."

But does this really explain anything? For instance, there are myriad negative book reviews in the literary world that chide authors for their style as well as for their ideas. The point is that Horowitz's works are not even negatively criticized. They are deliberately ignored.

Let me ask this: Could it be that this phenomenon is related to the reason why the mainstream press refused to say one word for years about the murders that the Black Panthers committed? Berman even tried — preposterously — to identify Horowitz and Collier as part of a criminal element of the Left, as though the New Left as a whole had not embraced the criminals.

Could the conversion of Horowitz into an unperson in the intellectual community of the Left be related to how the leftist keepers of the historical record have remained steadfastly determined to take their secrets to the grave? SDS leader and later California State Senator Tom Hayden and *Los Angeles Times* journalist Robert Scheer, who worked with the Panthers and promoted their agendas, have both, for instance, never written a word about Panther crimes in the more than thirty years since. Former SDS president Todd Gitlin's history of the

1960s fails to acknowledge Panther criminality or any of their murders. Horowitz was a witness to the crimes committed by these heroes of the Left , and as a leftist he acknowledges these crimes. Furthermore, as just noted, his conversion has involved a far different and fundamentally more acute character than most ex-leftists. He sees the roots of Stalinism *in the socialist idea itself* — and he has illustrated how this dynamic works, from the inside out, more powerfully than any other ex-leftist.

So could it not be for this reason that Horowitz has been written out of our cultural history? In other words, could it be that just as the Soviet regime consistently rewrote its own history and erased inconvenient individuals from its past, that the academic and literary Left, which determines the parameters of political discourse in our culture, diligently keeps Horowitz's work as far out of society's consciousness as possible?

It is true that Horowitz has a place in the popular culture and that is good. But in the intellectual culture, except for his work on universities, he remains invisible.

Your thoughts?

Hollander: You are right, Horowitz's sin is the thoroughgoing rejection not only of the practices but also the ideological foundations of the Left and this does distinguish him from people like Hitchens. I would not dispute that his excommunication or the hostility he has inspired has mainly or primarily political roots, but they are combined and colored by the personal aspects I mentioned earlier.

People who are so unwavering in their hostility to DH cherish what they regard as their youthful, 60s idealism; his critiques of this idealism are the most unforgivable. They identify their political beliefs with their past, their youth — their supposed youthful purity.

These attitudes also explain why critiques of the 60s you referred to earlier have been excluded from the college curriculum.

And of course there is a critical mass of such people, a whole generation or "cohort", who can give one another aid and comfort and support clinging to these nostalgic, comfortable beliefs.

FP: Absolutely — as your works *Political Pilgrims* and *Anti-Americanism* have crystallized Dr. Hollander, the leftist's vision is a direct outgrowth of the depersonalization and politicization of his own personal problems and neuroses. And the leftist's clinging to his own identity — which he himself has manufactured on a field of lies — is much more important to him than the truth.

Terzian: I think Hitchens' status can be explained two ways: First, and it's a banal point I concede, but his Englishness lends a certain personal quality that Americans admire and which DH can hardly approach. Secondly, and I speak as an acquaintance (and sometime admirer) of Hitchens', he is only a partial apostate: He remains a social democrat in the Orwellian tradition, with Islamic jihadism taking the place of Stalinism. It's one thing to break ranks on a question (Islamic jihadism) which crosses political lines; it's another to pointedly reject the Left and align oneself with the Right, as DH has done. CH strikes me as one of life's temperamental nonconformist while DH seems to be searching for a political home to share with others.

Attachment to the Left is a romantic instinct; adherence to the Right is a cerebral action. It is the difference between emotion and reason. Tom Hayden, Todd Gitlin, Robert Scheer et al fail to address their admiration for the Panthers because they continue to believe it was the correct thing to do at the time, and because they cherish the visceral sensation — sense of sanctimony, self-satisfaction, etc — that leftism yields.

DH has succeeded in growing up, and his heresy is the sort of rebuke to leftism that can only infuriate those still attached to the cult. Hence the personal attacks and violent language. I do make a distinction between the juvenile romanticism of academic socialists — Berman, Gitlin — and the psychosis of radical leftism. And while I remain mystified by DH's journey toward the Panthers, I admire his ability to analyze his circumstances honestly and take the steps that would not only upset a lifetime's convictions but relegate him to pariah status (in certain quarters).

As a journalist I tend to approach these subjects indirectly and address them with irony or sarcasm; DH is far more direct and declarative and willing to march into the line of fire. That is the sort of bravery that is seldom rewarded in one's lifetime. While it is true that '*Radical Son*' has been excluded from the canon, I would argue that it is far too early to expect a final verdict. We will have to wait until the 1968 generation has passed from the scene, at the very least, for scholars to begin to appreciate its value.

Murray: Berman's attack on DH strikes me as symbolic. The re-emergence of violent Islamism has woken up a good cross-section of Left and Right. On both (and all) sides some people 'get it' and others don't. Those of us who are seen to be on the Right are at something of a disadvantage here. Where the leftists who understand the threat are congratulated and applauded for making the leap, a lot of conservative-minded people are assumed to be the people who *of course* get it.

As a result, far more attention is paid, if I may, to the sinner that repents than the person who was right all along. This is in some ways as it should be (encouraging more leftists out of their mind-set). But people identified as being on the Right do suffer for it. The reason is that a number of leftists can only save what credibility they still have with their former comrades by attacking people known to be on the right. I find myself providing this role a bit myself where allies with whom there is not a lot of difference publicly distance themselves from you not because there is any real difference, but because demonstrating that they are not with a conservative means that they are not a Conservative — it's a signal to their comrades that they have not 'sold out' entirely. It's not especially nice to find yourself providing that role, but the advantage is that some people remain in the left even as they are aligned actually on the right. I think that's good. They can cause far more damage where they are.

As for the '68ers dying out. I think it's true that that's what's needed to get a fairer view of the generation. It will certainly be easier once the 'romantic' allure still felt by some survivors is subjected to the cold gaze of history. But I'm reminded of something that the great Michael Barone said at last year's Restoration Weekend. He said then that there's good news and bad news here: the good news is that the '68-ers are dying out; the bad news is that he's going with them. There are some amazing people to have come from that generation — people to whom those of us following recognize ourselves to be enormously indebted. We started out by looking at DH's book as a generational work. The history of that generation has barely begun to be written, but it has certainly already acquired one of its first, and most important, texts. It may not be on the syllabuses now. But it will be.

Anderson: I agree. Generational change will take care of the exclusion of DH from the intellectual history of the sixties. *Radical Son* is simply an irresistible find for some future historian. Jamie pointed out that Whittaker Chambers didn't get a biography until 40 years after his death. But what's 40 years! I'd say DH may have to wait *as little as* 40 years to begin to achieve his rightful place.

Returning to the contrast between DH and Christopher Hitchens, we failed to mention perhaps the most obvious explanation for Hitchens's remaining a darling of the liberal media after his partial apostasy: his rakish charm. Marry that wit and genuine learning of his to the dishevelled, inebriated, bad-boy panache of Hitchens and you have a kind of highbrow performance art that, on almost any subject, is sure to shock and entertain. People love audacity.

DH himself tells us in *Radical Son* that when he reentered the political fray after his big change, he "made a decision to speak in the voice of the New Left — outraged, aggressive, morally certain." But not especially charming. He says flat out that he wanted to see his former comrades made to squirm by being put on the receiving end of their own tactics.

DH might have had a different place in our political discourse if, when he adopted what he calls the "modest" aims of liberal politics, he had also adopted the modesty of tone of someone seeking to *persuade*, rather than one seeking to pulverize. Think of Bill Buckley at the height of his powers, deploying a sharp intellect in gracious and witty engagement with opponents. This is not to blame DH for the texture of his individuality — only to note that his hard edge has consequences. Never mind. I suspect it is less his steely polemics than his masterpiece, *Radical Son*, that will secure his place in history.

FP: Well, let's finish up here. In this last concluding round, let me ask this: if you were addressing young people today, what would you tell them that they could learn from *Radical Son*. Why should they read it? Dr. Hollander?

Hollander: Young people, or anybody, should read *Radical Son* for several reasons:

First of all, it is one of very few writings which chronicles and analyses disillusionment with radical leftist political ideas and ideals of the 1960s variety. It is also solid social history and a rare critical examination of the period. It is well written and radiates authenticity. Finally, *Radical Son* is likely to be a durable document of the timeless conflict between utopian social-political hopes and aspirations and the limits imposed on these aspirations by human nature and the endemic conflicts between various incompatible values and beliefs human beings entertain.

Terzian: I would counsel the young — I'm enough of a Boomer to reel at the sound of that phrase! — to read *Radical Son* for two reasons.

First, as a corrective to most accounts of its era. DH is writing about very specific times and places, but he was part of a larger whole, and *Radical Son* offers a perspective that is both honest and instructive not only about its times but about the conditions that bred those times.

Second, it should be read as a cautionary tale for true believers, enthusiasts, seekers of enlightenment or universal justice, utopia, and so on. As I have mentioned before, I am a journalist by nature as well as trade — an observer rather than participant — and my detachment (or aloofness or emotional disconnection or however it might be phrased) from the times in which I've lived is such that accounts like DH's are like dispatches from another country.

I think it's wise to inform the young, in plain terms, that this is a tough, complicated world, and that dedicating oneself to a cause or movement in pursuit of a perfection mankind has never achieved is to invite severe disappointment and disillusion.

Murray: They should read it firstly because it will educate them honestly about an era which has too often been written about dishonestly. But also because it will also provide many readers with a morale boost. Many young people reading this book will learn from it one of the most simple and important lessons of all — that they are not alone.

Anderson: In addition to all those good reasons, having to do with history and politics, they should read it to notice what the author found to be of true value, as he shed his illusions: family, friendship, courage, and the graces of the heart.

FP: Paul Hollander, Philip Terzian, Douglas Murray and Claudia Anderson, thank you for joining Frontpage Symposium.

[Jamie Glazov, Symposium: Radical Son: The Ten Year Anniversary, *Frontpagemag*, March 21, 2008.]

Part VI: Energy Independence

[13] Energy Independence and the Terror War

What is the best way for us to achieve energy independence? What is the urgency for us to do so in terms of our conflict with Islamofascism? To discuss this issue with us today, Frontpage Symposium has assembled a distinguished panel. Our guests are:

Robert "Bud" McFarlane, Ronald Reagan's National Security Advisor. Currently, he serves as Chairman and CEO of McFarlane Associates Inc., developing energy projects in third world countries and working to develop alternative fuels so as to reduce US reliance on foreign oil.

Robert Zubrin, the president of Pioneer Astronautics and also president of the Mars Society. For many years he worked as a senior engineer for Lockheed Martin. In addition, he is the author of the critically acclaimed nonfiction books *The Case for Mars, Entering Space, Mars on Earth*; the science fiction novels *The Holy Land* and *First Landing*; and articles in *Scientific American, The New Atlantis, The New York Times, The Washington Post, Mechanical Engineering,* and *The American Enterprise*. He has appeared on major media including CNN, CSPAN, the BBC, the Discovery Channel, NBC, ABC, and NPR. He is the author of the new book, *Energy Victory: Winning the War on Terror by Breaking Free of Oil.*

Gal Luft, one of America's most influential energy independence advocates. He is executive director of the Institute for the Analysis of Global Security (IAGS) a Washington based energy policy think tank and co-founder of the Set America Free Coalition, an alliance of national security, environmental, labor and religious groups promoting ways to reduce America's dependence on foreign oil. He specializes in strategy, geopolitics, terrorism, energy security and economic warfare.

Anne Korin, Chair of Set America Free Coalition.

and

Daveed Gartenstein-Ross, the vice president of research at the Foundation for Defense of Democracies and the author of *My Year*

Inside Radical Islam, which documents his time working for the extremist Al Haramain Islamic Foundation.

FP: Daveed Gartenstein-Ross, Robert Zubrin, Gal Luft, Anne Korin and Bud McFarlane, welcome to Frontpage Symposium.

Robert Zubrin, let's begin with you.

What kind of policy do you favor to create energy security?

Zubrin: I'm glad you used the words "energy security," not "energy independence." While admittedly, being energy independent would be an improvement on our current position, it is not good enough, because if the oil cartel still controlled the world market, they could still collapse our economy by collapsing that of our allies and trading partners like Japan and Europe, and they would still be harvesting trillions that they could use to finance jihad and the takeover of our corporations and media organizations.

So even if it were possible, walling ourselves in a defensive "energy independent" position would not suffice. Rather, we have to take the offensive and destroy the power of the oil cartel internationally. The key to doing that is to destroy the vertical monopoly that they have on the world's vehicle fuel supplies. The U.S. Congress could strike a devastating blow in this direction simply by passing a law requiring that all new cars sold in the United States be flex fueled — that is able to run on any combination of gasoline, methanol, or ethanol. Such cars are existing technology and only cost about $100 more than the same vehicle in non-flex fuel form.

If such a law were passed, it would make flex fuel the international standard for cars, as not only the Detroit Big 3, but all the foreign manufacturers would shift their lines over immediately in response. This would put 50 million cars on the road in the U.S. within 3 years capable of running on alcohol fuels, and hundreds of millions more worldwide. With such a market available, alcohol production and distribution facilities would multiply rapidly, and gasoline would be forced to compete at the pump against alcohol fuels produced in any number of ways from any number of sources everywhere in the world.

(Methanol, for example, can be produced from any kind of biomass, without exception, as well as from coal, natural gas, and recycled urban trash. There are many starchy or sweet crops that can be used to make ethanol, with cellulosic options increasingly viable as well.)

This opening of the fuel market would put a permanent constraint on OPEC's ability to raise fuel prices. Instead of being able to raise oil prices to $200/barrel, which they are already discussing, prices would be forced back down to $50/barrel, because that is where alcohol fuels become competitive. Then, once such an alcohol fuel infrastructure is well in place, we can proceed to roll the oil cartel right off the map by instituting tax and tariff policies that favor alcohols over petroleum. That's how we beat the Islamists.

If we don't do that, with our current imports of 5 billion barrels per year, they will use a $100/barrel price to tax us $500 billion per year (and rob the world at a rate of $1.2 trillion/year). The NY Times today had a front page article quoting leading economists as saying that this huge tax (more than triple the size of the current economic stimulus treasury give-back) is grinding our economy into recession. So it is, but it is worse than that. If they are allowed to keep taxing us in this way, they will use that enormous monetary power to not only massively grow their jihadi movement, but to take over most of the major corporations and media organizations in the U.S., Europe and Japan within a decade.

So not only our economy, but our independence is at stake. We need to break the oil cartel, and forceful action to create fuel choice internationally is the way to do it.

Luft: I share Robert's sense of urgency about reducing the strategic value of oil by opening the transportation sector to healthy competition, and fuel flexibility should indeed be the first item on our agenda. There is no reason why the $100 addition which allows cars to burn alcohol should not be — just like seat belts, air bags or rear view mirrors — a standard feature in every car sold worldwide. This would be a low premium insurance policy against future supply disruptions and a Band-Aid to stop the bleeding of our economy. But flex fuel alone would not be sufficient to solve our energy problem. In the U.S.

today we use annually roughly 140 billion gallons of gasoline and additional 60 billion gallons of petroleum diesel. We simply don't have the resource base to replace all of this with alcohol and bio-diesel, even if we tapped into our vast coal reserves and diverted all of our food crops into fuel production. So we need solutions beyond liquid fuels.

In order to achieve significant petroleum displacement we must begin to electrify the transportation sector by speeding the commercialization of plug-in hybrids and fully electric cars. Unlike in the 1970s, today only 2 percent of our electricity is made from oil. Almost all of our electricity is made from domestic energy resources like coal, nuclear power, natural gas and hydro. In other words, on the electricity front, unlike the Europeans who rely on imported natural gas for their light and heating, Americans are already energy independent. Using electrons for transportation instead of gasoline essentially means shifting from an imported resource which poses a national security threat to an array of abundant domestic energy sources. In addition, electricity is cheaper and cleaner than gasoline. It costs about 3 cents per mile to run a car on electricity—roughly one fifth of the cost of driving the same mile on gasoline. This cost differential protects us from a counterattack by OPEC.

The oil cartel will surely respond to the emerging alcohol economy by dropping crude prices to a level that would make ethanol and methanol economically unattractive. This is exactly what they did in the 1980s in response to a massive effort by Western countries to wean themselves from oil. Oil dropped to $8 a barrel and alternative fuels producers lost their shirts. If cars had full fuel flexibility, allowing them, in addition to burning alcohols, to also tap into the grid, OPEC would have to drop prices to $5 a barrel to compete with 3 cents per mile of electric drive. This is way below where they can afford to go considering their youth bulges and domestic economic conditions. This is why the commercialization of plug in hybrid electric vehicles, which allow us to drive the first chunk of our daily driving on electricity after which the car begins to burn liquid fuel, is so critical. Congress should therefore provide tax incentives to early adopters of plug in hybrids — just as it did in the case of regular hybrids — while facilitating the emergence of a viable battery industry in the U.S. A flex fuel plug-in hybrid will run approximately 500 miles on a gallon of gasoline. This could really pull the plug on OPEC.

Korin: The goal is indeed independence, not in the sense of autarky (not importing any oil) but in the sense of regaining ability to act independently, without need to kowtow or defer to petrodictators, chief among them the Saudi royal family, a family which controls a quarter of the world's oil reserves and essentially all swing capacity on the global oil market (the mafia never had it so good.) To regain our independence we must strip oil of its strategic value. Salt presents a compelling historical parallel. Salt was once a strategic commodity, control of which determined geopolitical power and ability to sway world affairs. With the advent of electricity and refrigeration salt lost its strategic status as it was no longer the only option for preserving meat. Oil's strategic value derives from its domination of the transportation sector, which in turn accounts for two thirds of oil consumption. As Gal noted, we essentially no longer use oil to generate electricity (an inconvenient fact that renders bizarre the protestations of many politicians that solar, wind, or nuclear can reduce oil demand.)

Stripping oil of its strategic value will require fuel competition in the transportation sector. Flexible fuel vehicles, as Robert noted, provide a platform on which fuels can compete. For a very modest premium, they enable a driver to choose amongst a variety of liquid fuels, made from a variety of feedstocks, from coal to agricultural material. It costs 50 cents a gallon to make methanol from coal. Methanol has about half the energy of gasoline, so that's one dollar per gasoline equivalent gallon. The US is the Saudi Arabia of coal. China and India also have a lot of coal, and indeed China is rapidly expanding its coal to methanol capacity.

We need to remove the ridiculous 54 cent a gallon import tariff on sugarcane ethanol. We don't tax oil imports, so why are we taxing imports of an alternative fuel? It's not because of the oil industry; it's because of corn ethanol protectionists who'd rather be big fish in a small pond than open the dam and turn the pond into a sea. As Gal notes, it is also critical to get electricity into the transportation fuel market. Flex fuel plug in hybrids will mean the Saudis will need to figure out how to monetize sand. Perhaps they can learn to blow glass.

Gartenstein-Ross: I am of the opinion that energy security is the most pressing challenge we face. It should be the top issue in the current presidential campaigns because our oil dependence is without a doubt our Achilles' heel, yet no candidate has been seriously pushing the issue. This comes on top of the systemic failure of our political leaders, including the Bush administration and the presidential administrations that preceded it, to curtail our dangerous dependence on oil. (Interestingly, the one real exception was the Carter administration's Fuel Use Act, which is a major reason that, as Luft and Korin note, only 2 percent of our electricity comes from oil today.) Energy security has a cognizable impact on virtually all the other major issues that our country now faces.

There is the economy. Today, more than three out of four Americans believe that the country is in recession — and it is not difficult to recognize that high energy prices are a primary driver. Oil prices have more than doubled in the past fifteen months, rising from around $50 a barrel in early 2007 to about $110 a barrel today. Such a dramatic rise in energy prices will of course harm the U.S. economy. As Zubrin stated, this equates to a $500 billion per year tax on the U.S. economy, affecting all sectors. We depend on long supply lines to transport agriculture to consumers, as well as the vast majority of products that you can buy off store shelves. All prices — the price of food, the price of consumer goods — are pushed upward by the rising price of oil.

There is terrorism and our international political adversaries. One distinctive characteristic of Islamic terror movements is that they explicitly find religious sanction for their actions. Their interpretation obviously is not shared by all Muslims, as the world would look much different if we were at war with over a billion people. What helps extremist interpretations of Islam gain a foothold? One clear answer is petrodollars. Numerous analysts have connected radicalization in various regions to extremist charities, mosques, and madrasas funded by oil money. Some of the charities funded by petro-dollars are "dual-use," not only propagating an extreme interpretation of Islam but also directly funding terrorist groups. Venezuelan president Hugo Chavez famously declared in his opening address to an OPEC conference in 2006 that "the American empire will be destroyed." Do we want to be dependent on political leaders like that because of their oil resources? The Bush administration has had more than seven years to steer the country's energy policy, yet its combined policies amount to slapping a few Band-Aids on a hemorrhaging wound. (This is of course not just the Bush administration's fault: as a country, we have had more than forty years to address this issue since the dangers of our oil dependence became crystal clear.) For example, the primary strategy of the Energy Independence and Security Act of 2007 is a new national mandatory fuel economy standard that, in President Bush's words, "will save billions of gallons of gasoline." But as Zubrin shows in his commendable book *Energy Victory*, conservation-based strategies are not, and will not be, sufficient. If we could duplicate the technical success that Corporate Average Fuel Efficiency (CAFE) standards achieved from 1975 through 1990, Zubrin writes, we would not cut our oil consumption at all. Instead, it would reduce our expected rate of increase of oil usage by only 2.2 million barrels a day, during a period when the world as a whole is likely to raise its consumption another 30 million barrels per day. *Whatever demand we eliminate would be replaced fifteen times over.*

President Bush has also congratulated himself on the ethanol policies that his administration has undertaken, but they are a far cry from the large market for ethanol that Zubrin's policy recommendations would spur. (By Bush's account, we produced 6.4 billion gallons of ethanol in 2007 versus the approximately 200 billion gallons of gasoline and petroleum diesel that we use annually.)

But fortunately, while our oil dependence is currently causing great harm, I don't think the immediate solutions are mysterious. I agree strongly with the recommendations put forward by Zubrin and Luft in this symposium. Fuel flexibility should be the first major policy we push for because it provides immediate relief from this grave problem, but we should also move toward electrification of the transportation sector. The bottom line is that we are worse off, and our enemies in a better position, for each day that action is delayed.

McFarlane: As the panel has made clear, we have the means at hand to overcome the vulnerability of our economy and the challenge to our very way of life that is posed by our reliance on foreign oil. It starts with mandating that all cars and trucks sold in the U.S. be flex-fuel, and then, that we accelerate the production of plug-in hybrid-electric and all-electric cars and trucks, and that we build them out of carbon composite materials as Boeing is doing today in its new 787 Dreamliner.

We cannot consider this as nice-to-have, P-C, green "someday" matter. This is a matter of grave urgency. Today, if an attack on any of a dozen very vulnerable Saudi oil processing facilities were successful, we would be facing oil at $200/barrel overnight. That would lead within weeks (not months) to the collapse of the Japanese economy, and before long to those of our European allies and ultimately of our own. And even if such an attack does not occur, consider the price we are paying for our reliance on foreign oil. Last year we spent over $300 billion on foreign oil. Think for a moment of what $300 billion could buy in terms of better schools, health care, highways and bridges, law enforcement, a partial solution to our sub-prime mortgage problems, and a dozen other domestic priorities. But that's just the beginning.

Think about the half trillion dollars we spend every year — yes, 'trillion' every year — on the defense budget, and that doesn't count the supplemental appropriations for the war in Iraq. At least $200 of that $500 billion pays for forces that are deployed in the Middle East or to protect lines of communication between here and there and to our allies in Europe and Japan. Add it up — $500 billion for defenses, another $300 billion to pay for foreign oil, and with the price now above $100/bbl, the total from now on will be at least 1 trillion every year — yes every year — until we start changing our ways.

Of course the foregoing costs are just the financial dimension. Far more important are the costs in human lives, families shattered by separation, and the loss of loved ones. This is truly an intolerable condition — one that is all the more unconscionable considering that we have the means at hand to overcome it.

Zubrin: I would like to make an additional point. As bad as $100 per barrel oil is for us, it is much worse for the poorer nations of the world. It is one thing to pay $100 per barrel for oil when you live in a country where the average person makes $40,000 per year. It is quite another if you live in a country where the average person makes $1,000 per year. To many third world countries, particularly in Africa, the effects of OPEC looting are not merely recessionary, but genocidal. Indeed, the jacked up oil price is nothing else than a huge regressive tax levied by the world's richest people on the world's poorest people.

Consider this: This year, Saudi Arabia's high-priced oil business will reap that nation's rulers over $300 billion. Much of this bounty will be wasted on a wild assortment of narcissistic luxuries. The rest go towards funding of network of over twenty thousand Wahhabi madrassas worldwide. There, millions of young boys will be instructed that the way to salvation is to kill Christians, Jews, Buddhists, animists, and Hindus, all as part of a global campaign to create reactionary theocratic states that totally degrade women and deny all political, religious, intellectual, scientific, artistic, or personal freedom to everyone.

Simultaneously, Kenya, a nation whose population of 36 million is half again as great as that of Saudi Arabia, will scrape up around $3 billion in export earnings, and use these funds to buy badly needed fuel, farm machinery, and replacement parts for equipment. (Kenya, incidentally, is not one of the world's fifty poorest nations. There are many others much worse off.)

Distributed elsewhere, the loot garnered by the Saudi terror bankers could triple the foreign exchange of 50 counties comparable to Kenya. Distributed elsewhere, the $1.3 trillion per year taxed out of the world economy by the all the OPEC tyrannies could lift the entire third world out of poverty.

By shifting to alcohol fuels, we can shift a very substantial amount of capital flows in precisely such a direction. Many third world countries are tropical nations with very high agricultural potential. Within a few years of the establishment of a flex fuel mandate, we will have a much larger domestic market for agricultural produce to make ethanol than American farmers can deliver to. That is a very GOOD thing. It means that we will be able to give them all the business they can handle, and still have market share left over, which we could open to Latin American and Caribbean ethanol, but dropping the current tariff. So countries like Haiti, which desperately needs an export income source, will be able to get it by growing sugar ethanol for export to the USA. In the same way, Europe would be able to drop its agricultural trade barriers, and open itself up to ethanol exported from Africa, and Japan likewise from South Asia. Effectively, we would be able to redirect about a trillion dollars a year that is now going to OPEC and send it to the global agricultural sector instead, with about half going to advanced sector farmers and half going to the third world. This would create an enormous engine for world development.

Ethanol has been criticized by certain opponents who have alleged that its production from corn takes away from the food supply, and that large irrigation requirements draw power that exceeds that provided by the ethanol. Such analyses, however, are false. When ethanol is made from corn, all of the protein in the corn is preserved for use as animal feeds, and virtually no ethanol corn grown in the USA is irrigated. In fact, for the expenditure of a given amount of petroleum, nearly ten times as much ethanol can be produced as gasoline.

World food prices have been rising recently, at a rate of 4 percent a year, and oil cartel propaganda organs have been quick to place the blame on bio-fuel programs. But these are false accusations. Despite the corn ethanol program, U.S. corn exports have not declined at all in recent years, and our overall agricultural exports this year are up over 23 percent. So it's not corn ethanol that is driving up global food prices, including those for fish, fruit, and every kind of crop. Rather it is high fuel costs, which have risen 40 percent over the past year due to vicious OPEC price rigging. Not only that, these high fuel costs are driving up the cost of not just food, but nearly every product that needs to be transported anywhere in the world. And again, the hardest hit victims are the world's poor.

For the sake of social justice, OPEC must be destroyed.

Luft: Since we all seem to agree that fuel flexibility in our cars is the lowest hanging fruit, let's talk about how to make this happen. In the past two sessions of Congress there was strong bipartisan support in both the Senate and the House for flex fuel legislation. More than 30 senators from Sam Brownback on the right to Ted Kennedy on the left co-sponsored a bill including a requirement that at least 50 percent of new cars be flex fuel.

Presidential candidates are also in agreement. Both Barack Obama's and John McCain's energy platform include strong flex fuel provisions. Obama campaign pledged that an Obama Administration would ensure that all new vehicles have FFV capability by the end of his first term in office.

Less clear is how the automakers would respond. While it is true that the Big Three previously pledged to make 50 percent of their cars flex fuel by 2012, no industry likes to be told what to do and we should not expect the automakers, to embrace a full mandate without a fight, particularly after their recent defeat in the battle over mandatory fuel efficiency standards. (The Big Three also resisted other mandated low cost features like seat belts and airbags.) The Japanese automakers, who don't have experience with this technology, are likely to be even less enthusiastic.

But considering the low cost of fuel flexibility and the simplicity of retooling the production lines, this is certainly something they can live with.

So it's basically in the hands of Nancy Pelosi and Harry Reid to make this vision of fuel choice come true. Instead of complaining about the "insane" profits of oil companies the Democratic leadership in Congress could serve America best by pushing flex fuel legislation and bringing it to a vote before the elections.

It is important to ensure that the legislation doesn't enable automakers to get away with making E-85 cars that can only accommodate ethanol. True fuel flexibility is one that enables all alcohols to compete. The cars should therefore be warranted to run on both ethanol and methanol. With such legislation presented before the

Senate all three senators who are running for president would be forced to endorse it, which means that the next president would be on board.

Extra $100 per car is less than the price of one barrel of oil, and equipping every car in the U.S. with the feature would cost roughly $20 billion over the next two decades, much less than what the Fed forked over one weekend to save Bear Sterns. The same Congress that spent billions on regulating an open standard for high definition TV should be able to give us an open fuel standard for our cars.

Korin: The Arab oil embargo in the Seventies led to massive Japanese automaker entry into the U.S. market. While U.S. automakers were building huge cars, the Japanese had the more efficient vehicles that appealed to consumers at a time of high gas prices. Today, other competitors wait in the wings should U.S. autos stall on the road to fuel choice. Not so long ago a Chinese automaker showed an under-$10,000 family sedan at the Detroit auto show. Take that car, make it a flex fuel plug in hybrid, and you have an under $20,000 fuel choice enabling family sedan. Coming soon to a Walmart near you.

The Chinese are not waiting for us to move toward alcohol fuels or electrification of transportation. We can lead the train or we can run after it, and absent the policies discussed above and summarized below, the latter is more likely every day.

To summarize, the three key policies for breaking oil's monopoly in the transportation sector, the sector from which oil's strategic value is derived, are: an Open Fuel Standard so most new cars sold in the U.S. will be gasoline-ethanol-methanol FFVs; repeal of the 54 cent a gallon tariff on ethanol imports; consumer tax credits for plug in hybrids (this is the policy that helped hybrids move past the early adopter hump.)

Gartenstein-Ross: There is broad agreement on this panel about the significance of the energy security problem that we face, as well as the steps that the government needs to take to address this critical issue; thus, I will keep my remarks atypically short. I offer an apology to Jamie if he's disappointed that this symposium lacks the fireworks of some of the previous symposia in which I have participated—but I don't think that's a terribly bad thing in this case, since energy security is an issue where acting in the near-term is more important than lengthy debate.

I will follow Luft's suggestion that we discuss how to make the fuel flexibility mandate happen. I agree with him that automakers are likely to fight against a full mandate, and also think it likely that iterations of this legislation will be offered that involve E-85 cars rather than true fuel flexibility. So it is critical to ensure that any legislation on fuel flexibility that is signed into law not be watered down through the legislative process or subjected to the kind of bureaucratic capture that too frequently occurs in this country. I know that a large number of conservative activists read FPM (although I do not see energy security as an issue that should break along partisan lines). Informed members of the public should serve as energy security watchdogs, demanding of our politicians the full implementation of policies necessary to counter our dangerous dependence on foreign oil.

McFarlane: Gal and Anne often make the point that we ought to be realistic politically in structuring our approach to new legislation — as is required to mandate Flex-Fuel vehicles. It does no good to be doctrinaire — and lose. Or as President Reagan once told me, "Bud, if you go over the cliff, flags flying, you still go over the cliff." Specifically, it does no good to take on the major oil companies. Indeed our point is not anti-oil, we will need oil for a long time and it is in all our interests for American oil companies to produce as much oil as they can for as long as they can.

Rather, our approach to the public and to members of both parties ought to be cast in terms of the political, economic and security costs of doing nothing — losses which are measured in trillions of dollars, thousands of lives, and the gradual control of American industries by foreign sovereigns.

We must also stress that the global war against Islamism — especially as its financial support grows in proportion to oil revenues flowing to the Persian Gulf — will someday go nuclear. Unless we get serious toward moving our four-part agenda, we may run out of time.

FP: Daveed Gartenstein-Ross, Robert Zubrin, Gal Luft, Anne Korin and Bud McFarlane, thank you for joining Frontpage Symposium.

[Jamie Glazov, "Symposium: Energy Independence and the Terror War," *Frontpagemag.com*, May 02, 2008.]

Part VII: Leftist Lies

[14] Romancing Opiates

Theodore Dalrymple has sparked a heated controversy with his new book, *Romancing Opiates: Pharmacological Lies and the Addiction Bureaucracy*. His argument that the official doctrine concerning drug addiction is mistaken and self-serving has provoked much criticism from various quarters. Today we invite Dr. Dalrymple to face some of his critics and we also invite a supporter of his views. We are joined by:

Theodore Dalrymple, a contributing editor to *City Journal* and the author of a collection of essays: *Our Culture, What's Left of It: The Mandarins and the Masses*. He is the author of the new book that serves as the topic for this discussion: *Romancing Opiates: Pharmacological Lies and the Addiction Bureaucracy*.

Chris Rutenfrans, a criminologist who formerly worked at the University of Nijmegen and the Department of Justice in the Netherlands. Since 1998 he has been one of the two editors of the famous supplement *Letter & Geest* (Letter and Spirit) in the daily newspaper *Trouw*.

Ron Fisher, an active illicit opiate user since 1994. After several attempts at detox, meetings and rehabilitation, like so many other opiate abusers, he kept on relapsing. To find any type of stable life without the chase for the drugs and the depression caused by its withdrawal or abstinence, he found it through long-term methadone maintenance. He is currently on a 150 mg a day dose. Having been off illicit (non-prescribed) drugs for 5 years, he maintains he enjoys the maximum benefit of getting a month's worth of take home-medication at a time.

and

Percy Menzies, Director of Assisted Recovery Centers of America. He has a master's degree in pharmacy and worked for DuPont Pharmaceuticals that developed naltrexone for the treatment of heroin addiction. His special responsibility was training physicians and counselors on the rationale for the development of naltrexone.

FP: Theodore Dalrymple, Chris Rutenfrans, Percy Menzies and Ron Fisher, welcome to Frontpage Symposium.

Theodore Dalrymple, let's begin with you. Illuminate for us your general thesis and argument.

Dalrymple: My general thesis is simple: that addiction is not an illness and treatment is therefore metaphorical rather than real. Mao Tse Tung threatened addicts with dire consequences if they did not stop, and they did stop. This suggests that there is a category difference between addiction and, say, cancer of the bowel.

Addiction is one answer to perennial existential problems — in my view not a very good answer, but I don't claim to have a perfect one — and so-called medical treatment is beside the point. It often does tangible harm, and in my view does harm in an intangible way as well by persuading addicts that they 'need' the help of professionals to stop. This, of course, is all to the advantage of a group of professionals.

FP: Percy Menzies, Theodore Dalrymple appears to be just stating a basic given, so what exactly is the problem? Humans are all plagued by a spiritual human hunger that cannot be filled by the physical world, yet the obsessive attempt to do just that often leads to addiction. So addiction is not necessarily an "illness" that can necessarily be cured by professionals' medication for it. And the assumption that they do have a cure can obviously make things worse. Right?

Menzies: Heroin use may begin as a voluntary action, but over a period of time the use becomes involuntary primarily through negative reinforcement. The withdrawal symptoms are not life-threatening but they are so uncomfortable that few patients stop voluntarily. The addiction is further sustained through Pavlovian Conditioning. Patients who are off opiates for a period of time will experience all the symptoms of acute withdrawal (conditioned abstinence) when they are exposed to the sights, sounds, people, places etc. of past drug use. At my clinic detoxed patients are required to ingest naltrexone under supervision every other day and attend counseling sessions and the results are amazing. Naltrexone debunks the theory that opiate addicts need replacement medications for the rest of their lives. I am surprised that Theodore Dalrymple makes no mention of naltrexone in his book.

Rutenfrans: In favor of Dalrymple's thesis are the experiences in the US when the Harrison Act made the use of opiates illegal in 1914. Before 1914 opiates, often in the form of laudanum, were used mainly by women, especially to ease the discomfort of menstruation. As the Harrison Act made these practices illegal, most women who, even less than men, don't like to be regarded as criminals, stopped the use of opiates immediately, without any medical or psychiatric or psychological support. How could this happen, when opiates are indeed as addictive as much people think?

Fisher: I do believe addiction is a disease. I do not think it is comparable to a standard disease like bowel cancer or a brain tumor, but than again, not all illnesses are apples to apples comparison.

Having suffered first-hand from addiction, what I find similar to addiction and any other disease is that addiction is insidious, progressive, and fatal if ignored. I beg to differ with Dr. Dalrymple's statement: "Mao Tse Tung threatened addicts with dire consequences if they did not stop, and they did stop." Where are the statistics of how many addicts there were at the beginning? How many stopped as a result? How many were killed? How many suffered in silence? How many stopped for a period of time only later to relapse? If they did stop because of this threat, does that negate completely that addiction is a problem? Using Mao's example of how he addressed addicts is not valid since the Communist regime of the time probably did not keep statistics of how many people were dealt with under the threat of dire consequences.

The same lack of statistics also applies to the reference Mr. Rutenfrans made of the Harrison 1914 Act making opiates illegal resulted in users quitting. Both examples with their inherent flaws and lack of statistics make part of the argument that addiction is not a disease, baseless.

Addiction is not an answer to perennial existential problems; it is in itself a perennial existential problem — one that has endured throughout the ages. The two main methods of dealing with opiate addiction for long term clean time recently have been 12 Step meetings and methadone maintenance treatment. Many addicts are helped without the so called medical treatment at all. That is the basis of 12 step program, addicts helping addicts. However, there are many addicts that have repeatedly failed with 12 step programs as I have.

Not knowing of any other way to deal with addiction effectively, I felt I was really running out of options and was suggested methadone maintenance treatment. It was not much of a choice since it was either that or ending up in a jail, psychiatric ward, or even dead. Surprisingly, methadone gave me the breathing room I needed to begin to think clearly. My obsession to use was removed. Methadone itself does not make one high but somehow blocks chemically the hunger one has for opiates. I began to be able to think clearly again. I was able to finally deal with the wreckage of my past and look forward to a future.

Dalrymple: I do not agree that conditioning makes people automata. If it were true that addicts really cannot help themselves, that they lose all volition in the matter, it would justify the most illiberal measures to help them, to prevent them from destroying themselves and so forth.

But the fact that millions of addicts, not just of opiates, have given up, merely by taking thought, suggests that conditioning is not very important.

As to various drug treatments, they all suffer from very similar drawbacks. Readers will be interested to know that in a recent edition of the Lancet, the 'epidemic' of fentanyl injection in the mid-west of America, which is claimed to have taken the lives of 'hundreds' was explained by the fact that fentanyl gives a stronger 'rush' of pleasure than other drugs — suggesting that the search for pleasure is at the root of the problem.

In a Lancet just two weeks previously, it was reported that buprenorphine has become the drug of abuse favoured by tens of thousands in the Republic of Georgia. All in the last 3 years, since addicts in France started selling their treatment to dealers to export it to Georgia (the drug was already the favourite opiate of abuse in Finland, thanks to the same source). At the very least, this suggests how deeply addicts value their treatment.

At the same time, in the New England Journal of Medicine, a trial was reported with a clever drug which combined buprenorphine with naloxone, so that, if injected, it precipitated withdrawal symptoms. A very clever drug combination, if I may say so.

Of 497 subjects (heroin addicts) recruited, 296 were excluded immediately because of their antisocial behaviour or use of other drugs, and 35 refused to take part. Of the rest, only 44 per cent completed the study (75 subjects) which lasted only 24 weeks, and whose criteria of success included not failing to obtain the prescription for longer than a week, and not missing more than 3 appointments. Given the fact that trials are more successful than treatment in 'natural' conditions, and the fact that addicts are well able and willing to fool doctors with urine samples and self-reports, this was hardly a therapeutic triumph, and is absolutely typical of the whole methodology of the treatment model, whichever pharmacological 'treatment' is used. It depends on the willingness of the so-called patients to take it, and according to the theory on which treatment is necessary, they have no will.

As to China, the figure I have taken is a commonly quoted one, though higher numbers are sometimes quoted. In any case, it doesn't matter for the sake of the argument whether the real figure is 1, 5, 10 or 100 million.

The methods used by the new regime are in many books on China.

As to personal experience, it is of very limited evidential value in a field in which the subjects are so given to deceit and self-deceit.

Menzies: I am surprised that Dr. Dalrymple dismisses conditioning as a contributing factor to addiction. All the drive states involved in the survival of the species, i.e. food, sex, shelter etc. are a function of conditioning. Schools are trying to reduce near epidemic levels of obesity by removing or limiting access to fatty and high-sugar food and thus extinguish the conditioning caused by the easy access to these foods.

Mao eliminated opium addiction through extreme coercion of both the users and the suppliers. Would Mao have succeeded if the flow of opium was unimpeded? Heroin addiction is back big time in China due to the heroin coming from Laos and Burma. Just yesterday, China announced that it is going to open 100 new methadone clinics to treat the addicts. I once again contend that price and access are the two biggest contributing factors to the spread of addiction. We can see this in countries like Georgia, Pakistan, Iran, etc.

Addiction by its very nature will lead to neuroadaptation and tolerance. The addicts will make futile attempts to reach new 'highs' by increasing the dose, frequency and when that does not work — poly drug use. Addicts learn very quickly to boost the effects by mixing other substances. 'Speedball' is a popular combination of heroin and cocaine that has killed tens of hundreds. The newest 'supercharger' is fentanyl and addicts will discover newer combinations to feed the narcissistic behavior.

Scientists learned many years ago that drugs that have even a mild addiction potential can cause havoc. This quest is on for drugs that have no addiction potential whatsoever. The best example is the treatment of alcoholism. The three drugs approved by the FDA — Antabuse, naltrexone and acamprosate are all non-addicting. We learnt this from the disastrous results of the past of treating alcoholism with addictive drugs like Laudanum, beer and, yes, Valium (Mother's Little Helper).

The antithesis is the treatment of addiction to opiates. This is based on an unproven and phony theory that opioid addiction causes irreversible 'metabolic lesions' that can only be treated with replacement therapy. As a result, the three most widely used drugs - methadone, LAMM and

259

buprenorphine are addicting have kept tens of thousands of patients dependent on these drugs for years and years.

This acceptance of replacement therapy is so well-entrenched and the use of methadone so widespread that I call this 'pharmacohegemony'. I am certain Mr. Fisher was not offered naltrexone as a viable treatment. Tens of thousands of patients and even physicians are just as ignorant about naltrexone.

Naltrexone was introduced in 1984 to protect detoxed heroin addicts from relapsing to heroin use when they returned home to the familiar surrounding of past drug use. A single 50 mg tablet of naltrexone will prevent heroin from activating the brain. It can best be described as a 48-72 hour 'vaccine' against all opiates. Other physicians have described naltrexone as an 'insurance' against opiate use.

We have treated hundreds of opiate addicts with naltrexone and counseling with extraordinary results. Most patients take naltrexone for a six month period. If they slip, they go back on it. To further enhance compliance, naltrexone is now available as a depot injection that lasts for a month. Indeed, when opiate addicts refuse naltrexone we know the reason - they want to go back to using heroin. We treat patients at our clinic only if they are willing to take naltrexone.

The rejection of naltrexone and similar non-addicting medications has left opiate addicts in a perpetual cycle of ineffective treatments and relapse.

I would be very interested in comments on naltrexone from the panel members.

Rutenfrans: I am not a medical doctor, so I cannot comment on naltrexone or whatever medicine is used to cure opiate addiction. I am convinced that by far the most important factor to stop an addiction is the will of the addict to stop. Experiments with mice have shown that nicotine is the most addictive drug, opiates the second most addictive, alcohol the third and cannabis the least addictive. Let's suppose this is also true for human beings. How can it be explained that in the last ten years millions of men and women in the western world stopped smoking, simply by the exercise of their free will? This fact seems to me strongly supportive of the thesis of Mr. Dalrymple.

Fisher: I agree with Mr. Dalrymple's statement, "I do not agree that conditioning makes people automata." I also do not think conditioning has much to due with addiction. You are biochemically prone to addiction or you are not. Many people can use opiates for pain relief purposes and come off without ill effects at the end of their treatment. However, those that are biochemically prone most likely by genetics, as the studies have shown, suffer withdrawal and the desire to return to the drug.

The statement that millions have stopped using drugs with the mere desire and will power is overstated. I have yet to meet anyone in the depths of addiction to make it out without some type of support group or harm reduction program. It just does not happen. The sad fact is most die, are sent to jail, or put away to some asylum. There are no "millions that just quit on their own."

Why are people able to quit nicotine and if they are able to do so, why not other addictions? Simple: the reward of using nicotine is not great enough, it does not dement your state of reason, and it does not get you high. How many people get pulled over for driving while under the influence of nicotine?

As far as the various results of other treatments, such as Bupronorphine, Naltrexone, LAAM, and methadone, there is only one so far with enough studies and results to show some amount of effectiveness and that is Methadone. Bupronorphine is still rather new and its attraction is that it is given under a physician setting instead of a clinic setting. This opens a door to abuse that is much harder to achieve under the methadone clinic system.

LAAM as an effective treatment option has proved risky due to the potential cardiac problems it can cause and is being phased out completely. As far as Naltrexone, I had the experience of taking it at one point after one of my hospital detoxes. The problem with Naltrexone is it does not actually ease withdrawal effects, deal with the cravings, or curb the long lasting anhedonia that follows for years

261

after heavy opiate abuse. The desire to stay with the Naltrexone treatment fades quickly. I was lucky I did not have Naltrexone implants which I was offered since the desire to use while on Naltrexone was so great I am sure I would have removed them under less than a sterile setting as many others have done.

The solution is to keep looking for an answer. To ignore the problem in itself is not a solution. I know it is frustrating to see those in harm reduction programs like methadone treatment that continue to use. The key is harm reduction, not elimination. By providing the methadone, it may reduce the amount of heroin or other opiates one uses and in many cases, eliminate illicit use completely. Dealing with the problem by being more realistic has proven to have better results than being idealistic.

Dalrymple: First, the question of genetics. I accept that, within a population, there may be some genetic predisposition to abuse drugs of various kinds (or, in the case of East Asians, not to take alcohol). But I do not think that you can explain the very large variation between populations by means of genetics. When I started work in the city, in which I spent the last part of my career, heroin addiction was very rare. By the end of my career, it was very common. (I don't think my presence was causally related to the increase). This huge increase cannot be explained genetically: in the 1950s there were at most a few score addicts, and by 2000, between 150 and 300,000.

My belief is that the whole rationale of treatment is flawed. It is true that, if you take the case of methadone, you can show that a certain small percentage do well on it. That is true; but it would also be true that if you gave money to burglars — and there would be a dose-response curve — some, not all, would stop burgling. That does not make burglary a disease. In any case, treatment is not the answer to the social problem and never will be: in England, for example, stopping one person from taking heroin is not like interrupting the transmission of TB; it is just transferring the problem to someone else, as the drug-dealer finds another willing client/dupe. This fits what has happened, at least in Britain.

Finally, Mr Rutenfrans is right: millions of people, especially in the middle-classes, have given up smoking because they have become convinced of the need to do so — among them my mother and my wife. Interestingly, criminals rarely give up.

The recurrence of opiate addiction in China could bear the interpretation given it, but it is also the case that the society is far less repressive and more individualistic now, and this bears out my fundamental point.

Menzies: The treatment of heroin addiction remains highly polarized. On one side are the passionate advocates of replacement treatment with methadone and on the other side are the equally passionate advocates of no intervention. The divisions along ideological lines has only contributed to the enduring stigma and left tens of thousands of patients with few treatment options.

In liberal societies, drug use is often seen as an expression of 'free speech' and those impacted by drug addiction; especially the disenfranchised are entitled to life-long 'pharmacological welfare'. This approach is based on an unproven theory that heroin addiction leads to irreversible 'metabolic lesions'. There is no doubt that a certain percentage of opioid addicts will do well on replacement therapy but it is preposterous to suggest that methadone is the only treatment. It is even more preposterous to suggest that since methadone has been used for forty plus years, it is the only effective treatment.

The near-epidemic levels of heroin and opioid use is directly related to availability and price. Wars and weak governments in the poppy growing regions and the smuggling routes has flooded European countries with heroin and caused even bigger problems for countries like Pakistan, Russia, Iran etc. Easy access to drugs, the sense of hopelessness, particularly among the young and unemployed, and societal views on drug use has created this situation. Therefore it is not surprising that our prisons are bursting with drug addicts. Twenty years ago, chronic pain was a relatively unknown disease. Now we are told that 65 million Americans suffer from chronic pain and most of them will need opioid pain medications. Small wonder, 36 million

Americans have used opioid pain medications for non-medical purposes. We are now seeing more and more people addicted to pain pills.

Tens of millions of people have experimented with drugs but only relatively small percentage of people will have difficulty getting off the drug and we have to focus our efforts on this group. We have tried incarceration, sloganeering – "Just Say No", replacement therapy, needle exchange, safe injection sites and none of them have worked to make a major impact on the problem.

I am shocked at the misinformation and the hostility towards naltrexone. We have detoxed hundreds of opioid patients on an outpatient basis at our clinic and started them on naltrexone with excellent outcomes. The key is explaining to the patients the rationale for the development of medication and its pharmacology. Way too often heroin addicts appear to know all about the neurobiology of addiction and this is classical example of: Little knowledge is dangerous!

We will succeed only when we put aside ideology and learn to use every medication approved for the treatment of opioid addiction.

Rutenfrans: Mr. Dalrymple finds it interesting that so many people have given up their addiction to nicotine, which indeed is a drug, while criminals rarely give up that addiction.

The explanation of that fact is that criminal behavior, smoking tobacco, using drugs and alcohol, and poverty are different manifestations of one and the same underlying characteristic: a low level of self-control. A person with a low level of self-control finds it difficult not to respond immediately to his needs. He is short-term directed. A person with a high level of self-control is able to quit a habit when it appears to be bad for his health, which has occurred with the habit of smoking in the last decades.

A person with a low level of self-control, for example a criminal, finds it more difficult to quit the bad habit of smoking. This explanation bears the danger of being interpreted deterministically. Even human beings with a low level of self-control are able to recognise that they have a low level of self-control. His self-consciousness of this characteristic can be the first step to do something about it. He can improve his level of self-control by exercise. I am convinced that we can help individual human beings to improve their level of self-control when we as a culture succeed to value self-control as high as the Asian cultures do (for example China and Japan), and as western culture used to do in the not so distant past.

Since the Second World War western culture has had the tendency to ridicule self-control. When so-called ordinary people in a television-show are asked what they value the most in their friends, lovers or partners, the unchangeable answer is: 'spontaneity'. A culture with a high level of spontaneity has also high levels of criminality and drug addiction.

Fisher: After failing traditional 12-step methods of treatment half a dozen times, I felt I really had no option left - death or methadone. Such was the stigma of methadone. I thought if one was on it; it would be akin to a zombie-like existence. Even detoxification (with the help of Naltrexone) would not take away the obsession or compulsion to use. I really did not know what to expect on methadone, though once I started, the compulsion to use went away and I did not feel high or that I was exchanging one drug for another. I felt liberated almost instantly. Though it worked well for me, I think Methadone should only be used after one has failed many times at other methods. One should educate oneself about the benefits and the drawbacks of methadone before ever submitting to a possible life time of drug maintenance.

Dr. Dalrymple has discounted many studies up to now, based on the excuse that they support the flawed treatment options that exist currently. But such studies proved long term opiate abuse causes damage to one's endorphin producing system. This blanket discount of studies also precludes one from seeing that each dollar spent in the U.S. towards methadone treatment has a payback on an average of $7.00 in saved government funded healthcare and costs of incarceration. It prevents one from seeing that methadone and other current treatment options have helped more than a small percentage suffering from addiction.

Traditional current treatment for addiction is through one of the various 12-step programs or harm reduction with use of Methadone, LAAM, or Bupronorphine. Though methadone originally was to be used to detoxify opiate addicted patients gradually, it has since transformed into a maintenance drug much like insulin for the diabetic.

There has been talk of hostility towards Naltrexone in harm reduction; however, there really is none since Naltrexone has its place in opiate detoxification. Detoxification and long term abstinence from illicit use are two different things, and unfortunately Naltrexone's long-term potential is not comparable to that of methadone. Addicts in general understand the neurobiology of addiction after countless years of trial and error of trying to kick the habit on their own usually without success. This is knowledge gained through experience, much like the dog in Pavlov's experiment. But a little bit of knowledge and explanation of pharmacology has never kept anyone clean.

There are no perfect solutions for drug treatment but to deny any and all successes that have been made so far or say to that the whole rationale of treatment is flawed is irresponsible — especially when no alternative is suggested. It takes no courage to criticize an imperfect approach. Those who have not suffered from addiction tend to suggest simplistic, non-tolerant, holier than thou approaches of "threaten the addict with death and they'll quit." But they really lack true understanding of the diversity of the human soul. Additionally, the constant belittling of addicts and treating them as less than human makes many of the critics of current treatment options, just that – critics — but they fail to make any real contributions or humane suggestions of dealing with the problem.

FP: Dr. Dalrymple, last word goes to you sir.

Dalrymple: I would say that the idea of treatment is the one that belittles addicts, since it suggests that, unlike other people, they cannot behave other than as they do. The same has been said of criminals.

They are then less than fully human. I am not so pessimistic about them. It is, besides, empirically mistaken.

However, so long as addicts tell lies to themselves and doctors, and doctors tell lies to addicts (and the whole idea of 'treatment' is a lie), the absurd *pas de deux* will continue.

FP: Theodore Dalrymple, Chris Rutenfrans, Percy Menzies and Ron Fisher, thank you for joining Frontpage Symposium.

[Jamie Glazov, "Symposium: Romancing Opiates," *Frontpagemag.com*, October 13, 2006.]

Part VIII: A Discussion on Faith

[15] A Discussion on Faith

In this special edition of Frontpage Symposium, we have assembled a distinguished panel to discuss the "new atheism" and the role of religion in political life. Our guests are:

Rabbi David J. Wolpe, the rabbi of Sinai Temple in Los Angeles and a teacher of modern Jewish religious thought at UCLA. He has been named the #1 Pulpit Rabbi in America (as reported in *Newsweek*). Rabbi Wolpe writes for many publications, including *The Jewish Week, Jerusalem Post*, and Beliefnet.com. He has appeared as a commentator on CNN and CBS This Morning and has been featured on the History Channel's *Mysteries of the Bible*. He is the author of the national bestseller *Making Loss Matter: Creating Meaning in Difficult Times*. His new book is *Why Faith Matters*.

Bruce Chilton, the Bernard Iddings Bell Professor of Religion at Bard College in Annandale-on-Hudson and Rector at the Church of St. John in Barrytown, New York. He is the author of many scholarly articles and books, including the acclaimed *Rabbi Jesus* and *Mary Magdalene*. He is the author of the new book, *Abraham's Curse: The Roots of Violence in Judaism, Christianity, and Islam*.

Raheel Raza, a leading Muslim reformer, award-winning writer, professional speaker, diversity consultant, documentary filmmaker and interfaith advocate. She is the author of *Their Jihad . . . Not My Jihad*. Visit her site at *RaheelRaza.com*.

Fr. Maurice Guimond, a Trappist monk at Our Lady of Calvary Abbey, in Rogersville, New Brunswick, Canada. He was superior of his community for ten years.

and

Michael Novak, an American Catholic philosopher, journalist, novelist, and diplomat. The author of more than twenty-five books on the philosophy and theology of culture, Novak is most widely known for his book, *The Spirit of Democratic Capitalism*. In 1994, he was awarded the Templeton Prize for Progress in Religion, which included a million-dollar purse presented at Buckingham Palace.

FP: Bruce Chilton, Rabbi David J. Wolpe, Raheel Raza, Fr. Maurice Guimond and Michael Novak, welcome to Frontpage Symposium. Rabbi Wolpe, could you start the discussion for us by touching on the "new atheism"?

Wolpe: The "new atheism" (new in quotes because you can read about it in Bertrand Russell) is based on two misapprehensions about human beings: one gives them too much credit, the other too little.

The excess of credit is the belief that we are capable of sustaining ourselves morally and philosophically without God. The justification for free will, the address for gratitude, the ultimate grounding for morality — all of these are bequeathed by a God greater than us. To believe we are the best thing going is a staggering hubris.

We belittle ourselves by thinking that because we are a tiny planet tucked away in a corner of the solar system, the Creator of all could not be in relationship to us. The universe is, as scientists frequently note, a compound of rare improbabilities; change one astronomical constant and we are dust. Yet consciousness has arisen, knows and celebrates itself and its world.

Atheism finds its ballast in materialism, the certainty that there is nothing other than stuff in this world. Because we have gotten so good at manipulating stuff through technology, there must be nothing else.

Not so; not wise.

We are better than we think, and less good. Those are good mistakes with which to start.

Chilton: The best-selling atheists of our time — Sam Harris, Christopher Hitchens, and Richard Dawkins — make out the case that religion equals violence and is in any case grounded in fantasy.

To make their argument work, they need to engage in logical sleight of hand. Religious wars have indeed been vicious, but the attempt to scapegoat religion for the ills of civilization turns a blind eye to secular tyranny, which since the Enlightenment has proved itself by far the most lethal, oppressive, and dehumanizing force on earth. And to dismiss whatever cannot be proven empirically as wishful thinking would rob humanity of the values they live by. Although all three writers are eloquent, they are philosophically shallow.

Yet in the political arena, this troika of atheists has probably done us some good. Their false certainty that God does not exist challenges the Fundamentalist confusion of statements of faith with statements of fact.

Voters are rightly interested, not in the false certainties of either religious or secular fundamentalism, but in how candidates ground their actions in the beliefs and philosophies that draw their commitments.

FP: Thank you, Bruce Chilton.

Fr. Maurice?

In your contribution, can you touch a bit on the phenomenon of secular tyranny that Dr. Chilton has raised?

Fr. Maurice: In my monastic world, faith is something which is very little talked about; maybe because we are too busy living it, or trying to. Yet even in our "protected" environment, atheism is sometimes a temptation, while Fundamentalism can be sought as a safe haven for those days when we do not feel like questioning our beliefs. Sometimes we would like to shrink God and His works to the size of our capacity to comprehend, a favorite challenge for science. But then, there is no God and we are left to ourselves, in the dark and in the cold.

What we have seen of the use of religion in the world of politics often appears as nothing more but a shameless scheme to draw votes. The politician will be tempted to side with the most popular issues, whether it be abortion, stem cell research, gay rights, prayer in schools, or whatever else, according to what he/she may get out of it, But like what Dr Chilton rightly says: "Voters are rightly interested ... in how candidates ground their actions in the beliefs and philosophies that draw their commitments."

I still shiver remembering a famous speech on 9/11 when we heard, in a same breath: "The Lord is my shepherd... This is WAR." Actually, the Psalms have accustomed us to that kind of speech. "Lord, be good to your people...and kill everyone else." Around that time, I was trying to imagine God leaning on his balcony and listening to the prayers of the great leaders, each piously kneeling by his bed and praying that his enemies be wiped out. The greatest religions have practically all had their holy wars, usually vicious and merciless. Isn't atheistic secularism just another religion which has its own saints, its own clergy and worshippers, its own creed and its own fundamentalism?

Raza: First, let me touch on the new atheism. I agree with Rabbi Wolpe that it's not really new. In the Muslim world it was attempted by Kamal Ataturk when he did away with all religious leaders — leading to the current backlash. In Pakistan, ex-President Pervaiz Musharraf made a bid for secularism and handed over hundreds of people (many innocent) to the U.S. and some of them landed in Guantanamo Bay without trial or justice.

In terms of the place of religion in political life, I find it ironic that even the most secular leaders invoke the name of God when it suits their purpose to get support from the religious masses. In some ways faith and politics are intertwined and based on a value system. They call it Judeo-Christian values in North America and in the Muslim world, these are called Islamic values.

However, there is a problem in the Muslim world in that it doesn't have elected representatives or democracy but self-appointed kings or propped-up dictators. Therefore in the religious institutions there is no organized clergy and accountability so the mosques are run independently and base their value system on outdated Sharia.

Currently, the Moulvi (the head of the mosque) has no master other than vaguely defined political organizations that he might adhere to. No license is necessary to set up a mosque. The ownership and management of mosques is not regulated. This creates a huge gap between theory and practice and the separation of church and state which is inherent to life in the West. Very often we see that instead of using the pulpit of the mosque to impart spiritual values and speak to the scripture and everyday life (as Islam is supposed to be a way of life), these self-appointed Moulvis take on harsh political tones and bring a combination of polemics and politics right into the mosque leading to the current Islamist agenda.

The only solution to this problem is that we must change the system of managing mosques and managing Moulvis to make them more responsive to the community if the objective of enlightened moderation is to be achieved. If the Moulvis were somehow bureaucratized into a hierarchy that could control their thinking, we would be closer to moderation.

Novak: In *The Universal Hunger for Liberty* I was concerned to report on my own experiences in studying the very high idea of the Divinity cherished by Islam — nothing human or non-divine could be said to be made in His image. His transcendence was too great for that. In desert cultures, particularly, where human life is so fragile, and can under harsh conditions suddenly wither and die like grass, the sense of God's omnipotence (and the perishability of human beings) must be very acute. A second point I noted is the absence of an active principle of development — a method for showing, e.g., that certain practices, formulations of doctrine, and ways of looking at things are subject to new evaluations, as knowledge increases throughout history. One can change these things while adhering with loyalty to foundational inspirations and distinctions. There is progress within vital religions.

In the last two centuries, it seems that Christians and Jews, at least, have done a much better job in assimilating the lessons to be learned from modern science, secular cultures, and democratic polities, than secularists have done, in being able to learn from the religious dynamics that still move their civilization. The Enlightenment (an artful term of raw bigotry - "We are the Enlightened, you dwell in

274

darkness") developed a literature of contempt for religious realities and persons. It was a contempt in which such words as "illusion," "delusion," and "neurosis" figured quite heavily as descriptions of their religious neighbors by the Enlightened.

The balance has begun to right itself nowadays. Various groups on both sides of this divide have begun, warily, to speak more forthrightly and more respectfully than earlier. Certain important clarifications have also been made. For instance, Christopher Hitchens insisted in one recent debate that his opponent could not pin him into the position of defending science (invaluable and noble as it is) as the only form of human knowing. In another debate, Hitchens drew attention to his own awareness of the sacred, the numinous, and the transcendent in human experience. One should not deprive him of such perceptiveness, he suggested, simply by ruling him out as an 'atheist.' On a third occasion, he said he had no difficulty with an awareness of God as the irradiating intelligence that infuses all things and the empowering, thrusting energy that courses through all things, and that propels development and progress. He has little trouble with deists, he said. The God of Abraham and Jesus is another matter altogether.

These clarifications are very important. One feels as though this debate is getting somewhere, and is most worth contributing to. It may have very good fruits, too, not only enriching our public life and our respect for one another in our differences, but also uniting us to defend liberty against the powerful forces that hate it, and mean to destroy it. These warriors of destruction are avaricious for our conversion to their version of their own religion — or our death. Even in their own religion, these haters and destroyers are a minority, who threaten to torture and kill those of their own co-religionists who openly despise them and resist them.

Wolpe: I would like to begin at the ending, with Michael Novak's report of Christopher Hitchens. I recently completed a series of three debates with Mr. Hitchens (the first two available on the web) and it occurs to me that debates can work both ways — clarifying and polarizing. That is important because we cannot afford greater polarization.

So as religious people we have to think about approaches to this subject that give others a way out. The crucial, embattled position is that of the religious moderate. I'm not fond of the 'moderate' term, because it suggests a less ardent faith; reminiscent of Muir's poem on Kafka "we the proximate damned, presumptive blessed" — not sooo religious, you know.

But the passionate center, if you will, must pull on both sides to recognize the worthiness inherent in the other. Showing the shades in each position is hardly a Talmudic, or Jesuitical, undertaking, in the dismissive sense of those words; the future of civilization rides on the ability to acknowledge the worthiness of the 'other.'

Some time ago I proposed renaming my own movement in Judaism, Conservative Judaism; I wanted to rebrand it "covenantal Judaism." My reasons for that aren't germane now, but the larger focus is: only if we see all human beings tied together, by covenant if you will, by other notions if you wish, might we have a chance to establish the dialogue that can save us. As Reza Aslan notes, it is the separation of synagogue/church/mosque and state that gives the breathing room for such a dialogue to emerge — as it has right here in Frontpage.

Chilton: Two conceptual confusions that are common and impede clarity have crept into our discussion.

"Atheist" and "secularist" are not synonyms. Mustafa Kemal Ataktürk wanted secular government, and he succeeded in bringing reform to Turkey, but his religious orientation remains a matter of dispute. Secular government — that is, a conception of law limited to this world, and not imposed with divine authority — permits religious liberty, and that is generally good for every religion.

The West takes pride today in its "democracy," but secular, democratic forms of government would not have emerged, except for the military stalemate among the religious factions of Europe during and after the Reformation. Secular democracies were and are often partial affairs, coexisting with claims of monarchy and religious establishment in Europe, and with frequent appeals to Christian values in America.

No single constitutional settlement is required for progress in Democracy, and no constitution guarantees democracy. Who would have predicted that at the beginning of the 21rst century, China would encourage the teaching of theology, while America would give us Abu Ghraib? Allowing for the volatility of recent events, I see no reason to be pessimistic about the emergence of secular democracies in historically Muslim lands, provided it is understood that their identities will make for a unique expression of democratic governance. Progress is not certain, but its prospects would be improved by reducing the military intervention and confrontation that has characterized Western policy toward Muslim countries for two hundred years (quite aside from the Crusades).

The second confusion involves the appeal to moderation and balance. Although they seem to be virtues, their power is limited to where interests are being negotiated. Outside that realm, they only obscure matters. I am sure Christopher Hitchens is capable of uttering sensible reflections, but the title of his book, *God is not Great: How Religion Poisons Everything*, means what it says. Moderation is good, but only in moderation, where accommodation, rather than commitment, is at issue.

But religious faith involves commitment, and that is part of its irreducible strength. Replacing faith with appeals to moderating reason is as flawed as the program of putting belief in the place of policy. Faith and reason belong to our constitution as human beings, and for the sake of our health neither should be denied. Reason just as naturally refines faith as faith provides reason with its moral compass. The relation between the two is not adversarial, as the excessive positivism of some Enlightenment thinkers proposed. Trying to rely on only faith produces superstition, while the siren song of serving reason alone has, in the history of conflicts since the Englightenment, landed entire countries in tyrannical dystopias.

Our best future lies, not in trying to negotiate away the differences between faith and reason into some muddled middle, but in permitting full, civil clarity in regard to both categorical beliefs and the negotiable claims of self-interest.

Fr. Maurice: Last week, my brother emailed me a YouTube link to an exquisite interpretation of Ennio Morricone's "The Mission," directed by the author. The oboe is just superb. Listening to such heavenly music, I was musing on why God doesn't bother with copyrights on his works. It is so much so that an can claim as his own any masterpiece out of his mind and hands, but the inspiration of which is most mysterious.

As a matter of fact, my feeling is that God has been and is rather wreckless in the way he has entrusted the whole Creation to Man, letting him do his own thing with it. When Man stands and says to his face: "I don't believe in you", or "I hate you", nothing happens. Man is not stomped on or demolished. Even when the Son was assassinated, nothing happened. And this appears to be a family trait: when Jesus on his way to Jerusalem planned a stop at a Samaritan village, the villagers let him know that he was not welcome. Two disciples, James and his brother John, suggested that they call for the fire from heaven to come down on these people to teach them a lesson. Jesus' response was a blunt "No way!"

Discussing faith, we have noted that some religions (or at least a number of their members) are particularly touchy about what people believe or not, and the way they live their faith. Heretics have been burned at stakes, gentiles have been imprisoned, believers of other faiths have been persecuted. Isn't this all God's fault? Shouldn't we blame him? After all, where are his writings? Didn't he entrust his Word to Man just as he did his Creation? Moses destroyed one set of the stones on which God had written his law, and we don't know what happened to the other. Later, Jesus spread his teachings like a sower his seed, never bothering to write even a single line. The only instance of any "writing" was in the dirt, not even words but traits, and nobody knows what they were, traits that were then trampled on by man and beast.

However, we haven't wasted any time and have managed to write mountains of books about God, his law, about heaven and hell, theology, Christology, ecclesiology, telling others what to believe and how to live. Unfortunately, we don't agree on everything. Wouldn't it be more simple if we could have fitted God nicely in a box with lock and key, so that we could control what is to be known and believed about him? For many of us, church people, control is the big thing.

I believe that God has infinitely more respect for Man. He is not a puppeteer. Rather than imposing himself, he wants us to seek him, together, sharing our faith, rather than imposing it on each other, while remaining always eager to learn from each other. Chances are we will never "see the end of him": the more we find, the more we thirst, the more we thirst, the more we search.

Raza: Here I am responding to all of you from the heart of the three Abrahamic faiths — Jerusalem. This is a place that oozes spirituality and peace. Ironically one would not think so if one were to look at this place in terms of politics. But for people who have faith, there is so much here that is hard to absorb.

In simple words, obviously atheism and secular culture have not worked for everyone because there is a thirst for spirituality — which we see manifest in how humanity (especially in the West) attaches itself to cults and programs that present some spiritual connection. So I believe that while dogma and religion can divide, it is the innate spirituality within us that guides us and keeps us rooted.

For me, this spirituality is manifest not in my faith alone (although I get a lot of guidance from Sufism) but in every tradition and every path. I believe in God, but I respect those who believe in some form of a Creator or a higher being. In essence, I connect immediately with those who radiate spirituality and have a hard time having dialogue with atheists and agnostics.

I want to thank Frontpage for giving us this chance for deep dialogue.

Novak: Each conversationalist made points worth carrying forward. Let me begin with Professor Chilton's good distinction between "secular" and "atheist." "Secular" is a word invented by Christians in the earliest centuries to distinguish "the City of God" from "the City of man." So I completely agree that "secular" is a positive term.

However, in our age a quite anti-religious movement has arisen in the United States (and in Europe) among people who call themselves secular, as in "secular humanism." The British Enlightenment was tutored by tradition and respect for the imagination and habits of the heart; the French by a very narrow form of "reason." The second, French form chose to banish religion as much as possible from public life. The first, British form took care to show respect, and even to give protection to the tradition and the well-cherished religion of the people.

The U.S. Constitution is both secular and religious. It barely alludes to Judaism and Christianity, but in the spirit of "Give to Caesar the things that are Caesar's, and to God the things that are God's." The Constitution defines Caesar's limits and divides Caesar's powers. Yet it also takes care to protect the conscious and the free exercise of public religion.

I agree with Rabbi Wolpe, Professor Chilton, Professor Raza, and Father Maurice in supporting diligent intelligent efforts to conduct public, civil arguments. It will take sympathetic understanding to get at many of the hidden issues that unnecessarily separate one faith from another, and people of faith from unbelievers. This painstaking understanding is to be done, not exactly by "moderation," but by willingness to be patient during the sometimes exhausting task of drawing distinctions. This achievement will also require willingness to hear and to respond to the acute questions of others.

Heart does speak to heart, if we allow it.

FP: Bruce Chilton, Rabbi David J. Wolpe, Raheel Raza and Fr. Maurice Guimond and Michael Novak, thank you for joining Frontpage Symposium.

[Jamie Glazov, "Symposium: A Discussion on Faith," *Frontpagemag.com*, January 9, 2009.]